READING SKILLS FOR CAREER SUCCESS

SELMA WILF

Phoenix College

PRENTICE HALL
Englewood Cliffs, New Jersey   07632

Library of Congress Cataloging-in-Publication Data

Wilf, Selma.
    Reading skills for career success / Selma Wilf.
      p. cm.
    Includes index.
    ISBN 0-13-761842-5
    1. Reading (Adult education)—United States. 2. Career education—
United States. I. Title.
LC5225.R4W55 1991
428.4′071′5—dc20
                                   90-47050
                                     CIP

Editorial/production supervision and
   interior design: Virginia Rubens
Cover design: 20/20 Services Inc.
Prepress buyer: Herb Klein
Manufacturing buyer: David Dickey

 © 1991 by Prentice-Hall, Inc.
A Division of Simon & Schuster
Englewood Cliffs, New Jersey 07632

Printed in the United States of America

10 9 8 7 6 5 4 3 2 1

ISBN 0-13-761842-5

Prentice-Hall International (UK) Limited, *London*
Prentice-Hall of Australia Pty. Limited, *Sydney*
Prentice-Hall Canada Inc., *Toronto*
Prentice-Hall Hispanoamericana, S.A., *Mexico*
Prentice-Hall of India Private Limited, *New Delhi*
Prentice-Hall of Japan, Inc., *Tokyo*
Simon & Schuster Asia Pte. Ltd., *Singapore*
Editora Prentice-Hall do Brasil, Ltda., *Rio de Janeiro*

To Morris S., Joel M., and Steven R. Wilf
Adele and Albert Steinbock
Lillie and Israel Wilf
Gerry and Leonard Parmet

Contents

PART ONE
Building Your Professional Vocabulary

PART TWO
Developing Blocks of Related Information

PART THREE
Simplifying Complex Material

PART FOUR
Reading Beyond the Written Word

PART FIVE
Addressing Career-Related Reading Tasks

Preface

The United States Department of Labor has predicted that more than 21 million new jobs will be added to the economy by the year 2000. Most of these jobs will require well-trained workers. In fact, employers have already begun requiring that employees have more sophisticated education and skills. The better jobs of the future will most likely demand education beyond high school.

Since there are and will continue to be tremendous changes in the American workplace, jobs which exist today may not be available in the future. With advances in technology, jobs that are undreamed of today may be important in the future. There probably will be greater mobility in relation to career changes, with fewer people spending their working years in a single job. This trend can already be seen in the number of people returning to school to retrain for new careers.

The ability to read well has been targeted as an essential skill for people looking for success in the workplace now and in the future. *Reading Skills For Career Success (RSFCS)* has been written to enhance the reading ability of those who need to read efficiently and effectively as they prepare for future careers and then later, as they move into the workplace. The thirteen reading skills included in *RSFCS* are ones which are applicable in any career, regardless of whether that career occurs now or in the future. Material used to teach these thirteen skills has been taken from textbooks published for 35 different careers. To cite just a few career sources, these include architecture, construction, retail sales, management, public relations, fire science, records management, and so on. In addition, the material in RSFCS includes information related to the workplace from government publications and articles from professional journals. In all cases, an attempt has been made to limit the materials to those which do not require an extensive vocabulary or background in a specific field.

RSFCS is divided into five major parts: Building Your Professional Vocabulary, Developing Blocks of Related Information, Simplifying Complex Material, Reading Beyond the Written Word, and Addressing Career-Related Reading Tasks. The format of *RSFCS* has been designed for a hands-on approach to reading skill mastery. A skill is explained and samples are examined. The reader then uses this information to complete Sample Practice exercises, and checks his or her own responses, thus receiving immediate feedback and an analysis of acceptable responses. Additional practice is provided in Skill Development Exercises. Finally, skills are transferred to the reader's own career-related material in the Skill Application sections. The emphasis in *RSFCS* is twofold: on skill practice and on skill application—both critical to skill mastery.

To the Student

HOW TO USE *Reading Skills For Career Success* MOST EFFECTIVELY

Reading Skills For Career Success will help you to master the kinds of reading skills you need now to do well in your classes and later when you are responsible for handling the large quantity of reading material that is typically found in most jobs.

I have written *Reading Skills For Career Success* in a specific format which, if followed, will help you to master the thirteen skills included in this textbook. Each skill is presented in exactly the same way, and you should go through each of the steps:

1. The skill is introduced and explained. Samples are included where appropriate. This is the place to read very carefully and to make sure that you understand what has been presented to you.

2. The Sample Practice section gives you the first chance to try the skill. When you have completed this practice, you check your own answers. This is the time to analyze your answers if they differ from those given and to make sure that you understand how to apply the skill. Since the answers follow directly after the Sample Practice, you may be tempted to peek at the answers rather than coming up with your own. Don't! The Sample Practice is an important part of the learning process—a step that should be followed carefully.

3. You are now directed to the appropriate Skill Development Exercise for additional practice in the skill just learned.

4. The Skill Application section offers you an opportunity to apply what you have learned to materials that you select. They are called "career materials" in this text and include your own textbooks, manuals, brochures, articles in professional journals, or just about any other written material related to the career of your choice.

The key to doing well in *RSFCS* is simple—be sure to master each skill before going on to the next one. Each skill is important for the ones that follow. For example, you will need the vocabulary skills presented in the first part of *RSFCS* throughout the book where you most likely will encounter terms you do not know. The skills in the second part of *RSFCS*, Developing Blocks of Related Information, are essential if you are to be able to work with the rest of the book. In the last part of the book, Addressing Career-Related Reading Tasks, you will need to use everything you have learned about reading skills up to that point. As you can see, this is the kind of textbook in which skills are yours to use immediately.

Acknowledgments

The author would like to thank the following people at Phoenix College for their help and encouragement in the writing of *Reading Skills For Career Success:* Dean of Instruction Mary Briden, David Frazier and Michelle Cox of the bookstore, Cliff Schweitzer, Coordinator of Career Planning and Placement, and all of the students who kept this project going with their positive reactions and contributions of material.

In addition, the author is grateful to J. Philip Miller, Editor in Chief for Humanities at Prentice Hall, for his continued support and confidence, and to Virginia Rubens, Production Editor, for all of her hard work on *RSFCS.*

Finally, the author greatly appreciates permission from the following sources for allowing use of their materials.

Chapter One

Page 2, 1: Reprinted with permission of Macmillan Publishing Company from *Retail Management* by Barry Berman and Joel R. Evans. © 1986 by Macmillan Publishing Company.

Page 2, 2: Wheton, Sherrill, *Interior Design and Decoration,* 14th Edition. New York: J. B. Lippincott Company, 1974, p. 654.

Page 3, Sample A: Sirota, David, *Essentials of Real Estate Investment,* 3rd Edition. Published by Real Estate Education Company/Chicago, a division of Longman Financial Services Inc. © 1988, 1984, 1978 by Longman Group USA Inc. All rights reserved.

Page 3, Sample A: Edwards, James Don, and Lynn Thorne, *College Accounting Fundamentals,* 2nd Edition. Homewood, IL: Richard D. Irwin, Inc., 1986, p. 4.

Page 4, Sample B: Johnson, Webster H., and A. J. Faria, *Creative Selling,* 4th Edition. Cincinnati, Ohio: South-Western Publishing Company, 1987, p. 19.

Page 4, Sample C: Powers, Thomas F., and Jo Marie Powers, *Food Service Operations: Planning and Control.* New York: John Wiley & Sons, 1984, p. 90.

SAMPLE PRACTICE—CONTEXT CLUES

Page 5, 1: Rader, M. H., and Linda A. Kurth. *Business Communication for the Computer Age.* Cincinnati: South-Western Publishing Company, 1988, p. 5.

Page 5, 2: Hackney/Cormier, *Counseling Strategies and Interventions,* © 1988, pp. 158, 162. Reprinted by permission of Prentice-Hall, Inc., Englewood Cliffs, NJ.

Page 6, 3: Powers, Thomas F., and Jo Marie Powers, *Food Service Operations: Planning and Control.* New York: John Wiley & Sons, 1984, p. 145.

Page 6, 4: Bovée, Courtland L., and William F. Arens, *Contemporary Advertising,* Second Edition. Homewood, IL: Irwin Publishing Company, 1986, p. 89.

Page 6, 5: Peurifoy, Robert L., and William L. Ledbetter, *Construction Planning, Equipment, and Methods,* 4th Edition. New York: McGraw Hill, 1985, p. 5.

SKILL DEVELOPMENT EXERCISE 1

Page 9, 1: Adapted from Johnson, Mina M., and Norman F. Kallaus, *Records Management,* 3rd Edition. Cincinnati: South-Western Publishing Company, 1982, p. 2.

Page 9, 2: Reprinted with permission of Macmillan Publishing Company from *Retail Management* by Barry Berman and Joel R. Evans. © 1986 by Macmillan Publishing Company.

Page 9, 3: Stone, Elaine, *Fashion Merchandising—An Introduction*, 4th Edition. New York: Gregg Division, McGraw Hill-Book Company, 1985, p. 65.

Page 10, 4: Carlson, Ronald L., *Criminal Justice Procedures*, 3rd Edition. Cincinnati: Anderson Publishing Company, 1978, p. 79.

Page 10, 5: From *Economics*, Fourth Edition, by James D. Gwartney and Richard L. Stroup, copyright © 1982 Harcourt Brace Jovanovich, Inc. Reprinted by permission of the publisher.

Page 10, 6: Watson, Don A., *Construction Materials and Processes*, 3rd Edition. New York: Gregg Division, McGraw-Hill Book Company, 1986, p. 161.

Page 10, 7: Brody, David Eliot, *Business and Its Legal Environment.* Lexington, Mass.: D. C. Heath and Company, 1986, p. 7.

Page 11, 8: Bruce Harwood, *Real Estate Principles*, 4/E, © 1986, pp. 18, 19. Reprinted by permission of Prentice-Hall, Inc., Englewood Cliffs, NJ.

Page 11, 9: Seitel, Fraser P., *The Practice of Public Relations*, 3rd Edition. Columbus, OH: Merrill Publishing Company, 1987, p. 147.

Page 11, 10: Mathis, Robert L., and John H. Jackson, *Personnel Human Resource Management*, 4th Edition. St. Paul: West Publishing Company, 1982, pp. 73, 74.

Chapter Two

Page 20, Sample B: *Webster's New World Dictionary of the English Language*, Second College Edition © 1977. Used by permission of the publisher, Simon & Schuster, Inc., New York, N.Y.

SAMPLE PRACTICE 2—APPLYING PVS

Page 21: *Webster's New World Dictionary of the English Language*, Second College Edition © 1977. Used by permission of the publisher, Simon & Schuster, Inc., New York, N.Y.

Chapter Three

Page 33, Sample A: Reprinted with permission of Macmillan Publishing Company from *Engineering*, 5th Edition by George C. Beakley, Donovan L. Evans, and John Bertrand Keats. Copyright © by George Beakley.

Page 34, Sample B: Adapted from Bovée, Courtland L., and William F. Arens, *Contemporary Advertising*, 2nd Edition, Homewood, IL: Irwin Publishing Company, 1986, p. 79.

Page 34, Sample C: Johnson, H. Webster, and A. J. Faria, *Creative Selling*, 4th Edition. Cincinnati: South-Western Publishing Company, 1987, p. 18.

SAMPLE PRACTICE—IDENTIFYING STATED MAIN IDEAS IN PARAGRAPHS

Page 35, 1: (Adapted) Bare, William K., *Introduction to Fire Science*. New York: John Wiley & Sons, 1978, p. 77.

Page 36, 2: (Adapted) Reprinted with permission of Macmillan Publishing Company from *Retail Management: A Strategic Approach*, 3rd Edition by Barry Berman and Joel R. Evans. Copyright © 1986 by Macmillan Publishing Company.

Page 36, 3: Author unknown, "A Guide to Business Credit and the Equal Opportunity Act." Washington, D.C.: Board of Governors of the Federal Reserve System, no date, pages not numbered.

Page 37, 4: Watson, Don A., *Construction Materials and Processes*. New York: McGraw-Hill, Inc., 1986, p. 144.

Page 37, 5: Silvestri, George T., John M. Lukasiowicz, and Marcus E. Einstein, "Occupational Employment Projections Through 1995." Washington, D.C.: U.S. Bureau of Labor Statistics, Bulletin 2197, March 1984. p. 44.

SKILL DEVELOPMENT EXERCISE 3

Page 41, 1: Reprinted with permission of Macmillan Publishing Company from *Retail Management* by Barry Berman and Joel R. Evans. © 1986 by Macmillan Publishing Company.

Page 41, 2: Stone, Elaine, *Fashion Merchandising—An Introduction*, 4th Edition. New York: McGraw Hill Book Company, 1985, p. 30.

Page 42, 3: Author unknown, The Communication and Office Training Center, Bureau of Training, U.S. Civil Service Commission, Washington, D.C.: No date, no page numbers.

Page 42, 4: Excerpt from *Contemporary Marketing*, Fifth Edition, by Louis E. Boone and David L. Kurtz, copyright © 1986 by The Dryden Press. Reprinted by permission of the publisher.

Page 43, 5: Adapted from Halbran, Jack, and George L. Frunzi, *Supervision, The Art of Management*, 2nd Edition. Englewood Cliffs, NJ: Prentice-Hall, © 1986, p. 23. Reprinted by permission.

Page 43, 6: Johnson, H. Webster, and A. J. Faria, *Creative Selling*, 4th Edition. Cincinnati: South-Western Publishing Company, 1987, p. 20.

Page 43, 7: Excerpts from *Management Concepts and Applications*, 2nd Edition by Leon Megginsen, Donald Mosely, and Paul H. Pietri, Jr. Copyright © 1986 by Harper and Row, Publishers, Inc. Reprinted by permission of the publisher.

Page 44, 8: Seitel, Fraser P., *The Practice of Public Relations*, 3rd Edition. Columbus, OH: Merrill Publishing Company, 1987, p. 148.

Page 44, 9: Waltz, Jon R., *Introduction to Criminal Evidence*, 2nd Edition. Chicago: Nelson-Hall, 1985, p. 12.

Page 44, 10: Rader, M. H., and Linda A. Kurth, *Business Communication for the Computer Age*. Cincinnati: South-Western Publishing Co., 1988, p. 136.

Chapter Four

Page 50, Sample A: American Academy of Orthopaedic Surgeons, *Emergency Care and Transportation of the Sick and Injured*, Third Edition. Chicago: American Academy of Orthopaedic Surgeons, 1981, p. 211.

Page 50, Sample B: Adapted from Huffman, Edna K., *Medical Record Management*. Berwyn, IL: Physician's Record Company, 1985, p. 236.

SAMPLE PRACTICE—IDENTIFYING IMPLIED MAIN IDEAS IN PARAGRAPHS

Page 52, 1: Joseph, Marjorie L., *Essentials of Textiles*, 4th Edition. New York: Holt, Rinehart and Winston, Inc., 1988, p. 74.

Page 52, 2: Author Unknown, "Building the High Tech Business: Positioning for Growth, Profitability, and Success," No Publisher, 1988, p. 11.

Page 53, 3: McCormac, Jack C., *Surveying Fundamentals*, © 1983, p. 3. Reprinted by permission of Prentice-Hall, Inc., Englewood Cliffs, NJ.

Page 53, 4: Pride, William, Robert Hughes, and Jack Kapoor, *Business*, 2nd Edition. Copyright © 1988 by Houghton-Mifflin, Company. Used with permission.

Page 54, 5: Adapted from Kolasa, Blain J., and Bernadine Meyer, *The American Legal System*. Englewood Cliffs, NJ: Prentice-Hall, Inc., 1987, p. 55.

SKILL DEVELOPMENT EXERCISE 4-1

Page 57, 1: Johnson, H. Webster, and A. J. Faria, *Creative Selling*, 4th Edition. Cincinnati, OH: South-Western Publishing Company, 1987, p. 267.

Page 57, 2: Dennis, Marshall W., *Mortgage Lending Fundamentals and Practices*, 2nd Edition. Reston, VA: Reston Publishing Company, 1983, p. 18.

Page 58, 3: Bruce Harwood, *Real Estate Principles*, 4th Edition, © 1986, p. 15. Reprinted by permission of Prentice-Hall, Inc., Englewood Cliffs, NJ.

Page 58, 4: Mathis, Robert L., and John H. Jackson, *Personnel—Human Resource*, 4th Edition. St. Paul: West Publishing Co., 1982, p. 237.

Page 59, 5: Hackney/Cormier, *Counseling Strategies and Interventions*. © 1988, p. 158. Reprinted by permission of Prentice-Hall, Inc., Englewood Cliffs, NJ.

Page 59, 6: Hackney/Cormier, *Counseling Strategies and Interventions*. © 1988, p. 158. Reprinted by permission of Prentice-Hall, Inc., Englewood Cliffs, NJ.

Page 59, 7: Watson, Don A., *Construction Materials and Processes*, 3rd Edition. New York: McGraw Hill Book Company, 1986, p. 37.

Page 60, 8: Ruff, Laura, and Mary K. Weitzer, *Understanding and Using MS DOS/PC DOS*. St. Paul: West Publishing Company, 1986, p. 84.

Page 60, 9: "Women Business Owners: Selling to Federal Government." Interagency Committee on Women's Business Enterprise, U.S. Small Business Administration, Office of Women's Ownership, 1984, p. 7.

Page 61, 10: Malamed, Stanley F., *Handbook of Medical Emergencies in the Dental Office*, 3rd Edition. St. Louis: C. V. Mosby Company, 1987, p. 1.

SKILL DEVELOPMENT EXERCISE 4-2

Page 63, 1: Excerpts from *Management Concepts and Applications,* 2nd Edition by Leon Megginsen, Donald Mosely, and Paul H. Pietri, Jr. Copyright © 1986 by Harper and Row, Publishers, Inc. Reprinted by permission of the publisher.

Page 63, 2: Adapted from *Mediamerica,* 4th Edition, by Edward Jay Whetmore. © 1989 by Wadsworth, Inc. Used with permission of the publisher.

Page 64, 3: Sirota, David, *Essentials of Real Estate Investment,* 3rd Edition. Chicago: Real Estate Education Company (Division of Longman Financial Service Institute, Inc.), 1988, p. 25.

Page 64, 4: Excerpt from *Contemporary Marketing,* Second Edition by Louis E. Boone and David L. Kurtz, copyright © 1977 by the Dryden Press, reprinted by permission of the publisher.

Page 64, 5: Halloran, Jack, and George L. Frunzi, *Supervision, The Art of Management,* 2nd Edition. Englewood Cliffs, NJ: Prentice-Hall, © 1986, p. 28. Reprinted by permission.

Page 65, 6: Porter, Kent, *Beginning With BASIC—An Introduction to Computer Programming.* New York: Plume Books, 1984, p. 5.

Page 65, 7: Adapted from Halloran, Jack, and George L. Frunzi, *Supervision, The Art of Management,* 2nd Edition. Englewood Cliffs, NJ: Prentice-Hall, © 1986, p. 29. Reprinted by permission.

Page 65, 8: Adapted from Carlson, Ronald L., *Criminal Justice Procedures,* 3rd Edition. Cincinnati, OH: Anderson Publishing Company, 1978, p. 71.

Page 66, 9: Adapted from "Automation of America's Offices," Congress of the United States, Office of Technology Assessment. Washington, D.C., p. 197.

Page 66, 10: Norris, Eileen, "Fingerhut Gives Customers Credit," *Advertising Age,* March 6, 1986, p. 15.

Chapter Five

Page 71, Sample A: Reprinted with permission of Macmillan Publishing Company from *Retail Management: A Strategic Approach,* 3rd Edition by Barry Berman and Joel R. Evans. Copyright © 1986 by Macmillan Publishing Company.

Page 72, Sample B: Adapted from Kolasa, Blain J., and Bernadine Meyer, *The American Legal System.* Englewood Cliffs, NJ: Prentice-Hall, Inc., 1987, p. 55.

Page 73, Sample C: Excerpts from *Management Concepts and Applications,* 2nd Edition by Leon Megginsen, Donald Mosely and Paul H. Pietri, Jr. Copyright © 1986 by Harper and Row, Publishers, Inc. Reprinted by permission of the publisher.

Page 74, Sample D: American Academy of Orthopaedic Surgeons, *Emergency Care and Transportation of the Sick and Injured,* Third Edition. Chicago: American Academy of Orthopaedic Surgeons, 1981, p. 112.

Page 75, Sample E: Watson, Don A., *Construction Materials and Processes,* 3rd Edition. New York: McGraw Hill Book Company, 1986, p. 37.

Page 76, Sample F: Author Unknown, *Women's Handbook—How the SBA Can Help You Go Into Business.* Washington, D.C.: Prepared by the Office of Management Assistance, U.S. Small Business Administration, Undated, p. 40.

Page 77, Sample G: Johnson, H. Webster, and A. J. Faria, *Creative Selling,* 4th Edition. Cincinnati: South-Western Publishing Company, 1987, p. 18.

SAMPLE PRACTICE: SELECTING DETAILS THAT SUPPORT THE MAIN IDEA

Page 78, 1: Author unknown, "A Guide to Business Credit and the Equal Opportunity Act." Washington, D.C.: Board of Governors of the Federal Reserve System, no date, no page.

Page 78, 2: Adapted from Joseph, Marjorie L., *Essentials of Textiles,* 4th Edition. New York: Holt, Rinehart and Winston, Inc., 1988, p. 74.

Page 79, 3: Adapted from: Author Unknown, "The 1988–89 Job Outlook," *Occupation Outlook Quarterly.* Washington, D.C.: Bureau of Labor Statistics, U.S. Department of Labor, Spring 1988, Volume 32 #1, p. 6.

Page 80, 4: Adapted from: Author Unknown, *Opportunity 2000, Creative Affirmative Action— Strategies For A Changing Workplace.* Washington, D.C.: U.S. Department of Labor, September, 1988.

Page 83, 5: Adapted from: Author Unknown, "Automation of America's Offices," Washington, D.C.: Congress of U.S., Office of Technology Assessment, undated, unpaged.

SKILL DEVELOPMENT EXERCISE 5-1

Page 83, 1: Halloran, Jack, and George L. Frunzi, *Supervision, The Art of Management,* 2nd Edition. Englewood Cliffs, NJ: Prentice-Hall, 1986, p. 28.

Page 84, 2: Ruff, Laura, and Mary K. Weitzer, *Understanding and Using MS DOS/PC DOS.* St. Paul: West Publishing Company, 1986, p. 84.

Page 84, 3: Mathis, Robert L., and John H. Jackson, *Personnel—Human Resource Management,* 4th Edition. St. Paul: West Publishing Company, 1982, p. 237.

Page 85, 4: Stone, Elaine, *Fashion Merchandising, An Introduction,* 4th Edition. New York: McGraw-Hill Book Company, 1985, p. 62.

Page 85, 5: Excerpt from *Contemporary Marketing,* Fifth Edition by Louis E. Boone and David L. Kurtz, copyright © 1986 by The Dryden Press. Reprinted by permission of the publisher.

Page 86, 6: McCormac, Jack C., *Surveying Fundamentals.* © 1983, p. 3. Reprinted by permission of Prentice-Hall, Englewood Cliffs, NJ.

Page 86, 7: Norris, Eileen, "Fingerhut Gives Customers Credit." *Advertising Age,* March 6, 1986, p. 15.

Page 86, 8: Adapted from Johnson, H. Webster, and A. J. Faria, *Creative Selling,* 4th Edition. Cincinnati, Ohio: South-Western Publishing Company, 1987, p. 20.

Page 87, 9: Porter, Kent, *Beginning with BASIC—An Introduction to Computer Programming.* New York: Plume Books, 1984, p. 5.

Page 87, 10: Waltz, Jon R., *Introduction to Criminal Evidence,* 2nd Edition. Chicago: Nelson-Hall, 1985, p. 12.

SKILL DEVELOPMENT EXERCISE 5-2

Page 89, 1: Reprinted with permission of Macmillan Publishing Company from *Retail Management: A Strategic Approach,* 3rd Edition by Barry Berman and Joel R. Evans. Copyright © 1986 by Macmillan Publishing Company.

Page 89, 2: Shrader, Robert L., *Electronic Communication,* 5th Edition. New York: McGraw-Hill Book Company, 1985, p. 686.

Page 90, 3: From *Economics,* Fourth Edition by James D. Gwartney and Richard L. Stroup, copyright © 1982 Harcourt Brace Jovanovich, Inc. Reprinted by permission of the publisher.

Page 90, 4: Reprinted with permission of Macmillan Publishing Company from *Engineering,* 5th Edition by George C. Beakley, Donovan L. Evans, and John Bertrand Keats. Copyright © by George Beakley.

Page 91, 5: Adapted from *Mediamerica,* 4th Edition by Edward Jay Whetmore. © 1989 by Wadsworth, Inc. Used with permission of the publisher.

Page 91, 6: Adapted from Oglesby, Clarkson H., *Highway Engineering.* New York: John Wiley & Sons, Inc., 1982, p. 60.

Page 92, 7: Adapted from Grant/Murray/David Bergeron, *Emergency Care,* 4th Edition Revised, © 1989, p. 9. Reprinted by permission of Prentice-Hall, Inc., Englewood Cliffs, NJ.

Page 92, 8: Adapted from Skidmore, Rex A., Milton G. Thackeray, and O. William Farley, *Introduction to Social Work,* 4th Edition. Englewood Cliffs, NJ: Prentice-Hall, Inc., 1988, p. 39.

Page 93, 9: Bittner, John, *Broadcasting—An Introduction.* Englewood Cliffs, NJ: Prentice-Hall, Inc., 1980, p. 247.

Page 94, 10: Mathis, Robert L., and John H. Jackson, *Personnel—Human Resource Management,* 4th Edition. St. Paul: Western Publishing Company, 1982, p. 72.

Chapter Six

Page 99, Sample A: Poe, Roy W., and Rosemary T. Fruehling, *Business Communication: A Problem-Solving Approach,* 2nd Edition. New York: McGraw-Hill Book Company, 1984, p. 4.

Page 100, Sample B: McCormac, Jack C., *Surveying Fundamentals.* © 1983, p. 7, 8. Reprinted by permission of Prentice-Hall, Englewood Cliffs, NJ.

Page 101, Sample C: International Fire Service Training Association, *Introduction to Fire Apparatus Practices,* Sixth Edition. Oklahoma: Fire Protection Publications, Oklahoma State University, 1980, pp. 7, 8.

SAMPLE PRACTICE: IDENTIFYING MAIN IDEAS IN SELECTIONS

Page 102, 1: Krefetz, Gerald, and Gittleman Film Associates, *More Than a Dream: Being Your Own Boss.* New York: American Management Associations, U.S. Department of Labor, Employment Training Administration, 1980, unpaged.

Page 103, 2: Watson, Don A., *Construction Materials And Processes*, 3rd Edition. New York: McGraw-Hill Book Company (Gregg Division), 1986, p. 63.

Page 104, 3: Adapted from: Author Unknown, "The State of Small Business: A Report of the President Transmitted to the Congress," Washington, D.C.: U.S. Government Printing Office, 1987, p. xxi.

Page 105, 4: Brown, Walter C., *Blueprint Reading for Construction*. South Holland, IL: The Goodheart-Willcox Company, Inc., 1987, p. 244.

Page 106, 5: Pride, William, Robert Hughes, and Jack Kapoor, *Business*, 2nd Edition. Copyright © 1988 by Houghton Mifflin Company. Used with permission.

Page 110, Sample D: Poe, Roy W., and Rosemary T. Fruehling, *Business Communication: A Problem-Solving Approach*, 2nd Edition. New York: McGraw-Hill Book Company, 1984, p. 4.

Page 111, Sample E: McCormac, Jack C., *Surveying Fundamentals*. © 1983, pp. 7, 8. Reprinted by permission of Prentice-Hall, Englewood Cliffs, NJ.

Page 112, Sample F: International Fire Service Training Association, *Introduction to Fire Apparatus Practices*, Sixth Edition. Oklahoma: Fire Protection Publications, Oklahoma State University, 1980, pp. 7, 8.

SKILL DEVELOPMENT EXERCISE 6

Page 119, 1: Stoltenber, John, "How to Use a Microphone Well," *Working Woman*, February, 1986, p. 79. Reprinted with permission from *Working Woman* magazine. Copyright © 1986 by Working Woman, Inc.

Page 120, 2: Edwards, Don James, and Lynn Thorne, *College Accounting Fundamentals*, 2nd Edition. Homewood, IL: Richard D. Irwin, Inc., 1986, pp. 6, 7.

Page 121, 3: Adapted from: Author Unknown, *Technology and the American Economic Transition—Choices for the Future*. Washington, D.C.: Congress of the U.S., Office of Technology Assessment, May, 1988, pp. 22, 23.

Page 122, 4: Excerpt from *Contemporary Marketing*, 5th Edition by Louis E. Boone and David L. Kurtz, copyright © 1986 by the Dryden Press, reprinted by permission of the publisher.

Page 123, 5: Adapted from Bovée, Courtland L., and William F. Arens, *Contemporary Advertising*, 2nd Edition. Homewood, IL: Irwin Publishing Company, 1986, pp. 79–81.

Chapter Seven

Page 129, Sample A: "Employee Benefits in Medium and Large Firms 1986." U.S. Department of Labor, Bureau of Labor Statistics, June 1987, p. 29.

Page 132, Sample B: "Handbook of Labor Statistics." U.S. Department of Labor, Bureau of Labor Statistics, 1985.

Page 134, Sample C: "Budget of U.S. Government, Fiscal Year 1990." Executive Office of the President of the United States. Washington, D.C.: U.S. Government Printing Office.

SAMPLE PRACTICE: ANALYZING GRAPHS

Page 136, Line Graph: "The Condition of Education." U.S. Department of Education, Center for Education Statistics, Washington, D.C.: U.S. Government Printing Office, 1986, Table 2-3.

Page 138, Bar Graph: "Employment and Earnings," *Workforce 2000—Work and Workers of the 21st Century*. U.S. Bureau of Labor Statistics, January 1987, p. 22.

Page 140, Circle Graph: Text from *Economics*, Fourth Edition by James D. Gwartney and Richard L. Stroup, copyright © 1982 Harcourt Brace Jovanovich, Inc. Reprinted by permission of the publisher. Graph from "Monthly Labor Review," U.S. Department of Labor, 1986.

SKILL DEVELOPMENT EXERCISE 7-1

Page 145, Line Graph: Adapted from Shank, Susan E., "Women and the Labor Market: The Link Grows Stronger." *Labor Monthly Review*, U.S. Department of Labor, March 1988, pp. 3,5.

Page 147, Bar Graph: "Economic Report of the President, Transmitted to Congress." Washington, D.C.: U.S. Government Printing Office, 1989, p. 135.

Page 149, Circle Graph: "Monthly Labor Review," U.S. Department of Labor, Bureau of Labor Statistics, June 1988, p. 5.

Page 153, Sample D—Table with text: "U.S. Industrial Outlook," 1988.

Page 155, Sample E—Flowchart with text: Blanchard, Robert E., *Introduction to the Administration of Justice*. New York: John Wiley & Sons, Inc., 1975, pp. 153, 154.

Page 157, Sample F—Diagram without text: "Current Business Reports, Monthly Retail Trade—Sales and Inventory." U.S. Department of Commerce, Bureau of the Census, April 1986.

SAMPLE PRACTICE: ANALYZING TABLES, FLOWCHARTS, DIAGRAMS

Page 159, Table: "Employee Cost Indexes and Levels 1975–1988." U.S. Bureau of Labor Statistics, December 1988, Bulletin 2319, p. 43.

Page 161, Flowchart: "Women Business Owners: Selling to Federal Government." Interagency Committee on Women's Business Enterprise, U.S. Small Business Administration, Office of Women's Ownership, 1984.

Page 164, Diagram: Grant/Murray/Bergeron, *Emergency Care*, 4th Edition Revised. © 1989, pp. 296, 297. Reprinted by permission of Prentice-Hall, Inc., Englewood Cliffs, NJ.

SKILL DEVELOPMENT EXERCISE 7-2

Page 169, Table: "Occupational Outlook Quarterly," U.S. Department of Labor, Bureau of Labor Statistics, Spring 1988, Vol. 32, Number 1, page 8.

Page 171, Flowchart: Sardinas, Joseph L., Jr., *Computing Today—An Introduction to Business Data Processing*. Englewood Cliffs, NJ: Prentice-Hall, Inc. © 1981, p. 371. Reprinted by permission.

Page 173, Diagram: Greene, Charles N., Everett E. Adam, Jr, and Ronald J. Ebert, *Management for Effective Performance*. Englewood Cliffs, NJ: Prentice-Hall, Inc. © 1985, pp. 336, 337. Reprinted by permission.

Chapter Eight

Page 182, Sample B: Stone, Elaine, *Fashion Merchandising—An Introduction*, 4th Edition. New York: Gregg Division, Mc-Graw Hill Book Company, 1985, p. 64.

SAMPLE PRACTICE: MAPPING PARAGRAPHS

Page 184, 1: Excerpt from *Contemporary Marketing*, 5th Edition by Louis E. Boone and David L. Kurtz, copyright© 1986 by the Dryden Press, reprinted by permission of the publisher.

Page 185, 2: Adapted from Grant/Murray/Bergeron, *Emergency Care*, 4th Edition Revised. © 1989, p. 98. Reprinted by permission of Prentice-Hall, Inc., Englewood Cliffs, N.J.

Page 186, 3: Johnson, H. Webster, and A. J. Faria, *Creative Selling*, 4th Edition. Cincinnati, Ohio: South-Western Publishing Company, 1987, p. 13.

SKILL DEVELOPMENT EXERCISE 8-1

Page 191, 1: Edwards, Don James, and Lynn Thorne, *College Accounting Fundamentals*, 2nd Edition. Homewood, IL: Richard D. Irwin, Inc., 1986, p. 5.

Page 192, 2: From *Economics*, Fourth Edition by James D. Gwartney and Richard L. Stroup, copyright © 1982 Harcourt Brace Jovanovich, Inc. Reprinted by permission of the publisher.

Page 193, 3: Skidmore, Rex A., Milton G. Thackery, and O. William Farley, *Introduction to Social Work*, 4th Edition. Englewood Cliffs, NJ: Prentice Hall, Inc., 1988, p. 7.

Page 194, 4: Gross, Lynne S., *See/Hear—An Introduction to Broadcasting*. Dubuque, IA: Wm. C. Brown Company Publishers, 1979, p. 253.

Page 195, 5: Mathis, Robert L., and John H. Jackson, *Personnel—Human Resources Management*, 4th Edition. St. Paul: West Publishing Company, 1982, p. 165.

Page 199, Sample D: Rosch, Paul J., and Kenneth R. Pelletier, "Designing Worksite Stress Management Programs," *Stress Management in Work Settings*. Washington, D.C.: U.S. Department of Health and Human Services, Centers for Disease Control, National Institute for Occupational Safety and Health, May 1987, p. 78.

SAMPLE PRACTICE: MAPPING SELECTIONS

Page 200, 1: Sirota, David, *Essentials of Real Estate Investment*, 3rd Edition. Chicago: Real Estate Education Company, Division of Longman Financial Services Institute, Inc., 1988, p. 22.

Page 202, 2: Needles, Belvard E., Henry R. Anderson, and James C. Caldwell, *Principles of Accounting*, 3rd Edition. Copyright © 1987 by Houghton Mifflin Company. Used with permission.

SKILL DEVELOPMENT EXERCISE 8-2

Page 207, 1: Adapted from Steinhoff, Dan, *Small Business Management Fundamentals.* New York: Mc-Graw Hill, Inc., 1978, pp. 108–111.

Page 208, 2: Adapted from Grant/Murray/Bergeron, *Emergency Care*, 4th Edition Revised. © 1989, p. 17. Reprinted by permission of Prentice-Hall, Inc., Englewood Cliffs, NJ.

Page 210, 3: Mathis, Robert L., and John H. Jackson, *Personnel—Human Resources Management,* 4th Edition. St. Paul: West Publishing Company, 1982, pp. 73, 74.

Page 212, 4: Carlson, Ronald L., *Criminal Justice Procedures*, 3rd Edition. Cincinnati, OH: Anderson Publishing Company, 1978, pp. 80, 81.

Page 214, 5: Naisbitt, John and Jerry Kline, "Careers of the Future," *Success*, January/February, 1987, p. 12. (The Naisbitt Group is located at 1850 K St., N.W., Ste. 1000, Washington, D.C. 20006)

Chapter Nine

Page 221, Data Processing Chart: Adapted by Stanley Goins from information in Parker, Charles S., *Understanding Computers and Data Processing: Today and Tomorrow with BASIC.* New York: Holt, Rinehart, and Winston, CBS College Publishing, 1984, pp. 319–331.

Page 223, Sample B: Kratcoski/Kratcoski, *Juvenile Delinquency*, 2/E. pp. 6, 7. Reprinted by permission of Prentice-Hall, Inc., Englewood Cliffs, NJ.

SAMPLE PRACTICE: CHARTING PARAGRAPHS

Page 225, 1: Excerpt from *Contemporary Marketing*, Fifth Edition by Louis E. Boone and David L. Kurtz, copyright © 1986 by The Dryden Press. Reprinted by permission of the publisher.

Page 226, 2: Roblee, Charles L., Allen J. McKechnie, and William Lundy, *The Investigation of Fires*, Second Edition. Englewood Cliffs, NJ: A Brady Book, Prentice-Hall, p. 123.

Page 227, 3: Thompson, *Macro-Economics*. Reading, MA: Addison-Wesley Publishing Company. 1988, p. 7.

SKILL PRACTICE 9-1

Page 231, 1: Excerpt from *Contemporary Marketing*, Fifth Edition by Louis E. Boone and David L. Kurtz, copyright © 1986 by The Dryden Press. Reprinted by permission of the publisher.

Page 232, 2: "Women and the Labor Market: the Link Grows Stronger," *Monthly Labor Review*, March 1988, page 5.

Page 233, 3: Bruce Harwood, *Real Estate Principles*, 4th Edition, © 1986, p. 17. Reprinted by permission of Prentice-Hall, Englewood Cliffs, NJ.

Page 234, 4: Inciardi, James A., *Criminal Justice*. Orlando, FL: Harcourt Brace Jovanovich, 1987, p. 50.

Page 235, 5: Huffman, Edna K., *Medical Record Management*. Berwyn, IL: Physicians' Record Company, 1985, p. 101.

Page 238, Sample C: Awad, Elias M., *Systems Analysis and Design*, Second Edition. Homewood, IL: Richard D. Irwin, Inc., 1985, p. 23.

SAMPLE PRACTICE: CHARTING SELECTIONS

Page 240, 1: Watson, Don A., *Construction Materials and Processes*. New York: McGraw-Hill Book Company, 1986, p. 486.

Page 241, 2: Adapted from Seitel, Fraser, *The Practice of Public Relations*, 3rd Edition. Columbus, OH: Merrill Publishing Company, Bell and Howell Information Company, 1987, pp. 26, 27.

SKILL DEVELOPMENT EXERCISE 9-2

Page 247, 1: Watson, Don A., *Construction Materials and Processes*. New York: McGraw-Hill Book Company, 1986, p. 323.

Page 248, 2: Good, L. Steven, and Terry M. Whalen, "Real Estate Auctions Benefit Buyers, Sellers," *Small Business Report*, July 1988, p. 50.

Page 250, 3: Adapted from Grant/Murray/Bergeron, *Emergency Care*, 4th Edition Revised. © 1989, p. 421. Reprinted by permission of Prentice-Hall, Inc., Englewood Cliffs, NJ.

Page 251, 4: Muller, Edward J., *Architectural Drawing and Light Construction*, Third Edition. Englewood Cliffs, NJ: Prentice-Hall, Inc., p. 258 © 1985. Reprinted by permission.

Page 253, 5: "The Vital Few and Other Great Management Ideas," Auren Uris, © 1986 John Wiley & Sons. Reprinted by permission of John Wiley & Sons, Inc.

Chapter Ten

Page 262, Sample A: Edwards, James Don, and Lynne Thorne, *College Accounting Fundamentals*, 2nd Edition. Homewood, IL: Richard D. Irwin, Inc., 1986, p. 4.

Page 263, Sample B: Waltz, Jon R., *Introduction to Criminal Evidence*, 2nd Edition. Chicago: Nelson-Hall, 1985, p. 9.

SAMPLE PRACTICE: SUMMARIZING PARAGRAPHS

Page 265, 1: Reprinted with permission of Macmillan Publishing Company from *Engineering* 5th Edition by George C. Beakley, L. Evans Donovan, and John Bertrand Keats. Copyright © 1986 by George Beakley.

Page 265, 2: McCormac, Jack C., *Surveying Fundamentals.* © 1983, p. 1. Reprinted by permission of Prentice-Hall, Englewood Cliffs, NJ.

Page 265, 3: "Technical Change and Its Labor Impact in Four Industries." U.S. Department of Labor, Bureau of Labor Statistics. Washington, D.C.: U.S. Government Printing Office, December 1988, Bulletin 2314, p. 31.

Page 266, 4: Reprinted with permission of Macmillan Publishing. Company from *Retail Management: A Strategic Approach*, 3rd Edition by Barry Berman and Joel R. Evans. Copyright © 1986 by Macmillan Publishing Company.

Page 267, 5: Congress of the U.S., "Automation of America's Offices." Washington, D.C.: Office of Technology Assessment, p. 196.

SKILL DEVELOPMENT EXERCISE 10-1

Page 271, 1: Halloran, Jack, and George L. Frunzi, *Supervision—The Art of Management*, 2nd Edition. Englewood Cliffs, NJ: Prentice-Hall, © 1986, p. 357. Reprinted by permission.

Page 271, 2: Giesecke, Mitchell, and Spencer Hill Dygdon, *Technical Drawing*. New York: Macmillan Publishing, 1980, p. 164.

Page 272, 3: Soll, Harriet Premack, *Women's Handbook—How SBA Can Help You Go Into Business*. Washington, D.C.: Office of Management Assistance, U.S. Small Business Administration, Undated, p. 3.

Page 272, 4: Hamilton, Eva May Nunelly, Eleanor Noss Whitney, and Frances Sienkiewicz, *Nutrition Concepts and Controversies*, Third Edition. St. Paul: West Publishing Company, 1985, pp. 78, 79.

Page 273, 5: Johnson, Mina A., and Norman F. Kallaus, *Records Management*, 3rd Edition. Cincinnati, OH: South-Western Publishing Company, 1982, p. 3.

Page 271, Sample C: Poe, Roy W., and Rosemary T. Frueling, *Business Communication: A Problem-Solving Approach*, 2nd Edition. New York: McGraw-Hill Book Company, 1984, p. 4.

Page 277, Sample D: Rosch, Paul J., and Kenneth R. Pelletier, "Designing Worksite Stress Management Programs," *Stress Management in Work Settings*. Washington, D.C.: U.S. Department of Health and Human Services, Centers for Disease Control, National Institute for Occupational Safety and Health, May 1987, p. 78.

Page 279, Sample E: Awad, Elias M., *Systems Analysis and Design*, Second Edition. Homewood, IL: Richard D. Irwin, Inc., 1985, p. 23.

SAMPLE PRACTICE: SUMMARIZING SELECTIONS

Page 281, 1: Mathis, Robert L., and John H. Jackson, *Personnel—Human Resources Management*, 4th Edition. St. Paul: West Publishing Company, 1982, pp. 73, 74.

Page 282, 2: Seitel, Fraser, *The Practice of Public Relations*, 3rd Edition. Columbus, OH: Merrill Publishing Company, Bell and Howell Information Company, 1987, pp. 26, 27.

Page 283, 3: Watson, Don A., *Construction Materials and Processes*, 3rd Edition. New York: McGraw-Hill Book Company (Gregg Division), 1986, p. 63.

SKILL DEVELOPMENT EXERCISE 10-2

Page 285, 1: Adapted from Krefetz, Gerald, and Gittleman Film Associates, "More Than a Dream: Being Your Own Boss." U.S. Department of Labor, Employment and Training Administration. New York, American Management Associations, 1980, unpaged.

Page 286, 2: Author unknown, "Group Decision Making—Approaches to Problem Solving," *Small Business Report*, July, 1988, p. 31.

Page 287, 3: Adapted from: Author unknown, "U.S. Industrial Outlook 1988—Medical Instruments." Washington, D.C.: U.S. Department of Commerce, 1988, p. 36.

Page 288, 4: Adapted from *Mediamerica*, 4th Edition, by Edward Jay Whetmore. © 1989 by Wadsworth, Inc. Used with permission of the publisher.

Page 289, 5: "The Competitive Edge," U.S. Small Business Administration, Office of Business Development, Washington, D.C., Undated.

Chapter Eleven

SAMPLE PRACTICE: SEPARATING FACT FROM OPINION

Page 295, 3: Adapted from Carlson, Ronald L., *Criminal Justice Procedure*, 3rd Edition. Cincinnati, OH: Anderson Publishing Company, 1978, p. 73.

Page 295, 4: Author unknown, *Automation of America's Offices*. Washington, D.C.: Congress of the United States, Office of Technology Assessment, 1987, p. 37.

SKILL DEVELOPMENT EXERCISE 11-1 PART A

Page 299, 1: Good, Steven L., and Terry M. Whalen, "Real Estate Auctions Benefit Buyers, Sellers," *Small Business Report*, July 1988, p. 50.

Page 299, 2: Author unknown, "Group Decision Making—Approaches to Problem Solving," *Small Business Report*, July 1988, p. 30.

Page 299, 3: Shank, Susan E., "Women and the Labor Market: the Link Grows Stronger," *Monthly Labor Review*. Washington, D.C.: Bureau of Labor Statistics, March 1988, p. 3.

SKILL DEVELOPMENT EXERCISE 11-1 PART B

Page 299, 1: Adapted from Blanchard, Robert E., *Introduction to the Administration of Justice*. New York: John Wiley & Sons, Inc., 1975, p. 113.

Page 299, 2: Edwards, James Don, and Lynn Thorne, *College Accounting Fundamentals*, Second Edition. Homewood, IL: Richard D. Irwin, Inc., 1986, p. 5.

Page 300, 3: Greene, Charles N., Everett E. Adam, Jr., and Ronald J. Ebert, *Management for Effective Performance*. Englewood Cliffs, NJ: Prentice-Hall, Inc., © 1985, pp. 235, 236. Reprinted by permission.

Page 300, 4: Adapted from *Mediamerica*, 4th Edition, by Edward Jay Whetmore. © 1989 by Wadsworth, Inc. Used with permission of the publisher.

Page 300, 5: Hamilton, Eva May Nunelly, Eleanor Noss Whitney, and Frances Sienkiewicz, *Nutrition Concepts and Controversies*, Third Edition. St. Paul: West Publishing Company, 1985, pp. 78, 79.

SKILL DEVELOPMENT EXERCISE 11-1 PART C

Page 301, C: Kriegel, Marilyn Harris, and Robert Kriegel, "How to Master Back-burner Thinking," Working Woman, January 1988, p. 46. Reprinted with permission from *Working Woman*. Copyright 1986 by Working Woman, Inc.

TRANSLATING GOBBLEDYGOOK

Page 319: Lowe, Sam, "Plain English," *Phoenix Gazette*, December 15, 1988, Section B, p. 1.

SAMPLE PRACTICE: TRANSLATING GOBBLEDYGOOK

Page 320, 1: Request for proposals, U.S. Department of Health and Human Services, Administration on Aging, 1990.

Page 321, 3: Shank, Susan E., "Women and the Labor Market: the Link Grows Stronger," *Monthly Labor Review*. Washington, D.C.: Bureau of Labor Statistics, March 1988, p. 3.

SKILL DEVELOPMENT EXERCISE 11-3

Page 324, 2: "Agreement Between United States Postal Service and American Postal Workers Union, AFL-CIO, National Association of Letter Carriers, AFL, CIO," 1984–1987, pp. 70, 71.

Chapter Thirteen

SAMPLE PRACTICE: READING REPORTS

Page 353, Printed with permission of Michael Oliver.

SKILL DEVELOPMENT EXERCISE 13-1

Page 359: Reprinted with the permission of Arthur Andersen & Co. Copyright 1988 Arthur Andersen & Co. All rights reserved.

SAMPLE PRACTICE: READING ARTICLES IN PROFESSIONAL JOURNALS

Page 369: Cornell, Richard D., "Examining Our Telephone Manners," *Supervisory Management*, March 1986, pp. 21–23. Reprinted with permission of the author.

SKILL DEVELOPMENT EXERCISE 13-2

Page 375: Gonzalez, Jose L., "Time Management . . . or Learning How to Say NO," *Management Accounting*, 1987, Volume LXVIII, Number 10.

Chapter One

Using Context Clues

Most professions have their own career-related vocabularies. For example, if you listen carefully to people in a career that is different from yours, you will probably hear them use terms with which you are unfamiliar. In fact, if the speakers use enough of their own career-related terms, you will probably be unable to follow their conversation. It may even sound as though they are speaking a foreign language.

The same thing may happen to you in your own field if spoken or written material includes a number of terms with which you are unfamiliar. If you come into contact with enough unknown specific terms or even the same terms repeated again and again, your comprehension of what you hear or read will be greatly diminished.

What can you do about understanding these unfamiliar career-related terms in your own field as you hear them spoken or when you come across them as you read? You can ignore an unknown term, hoping that it's not really an important one. Obviously, this is a poor idea since such an action seriously affects your ability to understand what is said or written. On the other hand, you can actively look for clues to the meaning of the term. When found and used effectively, such clues enable you to immediately make some sense out of what you hear or read, and you are able to continue listening or reading with adequate comprehension.

Sometimes a speaker or writer is aware of using terms which may prove difficult for the listener or reader, and will provide clues to the term's meaning. These clues are found in the words that surround the unknown term. They may be included in the phrase, sentence, or paragraph in which the term is found. The words surrounding the term are called its **context.** For example, if the term "engine" stands alone, it is not within context. However, when the same term is put into a sentence—"The steam engine was indeed an invention that changed American life"—all of the words around the word "engine" form the context in which it is used. While the context in this case is a sentence, a phrase or an entire paragraph also can be considered as context for a term.

Terms, as used in career-related information, may be single words or several words that are often used together. For example, the two words *disk drive* are usually used together when referring to computers. Thus, for vocabulary development purposes, they are considered to be a term. In printed material, you may find that terms are sometimes *italicized* or presented in **boldface print** to signify that they are important for you to know. This change of type style is the author's way of calling your attention to important terms.

There are several important advantages to being able to recognize and use context clues in both listening and reading situations. First, you will have immediate comprehension of the term and, thus, understand what you are hearing or reading. Second, your interpretation of the term will be specifically related to the field you are hearing or reading about. For example, the term "image" has a number of different meanings. In the dictionary, you may find as many as five meanings for this term—not one of which is related to a specific profession. Each of the following two definitions of "image" is found in context related to a specific occupation. Note how different these definitions are and how context clues can be of great value to you when you are trying to understand career-related information.

1. RETAIL MANAGEMENT: *Image* refers to how a [retail] firm is viewed by consumers and others.

2. INTERIOR DESIGN: During the design process, the planner must develop a design theme that will reflect the aims and goals of the organization. This theme is the corporate or client *image*, and the designer physically reflects this image in the quality and style of the environment.

When you compare these two definitions of the term "image," you find that those in retail management view image as something projected within a retail firm, while those in interior design view an image as something which must be created by the designer.

As mentioned before, speakers or authors sometimes realize that the listener or reader may be unfamiliar with terms they are using. Therefore, they may include any one of a number of context clues to help you define such terms immediately. When you encounter unknown terms as you read or listen, ask yourself this very important question: **Are there context clues to help me define this term?** Then be on the lookout for context clues.

Three kinds of clues which are often used in the term's context can aid listeners or readers. First, the definition of the term may be found in context. Second, there may be clues which give you examples of the term. Finally, the author or speaker may provide clues which explain the term to you. Examine the following samples for context clues which have been included by various authors as aids to interpreting the italicized terms.

SAMPLE A: Definition Clue

The actual **definition** of the term may be given in context. You need only listen or read carefully to locate it. Sometimes a speaker or author may simply state the definition beginning with "a *** is . . .," or may use other words that tell you the term is about to be defined or has just been defined for you. An illustration of this kind of definition clue in context is found in the following sentence:

> The rights of a widow in the property of her deceased husband are called *dower rights.* . . .

You need only read the sentence carefully to be able to define dower rights as the rights of a widow in the property of her deceased husband.

In other written material, you may find that the definition of a term is separated from the rest of the information by the use of commas, dashes, or parentheses. In the following sample of a definition clue, note that the author of an accounting textbook has defined two important kinds of accounting for you—management and governmental. In this case, dashes have been used to separate the definitions from the actual terms.

> . . .Two other important areas of accounting are *management accounting*—the accumulation and presentation of information for internal management purposes—and *governmental accounting*—the accumulation and presentation of information about the financial affairs of government agencies.

SAMPLE B: Example Clue

You may be given an **example** or examples of the unknown term. You must analyze the example(s), looking for a common characteristic. When you have determined what the examples have in common, you must apply this to interpreting the unknown term. In the following sample, note that missionary selling has not been directly defined for you.

> *Missionary selling* is not tied directly to a specific sale. The medical detail salesperson, one type of missionary seller, calls on doctors. The medical detailers do not sell—they describe products, their advantages, uses, research conducted, and they leave samples. It is hoped that doctors will prescribe these products for their patients and that druggists will buy and stock the products.

The author of this material has provided examples of the characteristics of missionary selling as done by the medical detail salesperson. Picture what this one type of missionary seller does with potential buyers. Next, generalize the results of the kinds of activities that are described. Missionary selling can then be defined as the kinds of activities which involve creating interest in new products and producing goodwill which will ultimately result in sales.

SAMPLE C: Explanation Clue

A speaker or author may give you an **explanation** of an unfamiliar term. By analyzing the explanation carefully, you are able to put together enough information to understand that term. Note, for example, that the author of the following material has not specifically defined the italicized term but provides enough information for you to picture in your mind what the term means.

> Different types of contracts are used when purchasing large quantities of food for commercial purposes. One type of contract, the *fixed price contract,* is most often used by very large (typically governmental) organizations. With this method, written specifications about the food are given to the potential supplier. The potential supplier then submits sealed bids (bids which will be opened at a precise time in the presence of all the bidders). The supplier who can provide the specified food at the lowest cost to the organization usually is awarded the contract.

If you read the sample material carefully, you find that the author has explained what a *fixed price contract* is. You can now mentally picture what this kind of contract involves. A *fixed price contract* is used for large food purchases and involves sealed bids from the potential supplier based on specifications about the food. The contract goes to the lowest bidder.

At times, speakers or writers may use more than one kind of context clue to aid you in term interpretation. For instance, a term may be defined and then explained, or it may be defined and then you may be provided with examples of the term to aid you in your comprehension of it.

When you use context clues as aids to defining an unknown term, you can easily check the appropriateness of your definition immediately. Use your definition in place of the term in its original context; the definition must make sense in that context.

For obvious practical reasons, the samples of context clues, the Sample Practice, and the Skill Development Exercise in this chapter are all presented in written materials. However, if you are alert to the possibility of context clues, it makes little difference whether information is encountered in spoken or written form. Simply apply the analytical skills required to identify clues in written context to what you hear. In other words, become a very careful listener as well as a very careful reader.

SAMPLE PRACTICE
Using Context Clues

> DIRECTIONS: *Examine the following samples of materials which include context clues to help you understand the italicized terms. Look carefully for context clues that provide a definition, example(s), or an explanation of the italicized term. Write your definition and the kind of clue in context that helped to define the term. Check your definition by using it in place of the italicized term; it must make sense.*

1.   *Technophobia*, or fear of technology, is becoming a commonplace communication barrier. Although technophobia may be associated with all kinds of technology, we are seeing its growing occurrence with the introduction of computers.

DEFINITION: _____

CLUE: _____

2.   Until the introduction of technology into most counselor training programs, the most frequent form of supervision was for the counselor to report to the supervisor, either in writing or verbally, what was transpiring in counseling, and for the supervisor to react to this information as presented. This method of supervision is called *self-report* because the counselor is in control of what he or she chooses to report about the counseling session or relationship. Self-reporting is still used

in supervision, though not as frequently as it once was, and not as often in the initial stages of counselor training.

DEFINITION: _____

CLUE: _____

3.   Shelf life is the amount of time you can reasonably expect the food product to maintain its quality if proper storage procedures are followed. The growth of spoilage microorganisms can be controlled by *processing* (canning, drying, salting, freezing, etc.), but for unprocessed foods, we must rely upon temperature controls and good sanitation.

DEFINITION: _____

CLUE: _____

4.   Most advertising relies heavily on copy—the words that make up the headline and message of the ad. People who create these words are called *copywriters.* Their work requires skill since they must be able to condense all that can be said about a product or service into just those points that are important and related to a given advertisement.

DEFINITION: _____

CLUE: _____

5.   Contractors frequently are required to furnish a *performance bond* for each project. This bond is a three-party instrument in which a bonding company (termed "surety") guarantees to the owner that the project will be built by the contractor in accordance with the contract. If for any reason, the contractor becomes unwilling or unable to complete the contract, the surety will take steps to engage another contractor to complete the contract or take such other steps as will be satisfactory to the owner. The cost of a performance bond depends upon the size of the project but will generally be in the range of 1 percent of the total project cost, provided the contractor has a good reputation and can get a performance bond.

DEFINITION: _____

CLUE: _____

Check your answers to the Sample Practice.

Sample Practice Answers

Your definitions do not have to match those given here word-for-word. However, the concepts should be similar and, of course, your definitions must pass the test of making sense when they are used in place of the original italicized words.

1. *technophobia:* fear of technology
   context clue: definition

   (The definition of technophobia is found right in context, separated from it by the use of commas.)

2. *self-report:* the type of supervision in which the counselor reports verbally or in writing to the supervisor, telling what happened in counseling, and the supervisor reacts to this information
   context clue: explanation

   (The author has explained what self-report is in counseling throughout the paragraph rather than stating a clear-cut definition. You must put the information together in order to arrive at an adequate definition.)

3. *processing:* methods of keeping food from spoiling, such as canning, drying, salting, freezing, etc.
   context clue: example

   (The author does not define processing but you get an idea of what is meant by analyzing the common characteristic of each process mentioned. They are all methods of keeping food from spoiling.)

4. *copywriters:* people who create words that make up the headline and message of an ad
   context clue: definition

   (In this case, the definition is not found in a single phrase or sentence. For clarity, the actual definition requires information from both of the first two sentences of the paragraph.)

5. *performance bond:* a three-party instrument in which a bonding company (termed "surety") guarantees to the owner that the project will be built by the contractor in accordance with the contract.
   context clue: definition

   (The italicized term is clearly defined within the context of the paragraph, beginning with "This bond is . . .")

Now go on to Skill Development Exercise 1 on page 9, which will give you additional practice in using context clues as aids to understanding unfamiliar terms.

Next, apply what you have learned about context clues to your own career materials in Skill Application Exercise 1 on page 13. To make this application a practical one, choose terms you really need to define as they appear in context.

Finally, begin to apply what you know about using context clues right here in this textbook. As you are presented with material from various careers, use your skill with context clues to help you understand unfamiliar terms.

SKILL DEVELOPMENT EXERCISE 1
Using Context Clues

DIRECTIONS: Ask **Are there context clues to help me define this term?**
*Use what you know about definition, example, and explanation context clues
to understand each of the italicized terms. Check your definitions by using
them in place of the italicized word. They should make sense in context.*

1.   As you walk through any office and observe carefully, you will
quickly note the great number and variety of records being used and
stored. Think of all the items that can be called office "records"—
papers, financial statements, books, bound reports, magnetic tapes,
photographs, microforms, manuals, works of art, and many more!
All of the activities dealing with the creation of these office records,
their maintenance for active use and in temporary storage, and their
destruction or permanent storage are called *records management.*

records management: _____

_____

2.   During each stage in the development of a retail strategy, management receives signals or cues as to the success of that part of the
strategy. These signals or cues are called *feedback.* Some forms of
positive feedback are increased sales, no problems with the government, employee satisfaction, and status in the community. Some forms
of negative feedback are declining sales, shoplifting, governmental in-
terference, excessive inventories, and consumer complaints.

feedback: _____

_____

3.   The oldest theory of fashion adoption is the *downward-flow theory* (or the "trickle-down theory"). It maintains that in order to be
identified as a true fashion, a style must first be adopted by people at the
top of the social pyramid. The style then gradually wins acceptance at
progressively lower social levels.

downward-flow theory: _____

_____

4.   Nonmonetary release (release that does not involve money) is based upon the defendant living up to specific conditions imposed by the court. Under this approach, the defendant is released on his own *recognizance* (a written promise to appear signed by the defendant under oath) . . .

recognizance: _____

_____

5.   *Investment goods* provide a "flow" of future consumption or productions service. Unlike food or medical services, they are not immediately "used." A house is an investment good because it will provide a stream of services long into the future. Business plants and equipment are investment goods because they, too, will provide productive services in the future. Changes in business inventories are also classed as investment goods, since they will provide future consumer benefits.

investment goods: _____

_____

6.   Lumber which has been individually pretested by nondestructive mechanical means, supplemented by visual grading in order to establish unit working stresses, is classed as *machine stress-related lumber* (MSR). Machines continuously measure strength and elasticity, and each piece is stamped with the proper strength and stiffness value as it leaves the machine.

machine stress-related lumber: _____

_____

7.   The court or jury will examine the facts (for example, as disclosed in notes and correspondence between plaintiff and defendant that covered a period of several weeks, together with the facts disclosed by testimony and exhibits at trial) and the court will apply the same legal principle in both the business law and nonbusiness law cases: to find *mutual assent*, the parties (plaintiff and defendant) must reach an agreement on the same bargain, on the same terms, and at the same time.

mutual assent: _____

_____

8.   Ownership of land normally includes the right to drill for and remove water found below the surface. Where water is not confined to a defined underground waterway, it is known as *percolating water.* In some states a landowner has the right, with neighboring owners, to draw his share of percolating water.

percolating water: _____

_____

9.   Everyone lives in a world of his or her own *stereotypical figures.* Ivy Leaguers, Midwesterners, feminists, bankers, politicians, and thousands of other characterizations cause people to think of certain specific images.

Public images, for example, are typecast regularly. The "dumb blonde," the "bigoted blue-collar worker," and the "shifty used car salesman" are the kinds of stereotypical figures our society—particularly television—perpetuates.

stereotypical figures: _____

_____

10.   *Technical problems* can prevent a message from conveying the intended meaning. If you were in a room talking with friends and a rock band was playing loudly, you might not accurately hear what was said. Likewise, any message can be interrupted by noise before it reaches the receiver. Both noise and physical barriers can be technical problems in oral communication. You cannot always assume that messages sent will be received as intended.

technical problems: _____

_____

SKILL APPLICATION 1
Using Context Clues

DIRECTIONS: Use any of your own career materials such as textbooks, manuals, professional magazines and so on. Find, duplicate, and attach five samples of an author's use of context clues. Underline the term and write its definition based on those context clues.

If all of your items come from one source, just fill in the blanks under the first SOURCE INFORMATION. If you take items from more than one source, fill in information for each item.

SOURCE INFORMATION 1

Title: _____

Author: _____

Place of publication: _____

Publisher: _____

Copyright Date: _____   *Page(s):* _____

SOURCE INFORMATION 2

Title: _____

Author: _____

Place of publication: _____

Publisher: _____

Copyright Date: _____   *Page(s):* _____

SOURCE INFORMATION 3

Title: _____

Author: _____

Place of publication: _____

Publisher: _____

Copyright Date: _____   *Page(s):* _____

SOURCE INFORMATION 4

Title: _____

Author: _____

Place of publication: _____

Publisher: _____

Copyright Date: _____   *Page(s):* _____

SOURCE INFORMATION 5

Title: _____

Author: _____

Place of publication: _____

Publisher: _____

Copyright Date: _____   *Page(s):* _____

Chapter Two

Applying the Professional Vocabulary System

In many cases, defining unfamiliar terms by using clues in context as you did in Chapter One may be sufficient for your immediate comprehension of career-related conversations and written material. Unfortunately, however, terms which are defined using clues in context have a tendency to serve for the moment and then are gone. The next time you see the same term in a different context, chances are that you will have to define it again.

Your own career-related terms are so important that they must become a part of your permanent vocabulary. If you ask yourself the question **Is this term important for me to know?** and the answer is yes, you must make a serious effort to master that term. If the term seems to be repeated often among professionals in your field, that is an indication that the term should be mastered. As was noted in Chapter One, authors frequently call your attention to important terms by having them appear in boldface print or italics. Master these terms!

When you "master" a term, it becomes yours. In other words, you are able to use that term appropriately in conversations, recognize the term when it is spoken by others, recognize and comprehend the term when you read it, and spell the term correctly when you need to use it in your own writing.

There is a system, the **Professional Vocabulary System (PVS)**, which will enable you to develop and extend your vocabulary. You will master terms that you select as being important to know. You can indeed make any term that you have heard or read become yours.

PVS is an economical system for mastering terms in several ways. It saves you time and energy since your time is spent only on terms you need and want to learn. It is also economical money-wise since all you need to effectively apply PVS is an up-to-date dictionary (or a glossary if your printed source has one) and a good supply of 3 × 5 cards.

There are two major parts to PVS. First, you must record information about the specific term on a 3 × 5 card, and second, you must master that information. You will want to record all you need to know about a term on a 3 × 5 card, so do it as soon as you can after you hear the term in conversation or as you encounter the term in written material. Don't wait—you need to work with the term right away so you can make sense out of what you have heard or read.

APPLYING PVS—PART ONE:
RECORDING INFORMATION ON A 3 × 5 CARD

On the front of the card:

1. Write the term you want to master in the middle of a 3 × 5 card. Be sure that the spelling is correct. (The correct spelling may be a problem when you make cards for terms you have heard but not seen. Check the dictionary or check with the person who originally used the term to make sure you are writing it correctly.)

2. Beneath the term, copy the context (phrase or sentence) in which the term appeared. You may use a phrase or a full sentence in which the term appears as context. Keep the context as brief as possible but make sure there is sufficient context to indicate how the term was originally used.

    If you use a phrase as original context, write three dots in front of and after the phrase to indicate that it was actually part of a full sentence.

    Enclosing context in parentheses improves the readability of the front of the card because it separates the term from the context. You now know exactly where context begins and ends.

    When you underline the term in context you draw attention to it within the phrase or sentence. You will find this very helpful when you test the term's definition to see if it makes sense and fits into the grammar of the context.

3. Write the dictionary pronunciation for the term in the upper right-hand corner. Copy the letters and marks very carefully; be sure to show how the term is divided into spoken syllables. (You only need to write the pronunciation if you are not sure how a term should be said correctly.)

On the Back of the Card:

4. Write the term's part of speech in the upper right-hand corner. Knowing if the term is a noun, verb, adjective, or adverb will help you to use the term correctly when speaking or writing.

5. Write the definition of the term. Be sure to select the definition that matches the term's use in context. A good way to check your definition is to insert it in the context you wrote on the front of the 3 × 5 card. The definition should fit in two ways. First, it should make sense in the context, and second, it should fit the grammar of the context.

6. Write your own sentence using the term. This step will give you practice in using the term and is a good way to assure that the term really becomes part of your own vocabulary. Check your sentence by inserting the definition in place of the term; it should make sense.

Make out a separate card for each term. Be sure that all of the information you write on the card is related to the specific term. This means that you must be especially careful about terms that have the same spelling but have more than one meaning, more than one pronunciation, or can be more than one part of speech. For example, the term *minute* can be an adjective that means very tiny or a noun that means one-sixtieth of an hour—i.e., a unit of time. The same spelling is pronounced differently depending upon which *minute* you mean. Your choice of pronunciation, meaning, and part of speech depends on how the term is used in the original context. What you write on the card should pass the test of making sense and fitting in with the grammar of that original context.

A sample 3 × 5 card showing the kind of information to be included and the placement of that information is found on the next page. You can use this sample as a guide when you fill out your own PVS cards.

SAMPLE A: PVS 3 × 5 Card Information

FRONT OF THE CARD

pronunciation
term
(context)

BACK OF THE CARD

part of speech
definition
your own sentence

SAMPLE B: Recording Information on a 3 × 5 Card

A sample 3 × 5 card has been made out for the term italicized in the following paragraph. Note the kind of information included on the card and the placement of that information. The dictionary entry from which the information was taken is also included so that you can refer to it.

In the United States, trade occurs most often between different *components* of the economy, which we can generally class as households (and the individuals within them), business and government. These components interact in a number of different ways. Individuals work for businesses and government. Businesses produce goods and services for households, government, and other businesses. Government taxes households and businesses and provides roads, national defense and laws regulating economic and noneconomic behavior. Viewed as a whole, economic interactions constitute an economic system.

com·po·nent (kəm pō′nənt) *adj.* [L. *componens*, prp. of *componere*, to compose < *com-*, together + *ponere*, to put] serving as one of the parts of a whole; constituent —*n.* **1.** *a)* an element or ingredient *b)* any of the main constituent parts, as of a high-fidelity sound system **2.** any of the elements into which a vector quantity, as force, velocity, etc., may be resolved on analysis —*SYN.* see ELEMENT

FRONT OF THE CARD

kəm pō´ nənts

components

(different <u>components</u> of the economy)

BACK OF THE CARD

noun

parts, elements

The rocket model had so many <u>components</u> that
Henry had to read the directions
very carefully.

In the paragraph used for Sample B, the term *components* is plural in context. Notice how the term, pronunciation, and definition have been adjusted to reflect that plural form. They must all match the use of the term in context. There are two definitions for *component;* one is an adjective and the other a noun. When you try to fit the definition into context, you find that it is the noun form that makes sense: "In the United States, trade occurs most often between different *parts* of the economy." The second term in the definition is "element" and, when used as a plural, also would fit into context. The other term, "ingredient," does not seem to fit so it has not been copied onto the card.

SAMPLE PRACTICE
Applying PVS

DIRECTIONS: Fill out a sample PVS card of your own. Read the following paragraph and make out a card for the italicized term **phenomenon.** *The card and dictionary entry are provided for you following the paragraph.*

There is sometimes such serious conflict within a company that employees are divided into one or more conflicting groups. One suggested way to reduce this conflict is to exchange individual members from one conflicting group with individual members from another group. However, this exchange usually does not work because of one particular *phenomenon*—employees do not change their loyalties. It has been found that such employee exchanges only serve to reinforce members' original attitudes—either positive or negative. The only people who are apt to have a change of attitude are those who were initially neutral. These formerly neutral members usually have such limited influence that they do not bring about any significant reduction of conflict between groups.

phe·nom·e·non (fi näm′ə nän′, -nən) *n., pl.* **-na** (-nə); also, esp. for 3 and usually for 4, **-nons**′ [LL. *phaenomenon* < Gr. *phainomenon*, neut. prp. of *phainesthai*, to appear, akin to *phainein:* see FANTASY] **1.** any fact, circumstance, or experience that is apparent to the senses and that can be scientifically described or appraised, as an eclipse **2.** the appearance or observed features of something experienced as distinguished from reality or the thing in itself **3.** any extremely unusual or extraordinary thing or occurrence **4.** [Colloq.] a person with an extraordinary quality, aptitude, etc.; prodigy

FRONT OF THE CARD

BACK OF THE CARD

Check the information on your card before going to the next part of PVS.

Sample Practice PVS Card

FRONT OF THE CARD

---

fi näm´ ə nan´

phenomenon

(. . . one particular <u>phenomenon</u>—
employees do not change. . .)

BACK OF THE CARD

---

noun

extremely extraordinary
thing or occurrence

your own sentence

Note that a phrase is used as original context and that dots are used to indicate that the phrase was actually part of a full sentence. The context has been enclosed in parentheses to improve the readability of the front of the card since it separates the term from the context. You can tell exactly where context begins and ends.

The term is underlined in context to draw attention to it within the phrase, and this makes it easier to test the definition of *phenomenon* you chose. You need to see if the definition makes sense and fits into the grammar of the context.

There are four definitions for the term *phenomenon*. When you read each definition carefully, it becomes clear that only the fourth definition will fit into context: one particular extremely extraordinary thing—employees do not change.

The sentence using the term is, of course, your own. Check your sentence to be sure that it makes sense when the definition is used in place of the term. (*Example:* Sighting a UFO is a phenomenon, an experience not shared by many people.)

APPLYING PVS—PART TWO: MASTERING INFORMATION ON THE 3 × 5 CARD

In the second part of applying PVS, you actively master the information you have recorded about the term. It is here that you do the majority of the work in the system. You will find that the time and energy invested here really do produce results. You will have terms that are yours; you will feel comfortable with them and, thus, you will be able to use them with ease.

Unlike the typical way of "studying" terms for mastery of their definitions, you don't have long lists of terms to be read over and over again. Instead of this single visual mode of learning, PVS requires you to use three additional kinds of stimuli to master terms: hearing, speaking, and writing. PVS requires writing the term and its definition when you fill in the 3 × 5 card, saying the term using the correct pronunciation, and listening as you say that term while learning it. In addition, you also recite the definition of the term aloud, adding hearing and repeating the definition as well as reading and writing it. Therefore, you are actually exposed to four ways of learning, and you are able to recognize the term when you hear it used by a speaker, or you recognize it in print, and you use it correctly in your own speaking and writing. You have truly mastered the term; it is an important addition to your ever-expanding professional vocabulary.

These steps can help you master the terms on your 3 × 5 cards:

1. Look at the front of the card and pronounce the term correctly.

2. Recite the definition of the term.

3. Check the back of the card to see if the definition you recited is correct.

4. Make two piles of cards. Put all of the cards with definitions that you know in one pile. Put cards with definitions that you don't know or aren't really sure of in the other pile.

5. Go over the cards in the "don't know" pile until you have mastered the definitions of these terms. Then move these cards to the pile of definitions you already know.

6. Review all of the cards frequently to reinforce what you have learned.

As your pile of 3 × 5 cards grows, you should use a file box and either a set of alphabet cards or homemade cards that can be used to separate the terms into categories of your own choosing.

Then file the cards in any of the following ways:

• alphabetical order, generally;

• alphabetical order by chapter in a career-related textbook if you are using PVS in a course;

• alphabetical order by category;

• any other system that makes sense to you.

In other words, the system you use to file your 3 × 5 cards is up to you—just as long as it makes sense to you, fits your specific needs, and provides easy access to terms when you need them. No matter how you file your cards, it soon will become obvious to you that you are developing your own personal dictionary—one which includes career-related terms that are important to you.

Now go on to Skill Development Exercise 2 on page 27, where you will have practice applying PVS to material which has been selected for that purpose. In addition, begin to apply PVS for unknown terms you encounter in this textbook, terms you feel you would like to master and use as part of your vocabulary.

When you apply PVS to terms you choose from your own career materials in Skill Application 2 (page 29), make this application truly practical by asking the vital question: **Is this term important for me to know?** If your answer is yes, apply PVS and begin to compile your own career-related dictionary.

SKILL DEVELOPMENT EXERCISE 2
Professional Vocabulary System

DIRECTIONS: Read the following selection from a criminal justice textbook. Note that some of the italicized terms are specific to that field while others are not. Choose ten of the italicized terms that you do not know. Apply PVS by filling out a 3 × 5 card for each of those terms. Remember to check your definitions by substituting them for the italicized terms. They should make sense in context and match the grammar within the paragraph. Also be sure to check your own sentences to see if they make sense when you insert the definition in place of the term.

All states allow *juveniles* to be tried as adults in criminal courts under certain *circumstances*. Some state juvenile *codes* specify that when a juvenile is accused of a serious *felony* offense, the juvenile court has no *jurisdiction* in the matter. The youth, regardless of age, must be tried in a criminal court.

A juvenile may also be tried in an adult court in cases of "*concurrent* jurisdiction." In such instances, which usually involve serious felonies, the *prosecutor* has the choice of filing charges against a youth in either the juvenile or the adult criminal court.

The *predominant* means by which cases involving juveniles come to adult criminal courts is through *judicial waiver*, or transfer from the juvenile court, which has original jurisdiction. Ten states do not *specify* a lower age limit at which juveniles' cases can be waived to adult courts, but for those states with a lower age limit, this age ranges from 14 to 16.

A well-*publicized* example of a juvenile case transferred to an adult court for trial was that of a 15-year-old charged with the first-degree murder of an elderly woman who had surprised him and another boy robbing her home. They killed her when she threatened to call the police. The boy was tried as an adult and found guilty of first-degree murder, in spite of his *contention* that he suffered from "television *intoxication*" as a result of long *exposure* to violent TV dramas.

1. juveniles
2. circumstances
3. codes
4. felony
5. jurisdiction
6. concurrent
7. prosecutor
8. predominant
9. judicial
10. waiver
11. specify
12. publicized
13. contention
14. intoxication
15. exposure

SKILL APPLICATION 2
Professional Vocabulary System

DIRECTIONS: Apply PVS to terms in your own career material such as textbooks, manuals, professional magazines, and so on. Choose terms that really are important to you.

1. *Make out ten 3 × 5 cards for terms you need to know. These terms may come from your reading in the field or from course lectures. Be sure to check your definitions in the term's context.*

2. *List each of the ten terms below and write its source. If the source is a lecture, indicate it as such. If the term comes from written material, write the title of the material, the author, and the page number where the term was found.*

YOUR PVS TERM: **SOURCE:**

1. _____   _____
                                   _____

2. _____   _____
                                   _____

3. _____   _____
                                   _____

4. _____   _____
                                   _____

5. _____   _____
                                   _____

6. _____   _____
                                   _____

7. _____   _____
                                   _____

8. _____   _____
                                   _____

9. _____   _____
                                   _____

10. _____   _____

Chapter Three

Identifying Stated Main Ideas in Paragraphs

Research on learning tells us that unrelated facts are difficult to remember, while related things or ideas are much easier to understand and retain. For example, think of the difficulty you might have if you tried to remember a randomly arranged list of as many as twenty to thirty different careers. However, if you rearranged that same list of careers into categories such as public service, business, fashion, health, and so on, and placed the items on the list under these categories, you would be surprised at how many careers you could remember. By grouping specific careers that are related to each other and to an overall career category, you make them easier to remember.

Likewise, the concept of relating information can be applied when you need to enhance your comprehension and retention of material associated with your own career. Here you analyze written materials in order to develop blocks of related information which include main ideas, detailed information to support these main ideas, and additional information from graphics or visual presentations.

The analysis of paragraphs is a good place to begin to learn how to develop blocks of related information, since paragraphs are relatively short and serve as the basic components within longer units of written materials. Before beginning to analyze paragraphs, however, it would be wise to define what it is that will be analyzed. What is a paragraph? Simply stated, a paragraph can be described as a group of related sentences that begins on a new line with an indented first word. In a well-written paragraph, sentences are related to each other because they all pertain to the same general topic. The author wants you to know something important about that topic. This important information about the topic is the paragraph's main idea.

There are two kinds of main ideas, **stated** and **implied.** Although both kinds of main ideas are used by authors, it is easier to become familiar with one kind of main idea at a time. Therefore, for our purposes, stated main ideas are stressed in this chapter while implied main ideas are covered in the following chapter. However, you will have an opportunity to work with both stated and implied main ideas at the end of Chapter Four.

The stated main idea is usually the broadest or most general sentence in the paragraph. It is supported by a number of specific details mentioned in other sentences in the paragraph.

The stated main idea may be located anywhere within the paragraph. Sometimes authors state the main idea in the first sentence and follow it with supporting details. However, authors may begin a paragraph with supporting details and then conclude with the main idea in the last sentence. In this situation, the main idea appears at the end of the paragraph. Occasionally, you may find the main idea somewhere in the middle of the paragraph. Regardless of the placement of the stated main idea within the paragraph, you can check to see if you have identified it correctly. Look at the rest of the sentences in the paragraph; all, or most, of these sentences should support your selected main idea by providing specific information about that main idea.

The first step in identifying the stated main idea is to read the paragraph carefully. The next step is to ask two important questions about the paragraph:

1. *What is the topic of the paragraph?*

2. *What does the author want you to know about that topic?*

Words, phrases, or ideas which are mentioned over and over again are clues to answering that first question. The answer will give you a very general idea of what the paragraph is about. The topic can usually be expressed in one or two words. Now, to answer the second question, you must analyze the sentences within the paragraph to find out what particular important information the author wants you to know about that topic. The sentence which contains that information is the paragraph's stated main idea.

When you answer the second question, express it in your own words in a complete sentence. Then refer back to the paragraph and look for a sentence which means the same thing as what you have just expressed in your own words. If the author has stated the main idea, you need only identify it in the paragraph by highlighting or underlining the sentence.

The following three sample paragraphs illustrate paragraphs with main ideas that appear at the beginning, middle, or end of the paragraph. Note how the stated main idea of each paragraph is identified by asking the two questions.

1. *What is the topic of the paragraph?*

2. *What does the author want you to know about that topic?*

In these sample paragraphs, I have given the answer to the second question, expressing it in my own words. While your wording might differ slightly, the answer must include the same concepts.

SAMPLE A: Main Idea at Beginning of the Paragraph

Employment may be secured by mechanical engineering graduates in almost every type of industry. Manufacturing plants, power-generating stations, public utility companies, transportation companies, airlines and factories, to mention only a few, are examples of organizations that need mechanical engineers. Experienced engineers are also needed in the missile and space industries in the design and development of such items as gas turbine compressors and power plants, air-cycle cooling turbines, electrically and hydraulically driven fans, and high-pressure refrigerants. In addition, mechanical engineers are also in demand in the development and testing of airborne and missile fuel systems, and electromechanical control systems.

What is the topic of the paragraph?

job opportunities for mechanical engineers

What does the author want you to know about job opportunities for mechanical engineers?

IN MY OWN WORDS: Many industries offer job opportunities for mechanical engineering graduates.

In Sample A, the author of the paragraph makes the general statement in the first sentence that there are job opportunities for mechanical engineering graduates and then goes on to describe the kinds of jobs that are available in the sentences that follow. The stated main idea, therefore, is the first sentence: "Employment may be secured by mechanical engineering graduates in almost every type of industry." Its wording is similar in concept to my own answer to the second question.

SAMPLE B: Main Idea at the End of the Paragraph

Individual department heads within the company sometimes tend to be more concerned with their budgets, problems, and promotions than with determining advertising which will benefit the firm as a whole. The potential power of repetitive advertising is often diminished because there is no uniformity in the advertising among divisions within the company. Rivalry between managers may become so fierce that it is virtually impossible to standardize styles, themes, or approaches to advertising. After one multidivision company decentralized its advertising, it had difficulty in just getting different product managers to use the same logo (company signature or trademark) in their ads. These are just some of the problems that arise when advertising departments within a company are decentralized.

What is the topic of the paragraph?

advertising within companies

What does the author want you to know about advertising within companies?

IN MY OWN WORDS: Decentralizing advertising departments within a company can cause problems.

In Sample B, the stated main idea is found in the last sentence, where the author of the paragraph has expressed approximately the same concept that I did. The author of the paragraph presents four different situations, or problems, that have occurred within a company and then states the main idea in the last sentence: "These are just some of the problems that arise when advertising departments with a company are decentralized."

SAMPLE C: Main Idea in the Middle of the Paragraph

Manufacturers, wholesalers, retailers, and service firms all employ order-takers. Nabisco Brands, a multi-billion dollar manufacturer of snack foods and related products, employs a large sales force of order-takers. The typical Nabisco salesperson will call and service ten to fifteen customers per day, generally supermarkets. On each call, the salesperson will straighten the Nabisco products on the store shelves, check for out-of-stocks, do some dusting and rearranging, and write up an order. From time to time the Nabisco salesperson will attempt to get advertising into the store, set up end-of-aisle displays, and encourage the retailer to engage in cooperative advertising programs with Nabisco.

What is the topic of the paragraph?

what a typical Nabisco salesperson does

What does the author want you to know about what a typical Nabisco salesperson does?

IN MY OWN WORDS: Typical Nabisco salespersons usually call on and provide services for a number of supermarkets each day.

In Sample C, the stated main idea is found in the middle of the paragraph. The first two sentences seem to serve simply as an introduction to the stated main idea: "The typical Nabisco salesperson will call on and service ten to fifteen customers per day, generally supermarkets." Once that main idea is stated, the writer goes on to give specific details about the typical Nabisco salesperson's services when calling on a customer.

SAMPLE PRACTICE
Identifying Stated Main Ideas in Paragraphs

DIRECTIONS: Read each of the following paragraphs carefully. Ask the two questions beneath each paragraph to help you identify the stated main idea and write the answers to these questions. Then underline or highlight the stated main idea in each paragraph.

1.   Among the uniformed fire departments, colors and symbols are used to denote rank and title. Gold and white are usually reserved for the chief officer, silver for the company officers, and dark blue for other ranks. In addition, the speaking trumpet is used on badges to further denote rank. Other symbols such as ladders, nozzles, and hydrants are used on badges for ranks below the officer level. Such uniform colors and the use of symbols make it easy to determine one's rank in a fire department. However, in certain areas of fire protection in some departments, uniforms are replaced by normal business clothing; yet, ranks are still used, even though they are not constantly displayed.

What is the topic of the paragraph?

What does the author want you to know about that topic?

IN YOUR OWN WORDS: _____

_____

_____

2.   Two selling techniques that are particularly applicable to retailing are selling up and suggestion selling. Selling up is the technique of convincing the customer to buy a higher-priced item than he or she originally intended. An automobile salesperson may convince a customer to buy a more expensive model than the person intended to buy. In a fancy clothing store, the salesperson may convince the customer that she cannot live without the dress that is far above what her budget says she can spend. Finally, selling up might be used in a furniture store when newly married customers are sold better furniture than they intended buying on their tight budget. By selling up, salespersons are able to earn higher commissions or achieve better sales figures.

What is the topic of the paragraph?

_____

What does the author want you to know about that topic?

IN YOUR OWN WORDS: _____

_____

_____

3.   Before approaching a lender, your first step is to prepare a cash flow forecast (a statement of the company's cash receipts and payments during an accounting period) to determine the financing needs of your business. Consider some important factors such as the purpose of the loan and how large a loan is needed. Also consider how long you will need the loan and how you will repay it. Once you have identified these factors, you are able to evaluate loan alternatives. Investigate these alternatives and select the loan and lender most appropriate for your financial needs. When you follow these specific planned steps, it is easier to approach a lender for aid in financing your business.

What is the topic of the paragraph?

_____

What does the author want you to know about that topic?

IN YOUR OWN WORDS: _____

_____

_____

4.   Lead is classed according to use either as an ingredient of a chemical compound or as a metal, either alone or alloyed with some other
metal. The chemical forms of lead most commonly encountered in the
construction industry are those used in the manufacture of paints and
primers. Lead carbonate, or white lead, is a white powder used mainly
as a stabilizer in exterior paints to provide toughness, elasticity, and
durability. Lead monoxide, or litharge, is a yellow powder used for
yellow pigments. Lead oxide, or red lead, is still one of the most effective
rust inhibiting primers or paint ingredients for structural steel.

What is the topic of the paragraph?

_____

What does the author want you to know about that topic?

IN YOUR OWN WORDS: _____

_____

_____

5.   The U.S. Bureau of Labor Statistics expects that a quarter of all
employment growth through 1995 will be in the category of "other
services." Within this category, the largest industry is business services
(a variety of things from business consultants to janitorial services)
which has a projected employment growth of 3.9 percent per year.
Professional services (legal, engineering, accounting, etc.) are expected
to add another 850,000 jobs. Financial and banking services are projected to have strong growth but "modest" employment gains of 1.9
percent per year or 21 percent in ten years. Obviously, job-seekers
should be aware of the opportunities for employment to be found in
"other services."

What is the topic of the paragraph?

_____

What does the author want you to know about that topic?

IN YOUR OWN WORDS: _____

_____

_____

Check the stated main ideas you have identified in the five paragraphs.

Sample Practice Answers

Your words in answering the two questions for identifying main ideas may differ slightly from those presented below. Keep in mind, however, that the concepts of the answers should be similar, and that they should lead you to identify the correct stated main idea in each of the five paragraphs. If your main ideas do not match those given, compare and analyze the differences in answers very carefully.

1. *What is the topic of the paragraph?*

   fire department rank and title

   What does the author want you to know about fire department rank and title?

   IN MY OWN WORDS: Fire departments use colors and symbols to show differences in rank and title.

   MAIN IDEA—FIRST SENTENCE: "Among the uniformed fire departments, colors and symbols are used to denote rank and title."

2. *What is the topic of the paragraph?*

   a technique known as selling up

   What does the author want you to know about selling up?

   IN MY OWN WORDS: Selling up is a technique which is used to get customers to spend more money.

   MAIN IDEA—SECOND SENTENCE: "Selling up is the technique of convincing the customer to buy a higher-priced item than he or she originally intended."

3. *What is the topic of the paragraph?*

getting a business loan

What does the author want you to know about getting a business loan?

IN MY OWN WORDS: There are steps to follow if you want to get a business loan.

MAIN IDEA—LAST SENTENCE: "When you follow these specific planned steps, it is easier to approach a lender for aid in financing your business."

4. *What is the topic of the paragraph?*

use of chemical forms of lead in the construction industry

What does the author want you to know about the use of the chemical forms of lead in the construction industry?

IN MY OWN WORDS: The chemical forms of lead are mainly used in the manufacture of paints and primers.

MAIN IDEA—SECOND SENTENCE: "The chemical forms of lead most commonly encountered in the construction industry are those used in the manufacture of paints and primers."

5. *What is the topic of the paragraph?*

employment growth projections in the "other services" category through 1995

What does the author want you to know about employment growth projections in the other services category through 1995?

IN MY OWN WORDS: The employment growth projections for "other services" category made by the U.S. Bureau of Labor Statistics shows growth through 1995.

MAIN IDEA—FIRST SENTENCE: "The U.S. Bureau of Labor Statistics expects that a quarter of all employment growth through 1995 will be in the category of 'other services.'"

Now go on to Skill Development Exercise 3 on page 41, which will provide you with additional practice in identifying stated main ideas in paragraphs.

Then apply what you have learned about identifying stated main ideas in paragraphs to your own career materials in Skill Application Exercise 3 on page 47.

SKILL DEVELOPMENT EXERCISE 3
Identifying Stated Main Ideas in Paragraphs

DIRECTIONS: Read each paragraph carefully. Ask the two questions to identify the stated main idea. Then underline or highlight the sentence that states the main idea of the paragraph. Beginning with paragraph six, ask the two questions in your head but do not write the answers unless you feel that you need to do so.

1.　　At the state and local levels, there are many restrictions placed on retailers. Zoning laws prohibit retailers from operating at certain locations and require building specifications to be met. Construction, fire, elevator, smoking, and other codes are placed on retailers by the state and city. Minimum resale laws require that specific items cannot be sold for less than a floor price. Blue laws limit the hours that retailers can conduct business. Other ordinances, called Green River laws, restrict direct-to-home selling. In addition, various licenses necessary for operation are under the jurisdiction of the state or city. Also, many states and municipalities are involved in consumer protection, and they police retailers from this vantage point.

What is the topic of the paragraph?

_____

What does the author want you to know about that topic?

IN YOUR OWN WORDS: _____

_____

_____

2.　　Where does the designer get ideas and inspiration for new fashions? The fashion designer gets ideas and inspiration everywhere! Through television the designer experiences all the wonders of the entertainment world. In films the designer is exposed to the influences of all the arts and lifestyles throughout the world. Museum exhibits, art shows, world happenings, expositions, the theater, music, dance, and world travel are all sources of design inspiration to fashion designers.

What is the topic of the paragraph?

_____

What does the author want you to know about that topic?

IN YOUR OWN WORDS: _____

_____

_____

3.   We cannot expect clerical staffs to increase at the same pace as the programs and activities which are their responsibilities. Instead, we must seek ways to get clerical jobs done with available resources. A way to best utilize available resources is to improve and update the skills of the clerical work force with training which goes beyond typing and shorthand. For example, secretaries and clerical employees should be trained in such areas as answering the phone correctly, meeting the public diplomatically, and dressing appropriately. Training in spelling accurately and proofreading conscientiously also needs to be included. In addition, this training should bolster the pride of workmanship in these employees.

What is the topic of the paragraph?

_____

What does the author want you to know about that topic?

IN YOUR OWN WORDS: _____

_____

_____

4.   The Wool Products Labeling Act of 1939 (requiring that the kind and percentage of wool in a product be identified), the Fur Products Labeling Act of 1951 (requiring identification of the animal from which the fur was derived), and the Flammable Fabrics Act of 1953 (prohibiting the interstate sale of flammable fabrics) formed the original legislation in this area. A more recent law—the Fair Packaging and Labeling Act, passed in 1967—requires the disclosure of product identity, the name and address of the manufacturer or distributor, and information concerning the quality of its contents. In 1971, the Public Health Cigarette Smoking Act prohibited tobacco advertising on radio and television. Thus, rules governing advertising and labeling constitute a sphere of marketing's legal environment.

What is the topic of the paragraph?

_____

What does the author want you to know about that topic?

IN YOUR OWN WORDS: _____

_____

_____

5.   A two-year survey of 1300 workers at ten industrial plants turned up a significant statistical relationship between job dissatisfaction and psychologically induced ailments. Workers describing themselves as unhappy with work often showed real cases of headache, fatigue, colds, and other common ailments. A nurse at Leesonal Corporation found that half of the 30 ailing machine operators she saw daily were just seeking relief from work. Her counterpart at Sprague Electric Company found more of his patients to be the unhappy clerks and factory hands than the more contented executives. A young Boston lawyer, who experienced chest pains in court and feared a heart attack, discovered it was merely a nervous stomach caused by hatred of her government job.

What is the topic of the paragraph?

_____

What does the author want you to know about that topic?

IN YOUR OWN WORDS: _____

_____

_____

6.   Think of the knowledge required when selling products like major appliances, photographic equipment, personal computers, televisions, and stereos to mention but a few. Customers will naturally ask questions and a salesperson must have good product knowledge to complete sales. For many retail selling jobs, considerable training is required. In some cases special training, such as the American Gem Society certificate program, must be completed to qualify for a retailing position. It is obvious, therefore, that many retail selling jobs require a great deal of knowledge and skill.

7.　　　Management, management concepts, and management techniques have always been used, either consciously or unconsciously. For example, Moses used the "span of management" and "delegation" principles in the exodus from Egypt around 1250 B.C. Yet management thought was slow to develop for several reasons. First, from the days of the Greek philosophers, through the Middle Ages, and even into the early modern period, business was not accepted as a respectable occupation. Second, early economists and political scientists were interested primarily in the national and international levels of analysis and did not concern themselves with the managerial or entrepreneurial aspects of business activities. Third, business people themselves did not aid in the development of management thought, since they considered their profession an art rather than a science, explaining that principles cannot be applied to management as they can to sciences. Fourth, business, up to the last third of the nineteenth century, was operated principally on a small personal basis as a sole proprietorship or partnership. Thus, there was little real incentive for management theory to develop.

8.　　　Marshalled properly, symbols can be used as effective persuasive elements. The Statue of Liberty, the Red Cross, the Star of David, and many other symbols have been used traditionally for positive persuasion. Indeed, in the Falkland Islands invasion by Argentina in 1982, England used the symbol of its Queen—and the honor of the Crown—to achieve public sentiment behind the war effort to win the islands back. Later that same year, a disgruntled antinuclear activist tried to hold the Washington Monument "hostage" as a symbol of a threatened nation. In the Mideast in the mid-1980s, Shiite fundamentalists burned the American flag as a symbol of the "American satan."

9.　　　Direct evidence is often referred to as "eyewitness" evidence. This is putting it too simply, however. Direct evidence is the product of a person's sensory perception and most people have perception from five senses: sight, touch, taste, smell, and hearing. The person who observed the accused pulling a revolver from his belt was giving direct eyewitness testimony. Had he also testified, "I heard three shots," he would have provided an example of what could be termed direct "ear-witness" testimony. The person who testifies, "It smelled like smoke," is a "nose-witness," and the person who testifies, "I felt his wrist and got no pulse," is a "touch-witness." "It tasted like bitter almonds" is, of course, an example of direct evidence based on the witness's sense of taste.

10.   Before you attempt to persuade someone to purchase a product, whether you are communicating orally or in writing, learn the facts about the product, the market, and the competition. Carefully research the subject, including reading any sales promotional literature that may be available from your competitors or from any other sources such as *Consumer Reports.* Use the product yourself and ask for feedback from other people who have used it. Learn about all the features of the product. Find out how it is constructed and from what materials. If possible, visit the factory that makes the product and observe the manufacturing or assembly process. You should also become familiar with the price, warranty, maintenance procedures, and the most common repair problems.

SKILL APPLICATION 3
Identifying Stated Main Ideas in Paragraphs

DIRECTIONS: *Choose two paragraphs with stated main ideas from your own career materials such as textbooks, manuals, professional magazines, and so on. Duplicate the paragraphs and paste them on this sheet with one paragraph on each side. Underline or highlight the main idea stated in each paragraph. Be sure to include the source information for each paragraph.*

PARAGRAPH 1 SOURCE INFORMATION

Title: _____

Author: _____

Place of publication: _____

Publisher: _____

Copyright Date: _____ *Page(s):* _____

PARAGRAPH 2 SOURCE INFORMATION

Title: _____

Author: _____

Place of publication: _____

Publisher: _____

Copyright Date: _____ *Page(s):* _____

Chapter Four

Identifying Implied Main Ideas in Paragraphs

Identifying both stated and implied main ideas as part of developing a block of related information begins with asking the two vital questions: **"What is the topic of the paragraph?"** and **"What does the author want me to know about that topic?"** Sometimes, however, when you express the answer to the second question in your own words, you may not find a sentence in the paragraph that is similar to your answer. In this instance, you are probably not dealing with a stated main idea. The author has not included a sentence that tells you what you are expected to know about the topic of the paragraph. When this occurs, you are dealing with an **implied main idea.**

In a paragraph that has an implied main idea, the author indirectly suggests or hints at what you need to know about the topic of the paragraph by giving details that point to a main idea rather than directly stating one. In such cases, you must read the details very carefully and look in the sentences that make up the paragraph for a common idea about the topic that links them together. Use this common idea as you express the answer to the second main idea question in a complete sentence. Your answer to the second question can be used as the implied main idea of the paragraph.

Just as you found with a stated main idea, your implied main idea will be a general statement in the paragraph and can be checked for accuracy. If all, or most, of the sentences in the paragraph support your general statement, you have correctly expressed the implied main idea.

Sample A is a paragraph with an implied main idea. Note how I've used my own words in a sentence to answer the second question and how that answer is the implied main idea. Keep in mind that your own answer may not match the sample answer exactly, but the concepts should be similar.

SAMPLE A

Lap seatbelts should be worn so that they are below the iliac crests of the pelvis. They should restrain the bony pelvis at the hip joint. If the seatbelt is too high and is fastened above the iliac crest, sudden deceleration or an abrupt stop of the vehicle may cause an injury of the abdominal organs or the great vessels as the belt squeezes them against the spine. Injuries of the pelvis and lumbar spine, including fractures of the pelvis and compression fractures of the lumbar vertebrae, have also occurred as a result of the improper use of seat belts.

What is the topic of the paragraph?

wearing lap seatbelts

What does the author want you to know about wearing lap seatbelts?

IMPLIED MAIN IDEA: It is important to wear lap seatbelts correctly.

Each sentence in the paragraph gives information about the topic, wearing lap seatbelts. The common idea is that each sentence either tells how to wear a lap seatbelt correctly or tells what can happen if you don't wear a lap seatbelt correctly. Since there isn't any general statement that tells you this is what you need to know about the topic of the paragraph, you can use this common thread to express the implied main idea in a complete sentence.

In working with the paragraph in Sample A, you can see how the sentences have a common idea so that you can answer the second question in a fairly specific manner. However, this is not always the case. Sometimes the sentences within a paragraph do not seem to have a common idea, and you cannot pinpoint exactly what the author wants you to know about the topic. When this situation occurs, the best you can do is to deduce that the author simply wants to give you general information, or facts, about that topic. Sample B presents a paragraph with this kind of situation.

SAMPLE B

Hospital medical staffs are made up of fully licensed physicians and may even include other licensed individuals who are nonphysicians but are permitted to provide patient care services. Medical staff members must apply for privileges from the governing body; and their applications are evaluated on the basis of education, experience, ethics, competence, and physical health status. By this selection process, the governing body entrusts the direct care and treatment of patients to those practitioners who are deemed competent to provide high quality patient care. The medical staff, as a whole, is directly accountable to members of the governing body for its actions.

What is the topic of the paragraph?

information about hospital medical staffs

What does the author want you to know about hospital medical staffs?

IMPLIED MAIN IDEA: This paragraph provides information about hospital medical staffs.

In Sample B, the first sentence talks about the persons who make up a hospital medical staff. The second and third sentences describe how such persons become members of the hospital medical staff. The last sentence tells you to whom a medical staff is accountable. Unlike a paragraph which has a stated main idea, there isn't any single sentence that pulls this diverse information together. Therefore, the answer to the second question must serve as the implied main idea. The diversity of the content in the sentences within Sample B makes it difficult to pinpoint a common idea; the only common idea is the reference to hospital medical staffs. A logical way to answer the second question is to say that the author of the paragraph wants you to know some information about hospital medical staffs. Since the answer to the second question is written in your own words, you might have expressed it slightly differently. You might have said that the author wants you to know some facts about hospital medical staffs or some characteristics of that group of hospital personnel. That is perfectly all right—the basic concept is the same as the one written above in answer to the second question.

In both Sample A and Sample B, all of the sentences in each paragraph support the implied main idea by giving information related to it.

SAMPLE PRACTICE
Identifying Implied Main Ideas in Paragraphs

DIRECTIONS: Read each of the following paragraphs carefully. Ask the two questions and write the answers. Your answer to the second question will be expressed in a complete sentence. This sentence is the implied main idea of the paragraph.

1.   Any type of detergent and any stain remover may be safely used for linen fabrics. Laundry additives also do little or no damage to this kind of fabric. If special finishes have been applied to the linen, care should be given to limit the temperatures used in ironing and to avoid the use of chlorine bleaches, particularly if a durable-press or wrinkle-resistant finish has been applied. Linen fabrics usually require ironing since they seldom come from the laundry or dry cleaning solvent without wrinkles. Because of its properties, linen does not soil quickly and, unless stained, seldom needs any bleaching. As with any textile product, the consumer should make certain that care label information is read and followed.

What is the topic of the paragraph?

_____

What does the author want you to know about that topic?

IMPLIED MAIN IDEA: _____

_____

_____

2.   The limited partnership is comprised of two types of partners: the general partner and the limited partner. The general partner is responsible for the day-to-day management of the business and, as in a regular partnership, has unlimited personal liability for any debt or legal actions against the partnership. In most states, the general partner may be an individual or a corporation. Depending on the partnership agreement, withdrawal of the general partner may cause the partnership to dissolve.

What is the topic of the paragraph?

_____

What does the author want you to know about that topic?

IMPLIED MAIN IDEA: _____

_____

_____

3.   Surveying is the science of determining the dimensions and contour (or three-dimensional characteristics) of the earth's surface by the measurements of distances, directions, and elevations. It also involves staking out the lines and grades needed for the construction of buildings, roads, dams, etc. In addition to these field measurements, surveying includes the computation of areas, volumes, and other quantities, as well as the preparation of necessary maps and diagrams. Surveying has many industrial applications: for example, setting equipment, assembling aircraft, laying out assembly lines, and so on.

What is the topic of the paragraph?

_____

What does the author want you to know about that topic?

IMPLIED MAIN IDEA: _____

_____

_____

4.   Direct marketing today occurs either in the form of a direct response, which requires a salesperson to complete the sale, or by direct order, is a sale made without a personal sales call. More broadly, direct marketing is the selling of products without the store, as with Avon or Amway products. Telemarketing, catalog shopping, personalized mailings, and trial offers are all ways to conduct direct marketing.

What is the topic of the paragraph?

_____

What does the author want you to know about that topic?

IMPLIED MAIN IDEA: _____

_____

_____

5.   The course of enacting federal legislation starts with a bill presented by a senator or a representative. Introduced bills are sent to a committee of the Senate or House of Representatives for consideration. After deliberation, perhaps including meetings and hearings by subcommittees, the bill may be amended or redrafted. The chairman of the committee or its members decide whether to send the bill for consideration by the entire Senate or House of Representatives. The Rules Committee determines the time for debate on the bill. If the bill is passed in both the Senate and the House of Representatives and there are no differences, the legislation goes to the President. If there are differences, it goes to a conference committee of members of both House and Senate for resolution. The approved bill may be signed by the President, or he may let it become law after an interval without signing, or he may veto it. The veto may be overridden by a two-thirds vote in the Senate and the House of Representatives.

What is the topic of the paragraph?

_____

What does the author want you to know about that topic?

IMPLIED MAIN IDEA: _____

_____

_____

Check your implied main ideas. Your wording of the implied main ideas probably will differ from mine. That is all right as long as the concepts match those presented. If your concept of any implied main idea does not match the one given, analyze the difference very carefully. Try to determine how I identified the implied main idea.

Sample Practice Answers

1. *What is the topic of the paragraph?*

   linen
   _____

   What does the author want you to know about linen?

   IMPLIED MAIN IDEA: Done properly, linen may be laundered or
   dry-cleaned with no damage.

2. *What is the topic of the paragraph?*

the general partners in a limited partnership

What does the author want you to know about general partners in a limited partnership?

IMPLIED MAIN IDEA: The general partner has a specific role in a limited partnership.

3. *What is the topic of the paragraph?*

uses of surveying

What does the author want you to know about surveying?

IMPLIED MAIN IDEA: Surveying is used for a number of different purposes.

4. *What is the topic of the paragraph?*

direct marketing

What does the author want you to know about direct marketing?

IMPLIED MAIN IDEA: Direct marketing is accomplished in several ways.

5. *What is the topic of the paragraph?*

a bill becoming a federal law

What does the author want you to know about a bill becoming a federal law?

IMPLIED MAIN IDEA: A bill must go through a number of steps before it is enacted into federal law.

Now go on to Skill Development Exercise 4–1 on page 57 for additional practice in identifying implied main ideas.

In reading your own career-related materials, you will find that main ideas can be either stated or implied, depending upon the individual author's writing style. It then becomes your responsibility as the reader to identify main ideas that have not been labelled "stated" or "implied" as they have been in Skill Development Exercises 3 and 4—1. Skill Development Exercise 4—2 on page 63 includes practice with both stated and implied main ideas in paragraphs that have not been labelled as such.

In Skill Application 4 on page 67 you will apply your skill in identifying main ideas to your own career-related material.

SKILL DEVELOPMENT EXERCISE 4–1
Identifying Implied Main Ideas in Paragraphs

DIRECTIONS: Read each paragraph carefully. Ask the two questions to identify the implied main idea. Write the answers for the questions and remember to state the answer to the second question in a complete sentence.

1.   If you suspect that a customer is hesitant to bring up an objection to the sale because it is trivial, say, "Mr. Elliott, objections may be trivial, or they may seem so small that a buyer would hesitate to mention them to a salesperson; but what may seem small to one person is important to another. If there is any problem that concerns you, even if you feel it would look small in the eyes of someone else, don't hesitate to mention it." The major objection is the one that appears large to the prospect, not necessarily to others. If you can get on common ground and discover where the problem lies, you can go ahead easily. Do not diminish the importance of the prospect's objection.

What is the topic of the paragraph?

_____

What does the author want you to know about that topic?

IMPLIED MAIN IDEA: _____

_____

_____

2.   Money market funds have become a new and strong competitor to financial institutions as savers seek the highest return on their funds. Savers can deposit as little as $1,000 and earn yields considerably higher than in traditional types of savings accounts. The money market funds also provide easy access to the saver's money through checks and credit cards. However, they do not provide either insurance or any protection against declining rates as other types of accounts do. Money market funds grew to over $181 billion in 1981 from $3 billion in 1975.

What is the topic of the paragraph?

_____

What does the author want you to know about that topic?

IMPLIED MAIN IDEA: _____

_____

_____

3.   When an object that was once personal property is attached to land (or a building thereon) so as to become real estate, it is called a *fixture*. As a rule, a fixture is the property of the landowner, and when the land is conveyed to a new owner, it is automatically included with the land. The question of whether an item is a fixture also arises with regard to property taxes, mortgages, lease terminations and hazard insurance policies. Specifically, real estate taxes are based on real property valuation. Real estate mortgages are secured by real property. Objects attached to a building by a tenant may become real property and hence become fixtures that now belong to the building's owner. Hazard insurance policies treat real property differently than personal property.

What is the topic of the paragraph?

_____

What does the author want you to know about that topic?

IMPLIED MAIN IDEA: _____

_____

_____

4.   The selection process for filling a job vacancy begins when a manager or supervisor sends a request to the company employment office, or [to] the staff member in charge of personnel, that an employee is needed. A job description, based on job analysis, identifies the vacancy. A job specification, which may also accompany the request, describes what kind of person is wanted to fill that vacancy. Employment or personnel specialists then use the job description and specifications to begin the recruiting process. The pool of applicants generated by recruiting activities must be narrowed down and one person selected to fill the job.

What is the topic of the paragraph?

_____

What does the author want you to know about that topic?

IMPLIED MAIN IDEA: _____

_____

_____

5.   *Morale* is the attitude of each individual in a group toward the group's purposes and goals. It is always present in some form although it may change from moment to moment. People are more apt to notice morale when it is conspicuously high or low. High morale develops over a long time, is difficult to maintain, and often is taken for granted. If morale is low, sometimes little else is noticed.

What is the topic of the paragraph?

_____

What does the author want you to know about that topic?

IMPLIED MAIN IDEA: _____

_____

_____

6.   In a recent supervision workshop, a videotape of a counseling session was shown in which the client teared up as she discussed a sensitive topic. When that happened, the counselor became very quiet and asked just one question for clarification. After the tape was viewed, a group of professional supervisors were asked to write down comments they would want to make to the counselor. Two of the supervisors focused on the segment of tape described above, but approached it from different angles. One said, "I wanted the counselor to say something to the client, to comfort her in some way." The other remarked, "I thought the counselor was threatened by the client's show of emotion. I would want to discuss this with her."

What is the topic of the paragraph?

_____

What does the author want you to know about that topic?

IMPLIED MAIN IDEA: _____

_____

_____

7.   Grade-beam foundations are widely used for residential construction, where permitted by local code, especially where basements are not required. A grade-beam is a reinforced concrete beam at ground level around the entire perimeter of the building. It is supported by a series of concrete piers extending down into undisturbed soil. The grade-beam

supports the load of the building, and the piers distribute this load to the foundation bed. This type of foundation is frequently used on sloping sites or in areas subject to earth slippage.

What is the topic of the paragraph?

_____

What does the author want you to know about that topic?

IMPLIED MAIN IDEA: _____

_____

_____

8.   Disk drives in personal computers are usually a part of the system unit. You may notice one or two disk drives for floppy disks. Your system may also have a hard disk drive. The disk drives will hold the disks for the software program that you use on the microcomputer as well as the disk that will store the data you create when using the system. The capacity of the disks that you can use to store your information will depend upon the type of disks that can be used in the disk drives. There is a wide variety of disk drive capacities and once again, your software requirements as well as storage needs will often dictate the choice that you make.

What is the topic of the paragraph?

_____

What does the author want you to know about that topic?

IMPLIED MAIN IDEA: _____

_____

_____

9.   Some corporations have begun home-based work programs, or allowed the option, in individual cases, to hold on to particularly valued workers. Some allow workers on retirement to continue part-time work from their homes. Others such as Control Data Corporation and Metropolitan Life began programs in order to offer employment to handicapped workers. A few corporations are reported to be turning to home-based work as a way of recruiting otherwise unavailable but highly

qualified workers, such as mothers of small children or suburban housewives.

What is the topic of the paragraph?

_____

What does the author want you to know about that topic?

IMPLIED MAIN IDEA: _____

_____

_____

10.   Life-threatening emergencies can and do occur in the practice of dentistry. They may happen to anyone: the dental patient, the doctor, members of the dental office staff, even a person who is simply waiting to accompany a patient home from the dental office. Although life-threatening emergency situations do not occur frequently within the typical dental practice, a number of factors may increase the rate at which these incidents arise. These include (1) the increasing number of older persons seeking dental treatment, (2) recent therapeutic advances by the medical profession, (3) the trend toward longer dental appointments, and (4) the increasing utilization and administration of drugs in the practice of dentistry. On the other hand, there are a number of other factors that the dental profession has at its disposal that will minimize the possibility of life-threatening situations occurring. Included are (1) the pretreatment physical evaluation of the dental patient, consisting of the patient-completed medical history questionnaire, physical examination of the patient, and the dialogue history, and (2) possible modification in dental therapy to decrease medical risk to the patient. It has been estimated that through the effective use of these procedures, all but about 10 percent of life-threatening situations can be prevented.

What is the topic of the paragraph?

_____

What does the author want you to know about that topic?

IMPLIED MAIN IDEA: _____

_____

_____

SKILL DEVELOPMENT EXERCISE 4–2
Identifying Stated and Implied Main Ideas in Paragraphs

DIRECTIONS: *Read each paragraph carefully. Ask the two questions to identify the stated or implied main idea of the paragraph.*

What is the topic of the paragraph?

What does the author want you to know about that topic?

If the main idea is stated, underline or highlight it in the paragraph. If the main idea is implied, write it in your own words below the paragraph.

1.   It is generally considered that the humanistic approach to management started as a result of the experiments conducted in the Hawthorne plant of the Western Electric Company, near Chicago, from 1924 to 1932. A series of studies there led to the discovery of new dimensions in the meaning of work, motivation, and organizational and interpersonal relationships. It was discovered that the powerful incentive toward increased production was not due to the physical working conditions or the financial rewards but a result of the Hawthorne effect, whereby workers felt important and appreciated because they were chosen as subjects for a scientific study.

MAIN IDEA (IF IMPLIED): _____

_____

_____

2.   Without copyeditors, newspaper articles would read strangely. No reporter hands in a story with every word spelled correctly, every punctuation mark in place, and every fact expressed clearly. Copyeditors clean up stories before they are set in type. This job is absolutely vital because readership studies indicate that spelling mistakes and grammatical errors detract from a story's credibility. The content may be correct, but if form is poor the reader is skeptical. Copyeditors usually write all the headlines and captions as well. You could honestly say that copyeditors are the unsung champions of the newsroom.

MAIN IDEA (IF IMPLIED): _____

_____

_____

3.   A limited partnership or syndicate is formed when a real estate promoter, assuming the liability and responsibility of a general partner or syndicator, purchases or takes an option to purchase an investment property. The public is then invited to participate as limited partners by buying ownership shares in various denominations. The result is a relatively large group of investors, often more than 100, who rely on the management expertise of the general partner for promised profits. The limited partners take a passive role in management and enjoy the security of protecting their other personal assets from liabilities incurred by the partnership. Any losses are limited to the extent of the individual's investment in the group.

MAIN IDEA (IF IMPLIED): _____

_____

_____

4.   A deteriorating economic environment adversely affects most marketers of goods and services. However, for some companies, the recent recession was good news. As inflation continues and production declines with corresponding growth in the level of unemployment, consumer buying patterns shift. Flour millers note that flour sales increase. Automobile repairs and home improvements also increase. Greeting card firms report that consumers buy fewer gifts, but more expensive cards. Hardware stores show higher sales. Decline is, of course, experienced by many other firms. Clearly, the economic environment has a sizable influence on the way marketers operate.

MAIN IDEA (IF IMPLIED): _____

_____

_____

5.   Today's jobs are not as likely to bring the same satisfaction earned by craftspeople such as the cabinetmakers or blacksmiths of the last century. Work skills are now linked to machine operations and what we make is mostly the product of other machines and other workers. The mechanized worker stands at a psychological distance from his or her work and is not identified with the end product. Often this type of employee is confined to a fixed work station and is expected to leave it only with permission—a restriction that can affect one's attitude toward work.

MAIN IDEA (IF IMPLIED): _____

_____

_____

6.　　　　BASIC is an acronym for Beginner's All-purpose Symbolic Instruction Code. It was originally developed at Dartmouth College in the 1960s as a tool for teaching principles of computer programming. Because it is quite easy to learn and oriented toward problem solving without much concern for machine details, it quickly spread beyond the college as a language especially suited for nonprofessional programmers and casual computer users. It became popular in commercial time-sharing and has spread rapidly with the rapid increase in the use of personal computers.

MAIN IDEA (IF IMPLIED): _____

_____

_____

7.　　　　Banks, retail stores, hospitals, and service industries are providing more white-collar jobs than ever before. Even in factories, the ratio of managers and engineers to production workers is growing. Research, design, marketing, and finance now provide more opportunities for white-collar people. Universally, white-collar work provides more prestige than blue-collar. The white-collar jobs are thought to give more individuality and are more likely to provide "middle class" status. Industrial psychology has found that a job title such as "staff assistant" may provide a sense of advancement to the employee who was doing almost the same job when it was called "chief clerk."

MAIN IDEA (IF IMPLIED): _____

_____

_____

8.　　　　The practice of releasing a defendant after his arrest and permitting him or remain free until trial is an ancient one. Under the English common law which established the pattern for American courts, defendants were released subject only to conditions designed to insure that a defendant would appear at his trial. One reason for this pretrial freedom involved fairness to the accused who, responsible for preparing his defense at his trial, was prevented from doing so if held in jail. A second reason involved the avoidance of imprisonment suffered by defendants eventually found not guilty in an era when some accused persons had to wait months for the judge to arrive and trial to begin.

MAIN IDEA (IF IMPLIED): _____

_____

_____

9.   "Selling to the Military" is a publication that gives information on how to get on Department of Defense bidders' lists. It also includes the addresses of major military purchasing offices. The publication includes a description of the federal government's system of specifications that will aid you in submitting bids. It provides information on military exchange services and bid opportunities in military research and development. This publication is available from the Superintendent of Documents.

MAIN IDEA (IF IMPLIED): _____

_____

_____

10.   Sears, Roebuck is the largest direct-mail marketer in the United States, followed by J.C. Penney. In a tie for third are Spiegel, Inc. and Fingerhut Corporation. Fingerhut executives say their success in selling electronics, garden supplies, and gift foods by mail stems from long-term customer relationships and easy credit. The firm targets individuals who are probably good credit risks and promotes selected items. If a customer's payment record proves reliable, more expensive items are offered in subsequent mailings. Fingerhut reinforces customer loyalty with special promotional items, sweepstakes, and awards.

MAIN IDEA (IF IMPLIED): _____

_____

_____

SKILL APPLICATION 4
Identifying Implied Main Ideas in Paragraphs

DIRECTIONS: Choose two paragraphs with implied main ideas from your own career materials such as textbooks, manuals, professional magazines, and so on. Duplicate the paragraphs and paste them on this sheet with one paragraph on each side. Write the implied main idea of each. Be sure to include the source information.

PARAGRAPH 1 SOURCE INFORMATION

Title: _____

Author: _____

Place of publication: _____

Publisher: _____

Copyright Date: _____   *Page(s):* _____

PARAGRAPH 2 SOURCE INFORMATION

Title: _____

Author: _____

Place of publication: _____

Publisher: _____

Copyright Date: _____   *Page(s):* _____

Chapter Five

Selecting Details That Support Main Ideas in Paragraphs

Once you have identified the stated or implied main idea of a paragraph, you have performed the first key step in developing a block of related information. You are now ready to examine the details in the paragraph and select those which support that main idea. For our purposes, we can say that a detail supports the paragraph's main idea when it provides additional and very specific information about that main idea. These details help you to understand and retain material; without them, main ideas are like the bones on a skeleton. They need to be fleshed out with additional information. Therefore, the examination of supporting details is considered to be the second key step to analyzing the organization of a paragraph and developing a block of related information.

You were able to identify the main idea of a paragraph by asking two essential questions:

1. *What is the topic of the paragraph?*

2. *What does the author want you to know about that topic?*

Now add a third, and final, question, which will enable you to identify details which support that main idea:

3. *What specific information in the paragraph supports the main idea?*

The answer to the third question helps you to select details which give you additional specific information about the main idea of the paragraph. Thus it can be said that the purpose of these details is to support the main idea.

One way to remember these three questions is to think of them as producing answers that result in a logical sequence. This sequence begins with the very general topic (first question), then narrows down to a main idea (second question), and finally narrows down even further to specific details which support that main idea (third question). As discussed earlier, the combined answers to the second and third questions are part of a block of related information.

Authors may use a number of different kinds of details to support main ideas. However, two specific kinds of details which often appear in textbooks and career-related materials are stressed in this chapter. These two kinds of details give you **examples** of the main idea or **reasons** for it. Details that are examples and reasons support the main idea of a paragraph by giving you very specific additional information about that main idea. Both stated and implied main ideas are supported by examples and/or reasons.

A main idea is not necessarily supported by both kinds of details. You may find paragraph main ideas which are supported by only one kind of detail—all examples or all reasons. Or you may find paragraph main ideas supported by any combination of the two kinds of details.

Before you actually begin to work with details in this chapter, you should be aware that sentences within the paragraphs have been numbered. This makes it easier to refer back to specific sentences as needed.

SUPPORTING DETAIL: EXAMPLE

Remember that the main idea is the most general sentence in the paragraph. If the main idea is implied, the sentence that you write is also a general one covering the common idea in the paragraph. An author may support either kind of main idea by giving specific examples of it. For instance, the broad main idea of a paragraph may state:

> A number of different kinds of products are manufactured at the Adams Corporation plants in Fort Wayne, Indiana.

Sentences that name and/or describe specific products would each serve as a detail that supports the main idea by providing an example of it:

- They make computers and computer-related products.
- They make television equipment.
- They make stereo components.
- They make compact audio disc players.

With such examples, the main idea is supported by specific information that enables you to get a better idea of what is produced at the Adams Corporation plant.

Example details frequently begin with "**for example**" or "**for instance**" so they are easily identified as such. If a detail doesn't have either of these phrases, you can check to see if it is an example of the main idea by inserting either phrase at the front of the detail. Check the above four details and you will find that either phrase can be inserted in front of each.

You worked with the following sample paragraphs A and B earlier, in Chapter Three and Chapter Four. They are now used to show how example details support main ideas. The stated main idea in Sample A has been italicized. The implied main idea in Sample B has been written in for you. Remember that the wording of this implied main idea may have differed slightly from yours since implied main ideas are written in your own words.

SAMPLE A: Stated Main Idea

(1) *At the state and local levels, there are many restrictions placed on retailers.* (2) Zoning laws prohibit retailers from operating at certain locations and require building specifications to be met. (3) Construction, fire, elevator, smoking, and other codes are placed on retailers by the state and city. (4) Minimum resale laws require that specific items cannot be sold for less than a floor price. (5) Blue laws limit the hours that retailers can conduct business. (6) Other ordinances, called Green River Laws, restrict direct-to-home selling. (7) In addition, various licenses necessary for operation are under the jurisdiction of the state or city. (8) Also, many states and municipalities are involved in consumer protection, and they police retailers from this vantage point.

1. Main Idea	5. Example
2. Example	6. Example
3. Example	7. Example
4. Example	8. Example

Note that each of the seven sentences that follow the stated main idea gives an example of state or local restrictions placed on retailers. The author could have written "for example" or "for instance" in front of each of these sentences. If you try these phrases in front of the seven examples, you will find that they make sense.

SAMPLE B: Implied Main Idea

(1) The course of enacting federal legislation starts with a bill presented by a senator or a representative. (2) Introduced bills are sent to a committee of the Senate or House of Representatives for consideration. (3) After deliberation, perhaps including meetings and hearings by subcommittees, the bill may be amended or redrafted. (4) The chairman of the committee or its members decide whether to send the bill for consideration by the entire Senate or House of Representatives. (5) The Rules Committee determines the time for debate on the bill. (6) If the bill is passed in both the Senate and the House of Representatives and there are no differences, the legislation goes to the President. (7) If there are differences, it goes to a conference committee of members of both House and Senate for resolution. (8) The approved bill may be signed by the President, or he may let it become law after an interval without signing, or he may veto it. (9) The veto may be overriden by a two-thirds vote in the Senate and the House of Representatives.

IMPLIED MAIN IDEA: A bill must go through a number of steps before it is enacted into federal law.

1. Example	4. Example	7. Example
2. Example	5. Example	8. Example
3. Example	6. Example	9. Example

The nine sentences in this paragraph each provide an example of a step a bill must go through before it becomes a federal law. You can write "for example" or "for instance" in front of each of these sentences and it will fit.

SUPPORTING DETAIL: REASON

Authors also frequently explain a main idea by giving a **reason** or **reasons** to support it. This kind of detail supposes that there is a question (Why?) between the main idea and the sentence, or detail, in the paragraph. If the detail explains the main idea by answering that question, the detail is a reason. In other words, the detail is giving a reason in support of the main idea. The "**Why?**" is not usually found in print. As you did with the terms "for example" and "for instance," you, the reader, must insert the "Why?" between the main idea and the detail. If the detail answers this question, the detail is a reason for that main idea.

The same main idea that was used to illustrate example details can now be used to demonstrate details that are reasons.

A number of different kinds of products are manufactured at the Adams Corporation plants in Fort Wayne, Indiana.

In this case, however, each sentence now should provide a reason why different kinds of products have been manufactured at that plant. Such details could include these sentences:

- There are facilities for producing different kinds of products.

- The company has found it profitable to manufacture a variety of products.

- The Board of Directors believes in product diversification.

- If one product loses popularity, the company can still show a profit because of the strong sales of the other products.

Sample paragraphs C and D are ones that you have already worked with and their main ideas have been identified. Sample C demonstrates how reason details can support a stated main idea while Sample D shows how reason details can support an implied main idea.

SAMPLE C: Stated Main Idea

(1) Management, management concepts, and management techniques have always been used, either consciously or unconsciously. (2) For example, Moses used the "span of management" and "delegation" principles in the exodus from Egypt around 1250 B.C. (3) *Yet management thought was slow to develop for several reasons.* (4) First, from the days of the Greek philosophers, through the Middle Ages, and even into the early modern period, business was not accepted as a respectable occupation. (5) Second, early economists and political scientists were interested primarily in the national and international levels of analysis and did not concern themselves with the managerial or entrepreneurial aspects of business activities. (6) Third, business people themselves did not aid in the development of management thought, since they considered their profession an art rather than a science, explaining that principles cannot be applied to management as they can to sciences. (7) Fourth, business, up to the last third of the nineteenth century, was operated principally on a

small personal basis as a sole proprietorship or partnership so there was little real incentive for management theory to develop.

1. _____	5. Reason _____
2. _____	6. Reason _____
3. Main Idea ___	7. Reason _____
4. Reason _____	

Note that in this sample paragraph, the author states that you will be given reasons in support of the stated main idea. The sentences with these reasons are numbered four through seven. You can insert a "Why?" between the main idea in sentence three and each of the sentences numbered four through seven, and the "Why?" makes sense since the detail answers that question. In other words, sentences four through seven each tell why management theory was slow to develop.

Also note that the first two sentences have not been selected as supporting details since they merely introduce the main idea stated in the third sentence but provide no specific information related to that main idea. Thus, sentences one and two are not considered as part of the block of related information.

SAMPLE D: Implied Main Idea

(1) Lap seatbelts should be worn so that they are below the iliac crests of the pelvis.   (2) They should restrain the bony pelvis at the hip joint.   (3) If the seatbelt is too high and is fastened above the iliac crest, sudden deceleration or an abrupt stop of the vehicle may cause an injury of the abdominal organs or the great vessels as the belt squeezes them against the spine.   (4) Injuries of the pelvis and lumbar spine, including fractures of the pelvis and compression fractures of the lumbar vertebrae, have also occurred as a result of the improper use of seatbelts.

IMPLIED MAIN IDEA: It is important to wear lap seatbelts correctly. ___

1. Example _____	3. Reason _____
2. Example _____	4. Reason _____

Sentences one and two are examples of proper placement of seatbelts. Sentences three and four tell you why lap seatbelts must be worn properly.

Thus, sentences three and four are related details that support the implied main idea by providing reasons for it.

SUPPORTING DETAIL: EXAMPLE OR REASON

On occasion, a detail may support the stated or implied main idea of a paragraph as either an example or a reason. Selecting and labeling this kind of detail becomes a matter of your perception of the written material. When a detail supports a main idea as either example or reason, either label will suffice. Sample E presents such a paragraph.

SAMPLE E: Supporting Example or Reason Detail

(1) Grade-beam foundations are widely used for residential construction, where permitted by local code, especially where basements are not required.   (2) A grade-beam is a reinforced concrete beam at ground level around the entire perimeter of the building.   (3) It is supported by a series of concrete piers extending down into undisturbed soil.   (4) The grade-beam supports the load of the building, and the piers distribute this load to the foundation bed.   (5) This type of grade-beam foundation is frequently used on sloping sites or in areas subject to earth slippage.

IMPLIED MAIN IDEA: Grade-beam foundations are used in residential construction.

1. Example
2. Example
3. Example
4. Example or reason
5. Example

In Sample E, sentences one, two, three, and five support the implied main idea by giving examples of the use of grade-beam foundations in residential construction. Sentence one gives an example of their use where permitted by local code, especially where basements are not required. Sentences two, three, and five are examples of their use, telling how they are used in construction. While sentence four also is an example of the use of grade-beam foundations in residential construction, it also tells why they are used. Thus, sentence four can correctly be identified as either an example or a reason. In either case sentence four belongs in your block of related information.

DETAILS THAT DO NOT SUPPORT THE MAIN IDEA

Sometimes an author may include a sentence that is a **restatement** of the main idea. Such a restatement does not actually support the main idea because it does not add information to what you already know. Instead, a restatement merely emphasizes what has been stated in the main idea by repeating it. The words are not necessarily the same as those in the main idea, but the concept is the same. If you get the feeling that the author is being repetitive, chances are that a restatement is being used for emphasis. Restatements are found only in paragraphs that have stated main ideas and should not be included in your block of related information.

Sample F presents a paragraph with a detail that is a restatement. The main idea and details have been identified for you.

SAMPLE F: Restatement Detail

(1) *If you think you have something to sell to a government agency—anything from paper clips to airplanes—make an appointment to see a Small Business Administration procurement officer.* (2) Federal procurement specialists in SBA field offices are prepared to assist you in the preparation of bids for prime contracts and subcontracts (contracts in which you supply required parts to the business which has been awarded the prime contract). (3) The procurement officers will—if you ask them—alert you to the federal agencies which buy the kinds of products or services you can supply. (4) These officers can also help you get your name on the bidders' lists, which are nothing more than another name for government agency "want" lists. (5) Thus, if you intend to become a seller to government agencies, don't neglect contacting an SBA procurement officer.

1. Main Idea _____
2. Reason _____
3. Reason _____

4. Reason _____
5. Restatement _____

Sentences two, three, and four support the stated main idea of the paragraph because they give you reasons why you should see the SBA procurement officer. Sentence five, however, has the same basic information as the main idea as stated in sentence one. The wording in sentence five may differ but the concept is the same: See an SBA procurement officer if you want to sell to government agencies. Sentence five is a restatement and should not be included in your block of related information.

Authors sometimes include details which do not support the paragraph main idea by providing specific information about that main idea. Such details may be used to introduce the main idea, as in Sample C above, or they may be used to make a transition from one paragraph to another. Sometimes a paragraph may include information that does not seem to fit with the main idea and with supporting details at all. For our purposes, we'll call these details **filler** since they fill up space without adding anything to what you need to know about the paragraph's main idea. Well-written materials should contain little, if any, filler. However, if it should happen to be included in your career materials, it is very important that you recognize filler for what it is. Simply remember to ask yourself, "What specific information in the paragraph supports the main idea?" If any detail doesn't add to your information about the main idea, don't be afraid to ignore it; filler has no place in your block of related information.

Sample G, which was used as a sample paragraph in Chapter Three, presents a paragraph with filler in it. The main idea and supporting details have been identified for you.

SAMPLE G: Filler

(1) Manufacturers, wholesalers, retailers, and service firms all employ order-takers.   (2) Nabisco Brands, a multi-billion-dollar manufacturer of snack foods and related products, employs a large sales force of order-takers.   (3) *The typical Nabisco salesperson will call on and service ten to fifteen customers per day, generally supermarkets.* (4) On each call, the salesperson will straighten the Nabisco products on the store shelves, check for out-of-stocks, do some dusting and rearranging, and write up an order.   (5) From time to time the Nabisco salesperson will attempt to get advertising into the store, set up end-of-aisle displays, and encourage the retailer to engage in cooperative advertising programs with Nabisco.

1. Filler
2. Filler
3. Main Idea
4. Example or reason
5. Example or reason

Sentence one is a very broad statement about order-takers. Sentence two introduces Nabisco Brands as an employer of a large number of order-takers. However, neither sentence one nor sentence two adds information to the stated main idea in sentence three. They do not support this main idea because they do not tell anything about what these Nabisco salespersons do on their service calls to customers. Compare sentences one and two to sentences four and five; sentences four and five do support the main idea of the paragraph by presenting examples of what the Nabisco Salespersons do as a service and by giving reasons why these salespersons call on the supermarkets. Note how sentences three, four, and five form a block of related information.

SAMPLE PRACTICE
Selecting Details That Support the Main Idea

DIRECTIONS: Read each of the following five paragraphs carefully. You have worked with some of these paragraphs before. The main ideas are identified in all of the paragraphs in order for you to concentrate on selecting details that support these main ideas. Write E if the detail is an example, R if the detail is a reason, and RE if the supporting detail is a restatement of the main idea. If the detail is filler, write F to indicate that it is unrelated to the main idea. I have written MI, where appropriate, to indicate Main Idea.

1. (1) Before approaching a lender, your first step is to prepare a cash flow forecast (a statement of the company's cash receipts and payments during an accounting period) to determine the financing needs of your business. (2) Consider some important factors such as the purpose of the loan and how large a loan is needed. (3) Also consider how long you will need the loan and how you will repay it. (4) Once you have identified these factors, you are able to evaluate loan alternatives. (5) Investigate these alternatives and select the loan and lender most appropriate for your financial needs. (6) *When you follow these specific planned steps, it is easier to approach a lender for aid in financing your business.*

1. _____	4. _____
2. _____	5. _____
3. _____	6. MI _____

2. (1) Any type of detergent and any stain remover may be safely used for linen fabrics. (2) Laundry additives do little or no damage to this kind of fabric. (3) If special finishes have been applied to the linen, care should be given to limit the temperatures used in ironing and to avoid the use of chlorine bleaches, particularly if a durable-press or wrinkle-resistant finish has been applied. (4) Linen fabrics usually require ironing since they seldom come from the laundry or dry-

cleaning solvent without wrinkles.   (5) Because of its properties, linen does not soil quickly and, unless stained, seldom needs any bleaching.   (6) As with any textile product, the consumer should make certain that care label information is read and followed.

IMPLIED MAIN IDEA: Done properly, linen may be laundered or dry-cleaned with no damage.

1. _____		4. _____
2. _____		5. _____
3. _____		6. _____

3.   (1) There is no easy solution for the problem of securing jobs for workers who are displaced because of declines in the industries in which they were formerly employed.   (2) Since these declining industries are often concentrated in specific areas of the country, many such workers will need to relocate.   (3) Displaced workers will require further training or education in order to find jobs similar to ones they have lost.   (4) Some of the displaced may not find similar employment anywhere and [may] remain unemployed because they do not have the education or training for [the] new kinds of jobs which are expected to emerge in the near future.

1. <u>MI</u>		3. _____
2. _____		4. _____

4.   (1) Both private and government employers are looking at new ways to schedule work.   (2) Flextime is the best known form of work scheduling.   (3) A German aerospace company was reportedly the first to use flextime, in 1967, to help employees cope with severe traffic congestion.   (4) The concept spread rapidly throughout Europe in the early 1970s, which was a time of low unemployment on the continent.   (5) Flextime came into wide use in the United States after having been tested in European businesses for over a decade. (6) Today, in America, an estimated 10 million workers in the private sector and an estimated 500,000 employees at 41 federal agencies participate in flexible time arrangements.

IMPLIED MAIN IDEA: This paragraph provides information about flextime and its use.

1. _____		4. _____
2. _____		5. _____
3. _____		6. _____

5.   (1) *The U.S. Bureau of Labor Statistics expects that a quarter of all employment growth through 1995 will be in the category of "other services."* (2) Within this category the largest industry is business services (a variety of things from business consultants to janitorial services), which has a projected employment growth of 3.9 percent per year. (3) Professional services (legal, engineering, accounting, etc.) are expected to add another 850,000 jobs. (4) Financial and banking services are projected to have strong growth but "modest" employment gains of 1.9 percent per year or 21 percent in ten years. (5) Thus, there should be employment opportunities to be found in "other services" through 1995.

1. MI _____   4. _____

2. _____   5. _____

3. _____

Check the details you selected in each of the paragraphs. Be sure to read the explanation provided for each paragraph. If your anwers are not the same as those given, analyze and compare the two answers very carefully.

Sample Practice Answers

1.   1. E _____   4. E _____

2. E _____   5. E _____

3. E _____   6. MI _____

Sentences one through five each support the stated main idea by presenting an example of a step to be followed in approaching a lender for a business loan.

2. **IMPLIED MI:**   Done properly, linen may be laundered or dry-cleaned with no damage.

1. E _____   4. E _____

2. E _____   5. E _____

3. E _____   6. E _____

In this paragraph, each sentence gives an example of a proper way to launder or dry-clean linen fabrics. Sentence one is concerned with the proper types of detergents and stain removers. Sentence two discusses ironing linen and chlorine bleaches. Sentence three continues to discuss the way to iron linen fabrics. Sentence four tells about the use of bleach. Sentence five makes an overall suggestion regarding the care-label information provided for consumers.

3.

1. MI _____	3. R _____
2. R _____	4. R _____

The main idea of the paragraph, found in sentence one, states that there is no easy solution for the problem of securing jobs for workers who are displaced because of declines in the industries where they were formerly employed. Sentences two through four each give a reason why the solution to this problem will be difficult. Sentences two and three discuss relocation and the need for additional education or training if the worker wants a similar job. Sentence four brings up the possibility of these workers not finding similar employment and remaining unemployed in the future.

4. **IMPLIED MAIN IDEA:** This paragraph provides information about flextime and its use.

1. F _____	4. E _____
2. E _____	5. E _____
3. E _____	6. E _____

Sentences two through six present information about flextime. Sentence two defines flextime while the other four sentences tell about the use of this system of scheduling work in Europe and in America. The only common idea in this paragraph is that information is given about flextime and its use. Sentence one is filler since it does not support the implied main idea with any information about flextime or its use.

5.

1. MI _____	4. E _____
2. E _____	5. RE _____
3. E _____	

The main idea of the paragraph, stated in sentence one, speaks of an expected growth in the category of "other services." Sentences two, three, and four each give an example of expected growth within segments of the "other services" category. Since sentence five repeats the concept stated in the main idea, it is a restatement.

Now go on to Skill Development Exercise 5–1 on page 83, which will provide you with an opportunity to focus on identifying supporting details. The paragraphs in this exercise are ones in which you have already identified main ideas. They come from Chapters Three and Four.

Then go on to Skill Development Exercise 5–2 on page 89 where you will work with new paragraphs. Here you will identify both main ideas (stated or implied) and related details to develop blocks of related information.

In Skill Application 5 on page 95, you are asked to apply all that you know about main ideas and details to your own career-related materials.

SKILL DEVELOPMENT EXERCISE 5–1
Supporting Details in Paragraphs

DIRECTIONS: You have worked with these paragraphs before and have already identified the main idea of each. If you need to, use Chapters Three and Four to fill in the main ideas. Write MI *next to the sentence number where the stated main idea is located or write the implied main idea below the paragraph. Then relate details to these main ideas. Identify related details as example (E) or reason (R). Mark details that do not support the main idea as restatement (RE) or filler (F).*

1.   (1) Today's jobs are not as likely to bring the same satisfaction earned by craftspeople such as the cabinetmakers or blacksmiths of the last century.   (2) Work skills are now linked to machine operations, and what we make is mostly the product of other machines and other workers.   (3) The mechanized worker stands at a psychological distance from his or her work and is not identified with the end product.   (4) Often this type of employee is confined to a fixed work station and is expected to leave it only with permission—a restriction that can affect one's attitude toward work.

MAIN IDEA (IF IMPLIED): _____

_____

_____

    1. _____   3. _____

    2. _____   4. _____

2.   (1) Disk drives in personal computers are usually a part of the system unit.   (2) You may notice one or two disk drives for floppy disks.   (3) Your system may also have a hard disk drive.   (4) The disk drives will hold the disks for the software program that you use on the microcomputer as well as the disk that will store the data you create when using the system.   (5) The capacity of the disks that you can use to store your information will depend upon the type of disks that can be used in the disk drives.   (6) There is a wide variety of disk drive capacities and once again, your software requirements as well as storage needs will often dictate the choice that you make.

MAIN IDEA (IF IMPLIED): _____

_____

_____

    1. _____   4. _____

    2. _____   5. _____

    3. _____   6. _____

3.   (1) The selection process for filling a job vacancy begins when a manager or supervisor sends a request to the company employment office, or [to] the staff member in charge of personnel, that an employee is needed.   (2) A job description, based on job analysis, identifies the vacancy.   (3) A job specification, which may also accompany the request, describes what kind of person is wanted to fill that vacancy.   (4) Employment or personnel specialists then use the job description and specifications to begin the recruiting process.   (5) The pool of applicants generated by recruiting activities must be narrowed down and one person selected to fill the job.

MAIN IDEA (IF IMPLIED): _____

_____

_____

    1. _____   4. _____

    2. _____   5. _____

    3. _____

4.   (1) Where does the designer get ideas and inspiration for new fashions?   (2) The fashion designer gets ideas and inspiration everywhere!   (3) Through television the designer experiences all the wonders of the entertainment world.   (4) In films the designer is exposed to the influences of all the arts and lifestyles throughout the world. (5) Museum exhibits, art shows, world happenings, expositions, the theater, music, dance, and world travel are all sources of design inspiration to fashion designers.

MAIN IDEA (IF IMPLIED): _____

_____

_____

1. _____   4. _____

2. _____   5. _____

3. _____

5.   (1) The Wool Products Labeling Act of 1939 (requiring that the kind and percentage of wool in a product be identified), the Fur Products Labeling Act of 1951 (requiring identification of the animal from which the fur was derived), and the Flammable Fabrics Act of 1953 (prohibiting the interstate sale of flammable fabrics) formed the original legislation in this area.   (2) A more recent law—the Fair Packaging and Labeling Act, passed in 1967—requires the disclosure of product identity, the name and address of the manufacturer or distributor, and information concerning the quality of its contents.   (3) In 1971, the Public Health Cigarette Smoking Act prohibited tobacco advertising on radio and television.   (4) Thus, rules governing advertising and labeling constitute a sphere of marketing's legal environment.

MAIN IDEA (IF IMPLIED): _____

_____

_____

1. _____   3. _____

2. _____   4. _____

6.   (1) Surveying is the science of determining the dimensions and contour (or three-dimensional characteristics) of the earth's surface by the measurements of distances, directions, and elevations.   (2) It also involves staking out the lines and grades needed for the construction of buildings, roads, dams, etc.   (3) In addition to these field measurements, surveying includes the computation of areas, volumes, and other quantities, as well as the preparation of necessary maps and diagrams.   (4) Surveying has many industrial applications: for example, setting equipment, assembling aircraft, laying out assembly lines, and so on.

MAIN IDEA (IF IMPLIED): _____

_____

_____

1. _____   3. _____

2. _____   4. _____

7.   (1) Sears, Roebuck is the largest direct-mail marketer in the United States, followed by J.C. Penney.   (2) In a tie for third are Spiegel, Inc., and Fingerhut Corporation.   (3) Fingerhut executives say their success in selling electronics, garden supplies, and gift foods by mail stems from long-term customer relationships and easy credit.   (4) The firm targets individuals who are probably good credit risks and promotes selected items.   (5) If a customer's payment record proves reliable, more expensive items are offered in subsequent mailings.   (6) Fingerhut reinforces customer loyalty with special promotional items, sweepstakes, and awards.

MAIN IDEA (IF IMPLIED): _____

_____

_____

1. _____   4. _____

2. _____   5. _____

3. _____   6. _____

8. (1) Think of the knowledge required when selling products like major appliances, photographic equipment, personal computers, televisions, and stereos to mention but a few. (2) Customers will naturally ask questions, and a salesperson must have good product knowledge to complete sales. (3) For many retail selling jobs, considerable training is required. (4) In some cases, special training, such as the American Gem Society certificate program, must be completed to qualify for a retailing position. (5) It is obvious, therefore, that many retail selling jobs require a great deal of knowledge and skill.

MAIN IDEA (IF IMPLIED): _____

_____

_____

1. _____   4. _____

2. _____   5. _____

3. _____

9. (1) BASIC is an acronym for Beginner's All-purpose Symbolic Instruction Code. (2) It was originally developed at Dartmouth College in the 1960s as a tool for teaching principles of computer programming. (3) Because it is quite easy to learn and oriented toward problem solving without much concern for machine details, it quickly spread beyond the college as a language especially suited for non-professional programmers and casual computer users. (4) It became popular in commercial time-sharing and has spread rapidly with the rapid increase in the use of personal computers.

MAIN IDEA (IF IMPLIED): _____

_____

_____

1. _____   3. _____

2. _____   4. _____

10.   (1) Direct evidence is often referred to as "eyewitness" evidence.   (2) This is putting it too simply, however.   (3) Direct evidence is the product of a person's sensory perception, and most people have perception in five senses: sight, touch, taste, smell, and hearing.   (4) The person who observed the accused pulling a revolver from his belt was giving direct eyewitness testimony.   (5) Had he also testified, "I heard three shots," he would have provided an example of what could be termed direct "ear-witness" testimony.   (6) The person who testifies, "It smelled like smoke," is a "nose-witness," and the person who testifies, "I felt his wrist and got no pulse," is a "touch-witness."   (7) It tasted like bitter almonds," is, of course, an example of direct evidence based on the witness's sense of taste.

MAIN IDEA (IF IMPLIED): _____

_____

_____

1. _____   5. _____

2. _____   6. _____

3. _____   7. _____

4. _____

SKILL DEVELOPMENT EXERCISE 5–2
Main Ideas and Supporting Details in New Paragraphs

DIRECTIONS: Identify the main idea of the paragraph. If the main idea is stated, underline it. If the main idea is implied, write it in your own words. Then show how details support that main idea. Write E if the detail is an example of the main idea or R if the detail is a reason for the main idea. If the detail does not support the main idea, leave the line blank. Check your main idea and supporting details by seeing if they form a block of related information.

1.   (1) Saks Fifth Avenue defines its target market as the upper-class, status-conscious consumer, whereas K-mart defines its target market as the middle-class, value-conscious consumer. (2) Factory outlets cater to price-conscious consumers, whereas small clothing stores concentrate on consumers interested in the personal touch. (3) National gasoline-station chains seek consumers who value a total car-service offering; small independent gasoline stations attract buyers interested only in the lowest prices for gasoline. (4) The key to success of each of these companies is their ability to define their customers and cater to their needs in a distinctive manner.

MAIN IDEA (IF IMPLIED): _____

_____

_____

      1. _____   3. _____

      2. _____   4. _____

2.   (1) Speaking too far from a transmitting microphone may result in weak, hard-to-hear signals. (2) Shouting into the microphone produces a distorted output signal that may be difficult to understand. (3) If there is considerable local noise, it may help intelligibility to cup the hands around the microphone and speak directly into it in a moderate voice. (4) Directing the front of the microphone away from noise sources helps.

MAIN IDEA (IF IMPLIED): _____

_____

_____

      1. _____   3. _____

      2. _____   4. _____

3.   (1) The United States has established some limitations on the right to strike.   (2) Several states limit the right of public employees to strike.   (3) The Taft-Hartley Act allows the president to seek a court injunction prohibiting a strike for 80 days when it is believed that the strike would create a "national emergency."   (4) During the 80-day period, work continues under the conditions of the old contract.   (5) If a settlement has not been reached during the "cooling off" period, however, employees again have the option of using the strike weapon.   (6) Strikes by federal employees are also prohibited by law.   (7) When the air-traffic controller's union called a strike during the summer of 1981, striking workers who refused to return to work were fired and eventually replaced.

MAIN IDEA (IF IMPLIED): _____

_____

_____

1. _____	3. ⎫ *	6. ⎫
2. _____	4. ⎬ _____	7. ⎭ _____
	5. ⎭	

* Consider sentences 3, 4, and 5 together as a single detail, since they logically go together, and consider sentences 6 and 7 as another single detail for the same reason.

4.   (1) In early America, wood was the primary source of energy. (2) Today the major source of energy is petroleum.   (3) Petroleum has replaced wood as America's most used source of energy.   (4) It is the most widely used of all energy sources because of its mobility and flexibility in utilization.   (5) Approximately three-fourths of the total energy needs of the United States are currently supplied by petroleum products, and this condition will likely continue for many years. (6) Petroleum engineering is the practical application of the basic sciences (primarily chemistry, geology, and physics) and the engineering sciences to the development, recovery, and field processing of petroleum.

MAIN IDEA (IF IMPLIED): _____

_____

_____

1. _____	4. _____
2. _____	5. _____
3. _____	6. _____

5.   (1) Television has become a vast resource, the ultimate educational device, not because it teaches traditional curricula, but because it supplies *roles*.   (2) Countless characters parade through our lives each day via TV: priests and politicians, doctors and lawyers, private detectives and public enemies, sex objects, and sex offenders. (3) Each character supplies us with bits of information about what his or her role is like.   (4) We have personal contact with a few people every day, but television gives us contact with a cast of hundreds.   (5) These roles may have a direct impact on how we perceive ourselves and our own roles in our personal day-to-day environment.

MAIN IDEA (IF IMPLIED): _____

_____

_____

    1. _____   4. _____

    2. _____   5. _____

    3. _____

6.   (1) As of today, public transit is predominantly a governmental function.   (2) Nine-tenths of the services are supplied by governmentally-owned agencies.   (3) Buses and para-transit vehicles such as vans and taxis all travel on government-supplied highways and streets.   (4) In 20 of the largest urban areas, governmental agencies operate heavy, commuter or light-rail facilities, augmented by buses.   *(5)* Indeed, governmental involvement in public transportation is widespread.

MAIN IDEA (IF IMPLIED): _____

_____

_____

    1. _____   4. _____

    2. _____   5. _____

    3. _____

7.   (1) As an Emergency Medical Technician, you will have to provide basic life support for patients because they cannot breathe adequately, have stopped breathing, have developed cardiac arrest, or have developed shock.   (2) You will have to provide care for patients having cuts, bruises, fractures, burns, and internal injuries.   (3) You will be called on to deal with heart attacks, strokes, respiratory illnesses, seizures, diabetic coma, insulin shock, childbirth, poisoning, drug abuse, and problems due to excessive heat and cold.   (4) In addition, you will have to provide care for patients suffering emotional or psychiatric emergencies.   (5) Some problems you encounter will be simple while others will be life-threatening.   (6) All situations will require professional-level emergency care.

MAIN IDEA (IF IMPLIED): _____

_____

_____

    1. _____   4. _____

    2. _____   5. _____

    3. _____   6. _____

8.   (1) In ancient China, there were refuges for the aged, the sick, and the poor, free schools for poor children, free eating houses for weary laborers, associations for the distribution of secondhand clothing, and even societies for paying expenses of marriage and burial among the poor and destitute.   (2) In India, especially after the time of Buddha, considerable activity was related to giving to beggars.   (3) A saint with his bowl was one of the traditions of the Orient, and the emphasis in the religious teachings upon the obligation of almsgiving not only made the holy men of that country a nuisance but also encouraged impostors.   (4) The Greeks had no regular charitable organizations, but they did have institutions for the unfortunate and the sick.   (5) Gifts and assistance were publicly distributed at the time of the great festivals by men who were candidates for public office.   (6) There were asylums for wounded soldiers and for abandoned children; and in Athens, a poor tax was levied and collected to help the destitute.   (7) The religion of the Hebrews laid great stress upon charity and helping those in

need.   (8) It is obvious, then, that social welfare was rooted in the distant past.

MAIN IDEA (IF IMPLIED): _____

_____

_____

1. _____   7. _____

2. ⎤ *
3. ⎦ _____   8. _____

4. ⎤
5. ⎬ _____
6. ⎦

* (Consider sentences 2 and 3 as a single detail as they logically go together, and consider sentences 4, 5, and 6 as another single detail for the same reason.

9.   (1) The BBC started in 1922 as the British Broadcasting Company, becoming a corporation in 1927.   (2) Today, it acts as an independent organization, although it receives its budget for overseas broadcasting from Parliament.   (3) The fees it collects from licenses are also determined by Parliament.   (4) Directed by a twelve-person board of governors appointed by the Queen, the corporation operates under the advice of a series of advisory boards, which include the General Advisory Council, National Broadcasting Councils for Scotland and Wales, and advisory bodies in such areas as religion, education, and local radio.   (5) Originally founded as a nonprofit, public corporation by Royal charter in 1927, the BBC does not receive income from advertising.

MAIN IDEA (IF IMPLIED): _____

_____

_____

1. _____   4. _____

2. _____   5. _____

3. _____

10.   (1) The success of a group is partially determined by the individual characteristics of group members.   (2) Age, sex, ethnic background, marital status, experience, and educational levels are important considerations.   (3) If the individual characteristics of group members are very similar, individual member satisfaction usually will be higher than in a group with diverse members.   (4) In homogeneous groups, members tend to be more friendly and have higher group spirit. (5) However, groups whose members have quite different characteristics (heterogeneous groups) tend to be more productive.

MAIN IDEA (IF IMPLIED): _____

_____

_____

1. _____   4. _____

2. _____   5. _____

3. _____

SKILL APPLICATION 5
Main Ideas and Supporting Details in Paragraphs

DIRECTIONS: *Choose two paragraphs from your own career-related materials. Duplicate the paragraphs and paste them on this sheet with one paragraph on each side. Number the sentences and then identify the main idea
and supporting details in each paragraph just as you did in Skill Development Exercise 5–2. Be sure to include the source information for each paragraph.*

PARAGRAPH 1 SOURCE INFORMATION

Title: _____

Author: _____

Place of publication: _____

Publisher: _____

Copyright Date: _____   *Page(s):* _____

PARAGRAPH 2 SOURCE INFORMATION

Title: _____

Author: _____

Place of publication: _____

Publisher: _____

Copyright Date: _____   *Page(s):* _____

Chapter Six

Identifying Main Ideas and Selecting Supporting Details in Selections

Much of the career-related reading you need to do probably involves materials that are longer than a single paragraph. You may need to read sections of chapters in textbooks, whole chapters in those textbooks, proposals, research, long memos, articles, and so on. For the sake of simplicity, in this textbook we will call any material longer than a paragraph a "selection."

As you read selections, it is very important that you develop the same kinds of blocks of related information you did when working with paragraphs. Identifying main ideas and details in selections is simply an extension of the analytical skills you developed in Chapters Three, Four, and Five.

It is sometimes more important for you to analyze the organization and content of a selection than of individual paragraphs, since it is here where you can possibly become lost in a sea of words. As you found out in working with paragraphs, packages of related information make is easier for you to understand and retain written material.

MAIN IDEAS IN SELECTIONS

To identify the main idea of a selection, use a slight modification of the two questions you used to identify main ideas in paragraphs. The questions now become:

1. *What is the topic of the selection?*

2. *What does the author want you to know about that topic?*

Words, phrases, or ideas which are mentioned over and over again in the entire selection are clues to answering the first question. As you found in working with paragraphs, the answer will give you a very general idea of what the selection is about. This answer to the first question, the topic, usually can be expressed in one or two words and leads you to the answer to the second question.

To answer the second question, you must carefully analyze the information presented within the paragraphs that make up the selection. The answer to the second question narrows down the answer to the first by giving particular information about the topic of the selection. The answer to the second question is the main idea of the selection. Express your answer to the second question in your own words for the same reason you did this when identifying the main idea of a paragraph: You will be able to recognize the stated main idea in the selection because its wording is similar to your words or, when appropriate, you will use your expressed answer as an implied main idea.

The main idea of a selection may be stated or implied. If it is stated, it is a sentence that may be found anywhere in the selection. As with single paragraphs, the most common writing style seems to state the main idea at the beginning of the selection. However, the stated main idea may also be found at the end of the selection or somewhere in the middle of it. The stated main idea may be an entire paragraph within the selection if a single sentence makes up that paragraph, or the stated main idea may be only a sentence within one of the selection's paragraphs. If the main idea of the selection is implied, be sure to express it in a complete sentence.

When you identify the main idea in a paragraph, you are able to check the accuracy of that main idea by analyzing sentences within the paragraph to see if they are related to it. You can check the main idea of a selection in the same way. The only difference is that you now check paragraph main ideas, rather than single sentences, to see if all, or most, of these paragraph main ideas support the main idea of the selection.

Sometimes a selection may have a title or a subtitle if it is part of a larger unit of material. Be careful of titles or subtitles: Sometimes they reflect the main idea of the selection, and sometimes they do not. They may even be the answer to the first main idea question, leaving you to then pinpoint what the author wants you to know about the selection's topic. You may find it better to ignore the title or subtitle until you have identified the main idea of the selection. Then decide how the main idea and the title (or subtitle) relate to each other.

Paragraphs within the selections in this chapter have been numbered to make it easier to refer to them.

The following three sample selections demonstrate how to identify the main ideas of selections. Sample A has a stated main idea while Sample B has an implied main idea. Sample C also has an implied main idea. In this case, however, the sample presents the kind of selection in which it is difficult to determine a common idea which then can be expressed in your own words as an implied main idea.

SAMPLE A: Stated Main Idea

BUSINESS COMMUNICATIONS IN YOUR FUTURE

(1) There are many reasons why you should know how to write effective business communications, regardless of the type of equipment to which you have access. In the first place, your value to the organization you work for will be greatly enhanced, which often means more rapid progress up the promotion ladder. Competent writers are not as plentiful as you might imagine, and those who write well stand out like a beacon.

(2) Second, those who can compose effective business letters make new friends and keep old ones for the organization, thereby increasing sales and profits, which all businesses need to survive.

(3) Third, good writers can save a great deal of time, effort, and money for an organization. Millions of dollars are wasted each year by people who write windy and garbled messages that exhaust and befuddle their readers.

(4) Finally, your rating as an employee—which hinges greatly on your skill in working harmoniously with the people around you—shoots up dramatically when you master the art of writing sensible, tactful, and finely honed memorandums.

What is the topic of the selection?

writing business communications

What does the author want you to know about writing good business communications?

IN MY OWN WORDS: There are reasons why you should be a writer of good business communications.

In answering the first question, note that the idea of writing good business communications is found in each of the four paragraphs in the selection. There is a sentence in the selection that expresses a concept similar to the one I've written. It is the first sentence of the first paragraph:

"There are many reasons why you should know how to write effective business communications, regardless of the type of equipment to which you have access." Therefore, Sample A does have a stated main idea to underline or highlight.

The title of the selection, "Business Communications in Your Future," is somewhat misleading. It suggests the sending and receiving of business communications instead of relating to the main idea of the selection, which is concerned with the reasons for writing effective business communication.

SAMPLE B: Implied Main Idea

OPPORTUNITIES IN SURVEYING

(1) There are few professions which need qualified people so much as does the surveying profession. In the United States, the tremendous physical development of the country (subdivisions, factories, dams, power lines, cities) has created a need for surveyors at a faster rate than our schools have produced them. Construction, our largest industry, requires a constant supply of new surveyors.

(2) There are hundreds of towns and cities throughout the United States where additional surveyors are needed. For a person with a liking for a combination of outdoor and indoor work, surveying offers opportunities. There are few other fields in which a qualified person can set himself up in private practice so readily and with such excellent prospects for success.

(3) It is necessary for a person going into private practice to meet the licensing requirements in his particular state. He may be able to do his initial work under the supervision of a registered surveyor until he qualifies for a license so that he can himself practice privately. Many people are able to hold other jobs and do surveying on holidays and weekends for licensed surveyors until they themselves can become registered.

(4) A large percentage of today's practicing surveyors reached their status by apprenticeships and self-study programs and perhaps have not had very much formal schooling in their field. Nevertheless, it is probable that this supply of surveyors will not be sufficient in the future.

What is the topic of the selection?

surveyors

What does the author want you to know about surveyors?

IN MY OWN WORDS: There are job opportunities for professional surveyors.

In the selection, the term "surveyor" is used over and over again, thus leading you to the answer to the first question. Each of the paragraphs in the selection discusses job opportunities for professional surveyors. However, there isn't a single sentence or even several sentences which express the particular information about surveyors that the author wants you to know. You must, therefore, use your answer to the second question as the implied main idea of the selection.

The selection in Sample B is part of a textbook chapter and includes a subtitle. However, the subtitle does not actually reflect the main idea of the selection; it is too broad. "Opportunities in Surveying" leads one to ask what kinds of opportunities are being referred to by the author. The selection primarily discusses job opportunities.

SAMPLE C: Implied Main Idea

FIRE DEPARTMENT PUMPERS

(1) Present recognized capacities of pumps for fire department pumpers are 500, 750, 1,000, 1,250, 1,500, 1,750, and 2,000 gallons per minute (gpm), although some larger capacity pumpers have been built. A fire department pumper must also be provided with adequate inlet and discharge pump connections, pump and engine controls, gauges and other instruments.

(2) Some fire department pumpers are referred to as triple combination pumpers, which means they have a water tank, fire pump, and hose compartment. A triple combination pumper will usually carry an extension ladder, a roof ladder, forcible entry tools, hose appliance, and other accessories. The three components of a triple combination pumper may vary with each manufacturer's design or with specifications as written by the purchaser.

(3) The main purpose of a fire department pumper is to provide adequate pressure for fire streams. The water it supplies comes from the apparatus tank, a fire hydrant, or a static supply.

What is the topic of the selection?

fire department pumpers

What does the author want you to know about fire department pumpers?

IN MY OWN WORDS: This selection presents information about fire department pumpers.

The term "fire department pumper" is repeated over and over again in the selection so that it is easy to see this is the topic of the selection and the answer to the first question. When you ask the second question, it is difficult to pin down exactly what the author wants you to know about these fire department pumpers. There isn't any common idea that goes through the selection; it seems to present a number of different facts about the fire department pumper. The answer to the second question, expressed in your own words, thus becomes the implied main idea of the selection.

The title of the selection reflects the answer to the first question but is too broad to serve as the main idea of the entire selection.

SAMPLE PRACTICE
Identifying Main Ideas in Selections

DIRECTIONS: Read each of the following selections carefully. Ask the two questions to identify the stated or implied main idea of the selection. If the main idea is stated, underline or highlight it in the selection. If the main idea is implied, write it in your own words below the selection.

1. CHOOSING A BUSINESS

(1) If you are serious about becoming a small business owner, the very first thing you should do is to engage in a period of investigation. Once you have generally defined the kind of business you would like to own, you need to examine what is involved in such a venture. The investigation will help you to determine if this is the kind of business in which you want to invest your time, energy, and money. The time spent investigating a potential kind of business can help you to avoid later disappointments and problems.

(2) Begin your investigation by getting all the facts which are readily available about the kind of business of your choice. Find out where the trade association is, what it publishes, and what assistance it offers. Look at all the magazines, newspapers, and newsletters written about that kind of business.

(3) Clarify the business's objectives. Understand exactly what the business is going to produce or what service it will render. Since no two businesses, even in the same field, are alike, try to determine how yours will be different.

(4) Visit businesses of this type to get a firm idea of how they operate. Talk to the owners and frankly discuss how business is and whether it is profitable. Ask about sales volume and how long it took for the business to become profitable. Inquire about the desirability of the location. Include questions on what mistakes were made at the start.

(5) Collect as much information as possible from other sources, even the competition. Visit the Chamber of Commerce as well as state and city development agencies. Talk with local associations and business groups. Interview potential customers. Ask for information and opinions from persons employed in local banks.

(6) Interpret the information with a view towards understanding the community's composition and how the needs of your potential customers can best be served. This information should tell you where to locate the business. It will also help you to plan on the kind of physical plant or store you need to provide the necessary work space and/or sales area.

(7) Finally, prepare an informal study which weighs the pros and cons from the materials you have collected during your investigation. Estimate the investment required: how much money you will need to function for one month, three months, six months, and a year. Estimate the profit possibilities: How much money can be expected from sales and how much will be left for earnings after expenses. Construct a table of income and expenses on a monthly basis for a year, determining where the break-even point is.

What is the topic of the selection?

_____

What does the author want you to know about that topic?

MAIN IDEA (IF IMPLIED): _____

_____

_____

_____

_____

2. BRICK

(1) Building bricks are solid masonry units composed of inorganic nonmetallic materials hardened or burned by heat or chemical action. Building brick may be solid or it may have cored openings not to exceed 25 percent of its volume. Bricks are produced in a wide variety of colors, shapes, and textures.

(2) Recent excavations in Egypt have shown that the ancient Egyptians used sun-dried and kiln-burned bricks for houses and palaces of nobility. In the Babylonian civilization (4000 B.C.), which developed in the valley of the Tigris and Euphrates Rivers, the thick mud and clay laid down by these rivers was well suited for brick, which thus became the usual building material for this civilization. Palaces and temples were constructed of sun-dried brick, faced with brilliant kiln-burned glazed brick.

(3) The Romans also made wide use of brick in conjunction with a very efficient mortar. The Roman bricks were comparatively thin for their length. They were laid in thick beds of mortar in several patterns. After the fall of the Roman Empire the art of brickmaking was lost throughout Europe until the beginning of the fourteenth century. The first brick buildings on the North American continent were erected in 1633 on Manhattan Island with bricks imported from Holland and England.

What is the topic of the selection?

_____

What does the author want you to know about that topic?

MAIN IDEA (IF IMPLIED): _____

_____

_____

_____

_____

3. SMALL BUSINESSES

(1) Recent research suggests that the role of small businesses in the U.S. economy has changed over the past few years. Small businesses are presently involved in activities that help bring stability and higher productivity to the U.S. economy.

(2) Small businesses aid the economy by playing an innovative role in the development and introduction of new goods and services to the marketplace. Many small firms are important suppliers of specialized goods and services. As such, they increase the variety of goods and services from which consumers can choose.

(3) Many small businesses act as market demand "shock ab-

sorbers." By employing flexible production technologies, small firms are able to meet short-term variations in demand. Thus, small firms help assure that temporary increases in demand are satisfied, without sharp price increases.

(4) Small businesses are more likely than large firms to employ less skilled workers and individuals with no prior work experience. This practice improves the prospects of these workers for sustained employment, thereby providing on-the-job training and employment history. Therefore, small businesses help to increase and expand the capacity of the U.S. economy by adding productive workers to the labor force.

(5) Thus it can be said that small businesses add much to the U.S. economy. They serve as innovators, introducers of new products and services to consumers, and employer/trainers of less skilled workers. All of these activities increase and strengthen the economy of this country.

What is the topic of the selection?

_____

What does the author want you to know about that topic?

MAIN IDEA (IF IMPLIED): _____

_____

_____

_____

_____

4. FOOTINGS

(1) Footings are the "feet" placed in the ground upon which the foundation walls and entire building load rests. The footing size is determined by architects and engineers, based on the type of soil (determined by tests) and the weight of the building.

(2) Footings also are required under a building's support columns. These footings frequently are wider and thicker than footings for foundation walls because the column loads are concentrated in one spot. Fireplace chimneys and similar concentrations of weight also require larger footings.

(3) Footings are located from strings attached to batter boards that are set back from the excavation for the building. The footings may be trenches cut into the floor of the excavation or they may rest on the excavation floor. In the latter case, boards are used to form the sides of the footings, to the proper width and adjusted for the correct height.

(4) Footings must rest on undisturbed earth, and steel reinforcing rods usually are placed in the footings. This is especially important where footings must pass over previously disturbed earth due to the installation of a drain pipe or other excavation.

What is the topic of the selection?

_____

What does the author want you to know about that topic?

MAIN IDEA (IF IMPLIED): _____

_____

_____

_____

_____

5.   CAUSES OF PRODUCTIVITY DECLINES

(1) No one is certain why declines in productivity have occurred in the United States. Several factors, however, have been cited as possible causes for this decline in productivity. First, in recent years the United States has experienced major changes in the composition of its work force. In particular, many women and young people have entered the work force for the first time. The majority of these new entrants have relatively little work experience. Therefore, their productivity might be lower than the average. As they develop new skills and experience, their downward influence on productivity trends should be minimized.

(2) Another potential cause of stagnation in productivity is recent changes in industrial composition. By industrial composition we mean the relative numbers of workers in various industries. Specifically, many workers moved from agricultural jobs (which are low in productivity) during the period beginning shortly after World War II and ending in the mid-1960s. This movement alone gave a boost to productivity growth. When it ended, productivity growth slowed down again.

(3) There has also been a shift in the ratio of capital input to labor input in American industry. During the last decade, businesses have slowed their rate of investment in new equipment and technology. As workers have had to use increasingly outdated equipment, their productivity has naturally declined.

(4) Another factor that may have contributed to the decline in productivity growth is a decrease in spending for research and development. The amount of money spent for research and development by

government and industry has been falling since 1964. As a result, there have been fewer innovations and fewer new products.

(5) Finally, increased government regulation is frequently cited as a factor that has affected productivity. Federal agencies such as the Occupational Safety and Health Administration (OSHA) and the Food and Drug Administration are increasingly regulating and intervening in business practices. Goodyear Tire and Rubber Company recently generated 345,000 pages of computer printout weighing 3200 pounds to comply with one new OSHA regulation! Further, the company spends over $35 million each year solely to meet the requirements of six regulatory agencies. These resources could increase productivity if they were invested elsewhere.

What is the topic of the selection?

_____

What does the author want you to know about that topic?
MAIN IDEA (IF IMPLIED): _____

_____

_____

_____

Check the main ideas you have identified in the selections. Your words in answering the first question for identifying main ideas may differ slightly from those presented below. Keep in mind, however, that the concepts of the answers should be similar and that they should lead you to underlining the correct stated main idea or to expressing the implied main idea in your own sentence. Also, remember that your wording of these implied main ideas may vary slightly from those presented below but that the concepts must match. If your main ideas do not match those given, compare and analyze the differences in answers very carefully.

Sample Practice Answers

1. *What is the topic of the selection?*

    investigating a business

What does the author want you to know about investigating a business?

The main idea of the selection is stated in the first sentence of the first paragraph: "If you are serious about becoming a small business owner, the very first thing you should do is to engage in a period of investigation." The author then goes on to tell you how to conduct this investigation in the other paragraphs.

2. *What is the topic of the selection?*

building bricks

What does the author want you to know about bricks?

IMPLIED MAIN IDEA IN MY OWN WORDS: Building bricks have been used for a very long time. Two of the three paragraphs support this main idea.

3. *What is the topic of the selection?*

small businesses

What does the author want you to know about small businesses?

The main idea is stated in the first paragraph: "Small businesses are presently involved in activities that help bring stability and higher productivity to the U.S. economy." Each of the other four paragraphs tells about these activities.

4. *What is the topic of the selection?*

footings

What does the author want you to know about footings?

IMPLIED MAIN IDEA IN MY OWN WORDS: This selection tells about the use of footings to support buildings.

5. *What is the topic of the selection?*

the decline in productivity in the U.S.

What does the author want you to know about the decline in productivity in the U.S.?

> The selection main idea is stated in the second sentence of the first paragraph: "Several factors, however, have been cited as possible causes for this decline in productivity." Each of the four paragraphs that follow mentions causal factors.

Note that the titles of selections two, three, and four all answer the first question; each thus provides you with the topic of the selection. The title of selection one, "Choosing a Business," is misleading since the selection discusses a period of investigation which is important after you have selected the kind of business you want to go into. The title of selection five, "Causes of Productivity Declines," comes close to the main idea of the selection.

DETAILS IN SELECTIONS

As you found when working with main ideas and supporting details in paragraphs, both are essential components in packages of related information. The same concept applies to selections—main ideas in selections also must be supported by details. These details are identified by asking a modified version of the third question you asked to find details that support the main idea of a paragraph:

3. *What specific information in the selection supports the main idea?*

Selection main ideas are usually supported by the same two types of details that supported paragraph main ideas: **examples** and **reasons.** These two details perform the same functions in selections as they do in paragraphs. They provide additional and very specific information about the stated or implied main idea of the selection.

Supporting details in a selection are identified in the same way they are in paragraphs. Use "for example" or "for instance" to help you identify example details. Insert a "Why?" in front of a detail you think is a reason for the main idea. If the detail answers this "Why?" question, it is a reason.

Be alert for details that do not support the main idea of the selection. As you found in working with paragraphs, there is no place in a block of related information for restatements or filler.

In working with selections of any length, it is too cumbersome and time-consuming to identify and relate each and every detail to the selection main idea. Instead, allow the stated or implied main idea of each paragraph to represent that paragraph. Identify that representative as a detail and check to see how it supports (or doesn't support) the overall selection main idea.

The same three selections used earlier to demonstrate how to locate a main idea in such materials supporting appear below to show you how to identify related details. In Sample D, the stated main idea of the selection is italicized , and in Samples E and F I've written the implied main idea under the selections in my own words. In all three samples, stated paragraph main ideas are presented in boldface print so you can clearly see how paragraph main ideas can represent the paragraph and relate to the selection main idea.

SAMPLE D: Stated Main Idea and Details

BUSINESS COMMUNICATIONS IN YOUR FUTURE

(1) *There are many reasons why you should know how to write effective business communications, regardless of the type of equipment to which you have access.* **In the first place, your value to the organization you work for will be greatly enhanced, which often means more rapid progress up the promotion ladder.** Competent writers are not as plentiful as you might imagine, and those who write well stand out like a beacon.

(2) **Second, those who can compose effective business letters make new friends and keep old ones for the organization, thereby increasing sales and profits, which all businesses need to survive.**

(3) **Third, good writers can save a great deal of time, effort, and money for an organization.** Millions of dollars are wasted each year by people who write windy and garbled messages that exhaust and befuddle their readers.

(4) **Finally, your rating as an employee—which hinges greatly on your skill in working harmoniously with the people around you— shoots up dramatically when you master the art of writing sensible, tactful, and finely honed memorandums.**

What specific information in the selection supports the main idea?

Paragraph 1. <u>MI/Reason</u>   Paragraph 3. <u>Reason</u>

Paragraph 2. <u>Reason</u>   Paragraph 4. <u>Reason</u>

Notice that the first paragraph contains both the main idea of the selection and the main idea of the paragraph. Be aware that this does not necessarily occur; it is simply the author's style in this case.

The author states in the main idea that there are reasons why it is important for you to know how to write effective business communications, and then goes on to give you four reasons. The first reason appears in the same paragraph as the stated main idea. Paragraph three has a stated main idea. This main idea supports the selection main idea since it is a reason why you should know how to write effective business communications, regardless of the type of equipment to which you have access. Paragraphs two and four each consist of only one long sentence, and they also are reasons which support the main idea of the selection.

SAMPLE E: Implied Main Idea and Details

OPPORTUNITIES IN SURVEYING

(1) **There are few professions which need qualified people so much as does the surveying profession.** In the United States, the tremendous physical development of the country (subdivisions, factories, dams, power lines, cities) has created a need for surveyors at a faster rate than our schools have produced them. Construction, our largest industry, requires a constant supply of new surveyors.

(2) There are hundreds of towns and cities throughout the United States where additional surveyors are needed. For a person with a liking for a combination of outdoor and indoor work, surveying offers attractive opportunities. There are few other fields in which a qualified person can set himself up in private practice so readily and with such excellent prospects for success.

(3) It is necessary for a person going into private practice to meet the licensing requirements in his particular state. He may be able to do his initial work under the supervision of a registered surveyor until he qualifies for a license so that he can himself practice privately. Many people are able to hold other jobs and do surveying on holidays and weekends for licensed surveyors until they themselves can become registered.

(4) A large percentage of today's practicing surveyors reached their status by apprenticeships and self-study programs and perhaps have not had very much formal schooling in their field. Nevertheless, it is probable that this supply of surveyors will not be sufficient in the future.

IMPLIED MAIN IDEA: There are job opportunities for professional surveyors.

What specific information in the selection supports the main idea?

Paragraph 1:   Reason _____

Paragraph 2:   Example _____

Paragraph 3:   Example _____

Paragraph 4:   Reason _____

The first paragraph's stated main idea gives a reason why there are job opportunities: The profession needs qualified people. The second paragraph's implied main idea (Surveyors can work in the profession in different ways) stresses the job opportunities which exist for surveyors. The third paragraph's implied main idea (There are job opportunities in surveying while one is meeting licensing requirements for private practice) offers another example in support of the selection main idea. The fourth paragraph is an unusual one since it consists of two rather distinct ideas: The first sentence discusses the education of a large percentage of surveyors, and the second sentence mentions that there will not be a sufficient supply of surveyors in the future. The implied main idea of this paragraph (In the future, there will probably not be a sufficient supply of surveyors who have been trained by apprenticeships and self-study programs) supports the main idea of the selection as a reason why there are job opportunities for surveyors. This main idea tells you that there will be job opportunities in the future because there isn't a sufficient supply of surveyors. This paragraph main idea supports the selection main idea by giving a reason why there are job opportunities.

SAMPLE F: Implied Main Idea and Details

FIRE DEPARTMENT PUMPERS

(1) Present recognized capacities of pumps for fire department pumpers are 500, 750, 1,000, 1,250, 1,500, 1,750, and 2,000 gallons per minute (gpm), although some larger capacity pumpers have been built. A fire department pumper must also be provided with adequate inlet and discharge pump connections, pump and engine controls, gauges and other instruments.

(2) Some fire department pumpers are referred to as triple combination pumpers, which means they have a water tank, fire pump, and hose compartment. A triple combination pumper will usually carry an extension ladder, a roof ladder, forcible entry tools, hose appliance, and other accessories. The three components of a triple combination

pumper may vary with each manufacturer's design or with specifications as written by the purchaser.

(3) The main purpose of a fire department pumper is to provide adequate pressure for fire streams. The water it supplies comes from the apparatus tank, a fire hydrant, or a static supply.

IMPLIED MAIN IDEA: This selection presents information about fire department pumpers.

What specific information in the selection supports the main idea?

Paragraph 1: Example

Paragraph 2: Example

Paragraph 3: Example

The first paragraph has an implied main idea: The paragraph describes the fire department pumper. The second paragraph also has an implied main idea: The paragraph describes the triple combination pumper. The third paragraph is rather meager and it, too, has an implied main idea: The paragraph gives information about the purpose of the fire department pumper and its water supply. Thus, the three implied paragraph main ideas support the main idea of the selection as examples of information about the fire department pumper.

SAMPLE PRACTICE
Selecting Supporting Details in Selections

DIRECTIONS: Refer to the Sample Practice entitled "Identifying Main Ideas in Selections" on page 102. You have already found the main ideas of these selections and checked your answers for accuracy. Now show how the details in each case (main ideas of paragraphs within the selection) support the main idea. If the detail is an example, write E; if the paragraph is a reason, write R. If the author has included a restatement, write RE, and write F if a paragraph is filler.

1. *What specific information in the selection supports the main idea?*

Paragraph 1. _____   Paragraph 5. _____

Paragraph 2. _____   Paragraph 6. _____

Paragraph 3. _____   Paragraph 7. _____

Paragraph 4. _____

2. *What specific information in the selection supports the main idea?*

   Paragraph 1. _____

   Paragraph 2. _____

   Paragraph 3. _____

3. *What specific information in the selection supports the main idea?*

   Paragraph 1. _____   **Paragraph 4.** _____

   Paragraph 2. _____   **Paragraph 5.** _____

   Paragraph 3. _____

4. *What specific information in the selection supports the main idea?*

   Paragraph 1. _____   **Paragraph 3.** _____

   Paragraph 2. _____   **Paragraph 4.** _____

5. *What specific information in the selection supports the main idea?*

   Paragraph 1. _____   **Paragraph 4.** _____

   Paragraph 2. _____   **Paragraph 5.** _____

   Paragraph 3. _____

Check your details. Compare your answers with those given and analyze any which do not match. Be sure to read the explanation under each selection's answers.

Sample Practice Answers

1.   **Paragraph 1.** MI   **Paragraph 5.** E

   Paragraph 2. E   **Paragraph 6.** E

   Paragraph 3. E   **Paragraph 7.** E

   Paragraph 4. E

Paragraphs two through seven each support the main idea by giving an example of what to do in the investigative period. Each paragraph has its main idea stated in the first sentence.

2. **IMPLIED MAIN IDEA:**   Building bricks have been used for a very long time.

   Paragraph 1. F

   Paragraph 2. E

   Paragraph 3. E

In this selection, the author starts out with an implied main idea in paragraph one—i.e., this paragraph describes brick. There is a change of direction in both paragraphs two and three where the topic is now a history of the use of brick. The implied main idea of the second paragraph (Brick was used in ancient Egypt and Babylonia) and the implied main idea of the third paragraph (Brick was used in Rome and again in America in the 17th century) both support the selection main idea. Both of these main ideas are examples of bricks being used for a very long time.

The major portion of the selection is concerned with illustrations of the use of bricks over time, beginning with ancient Egypt in the first paragraph and concluding with the use of bricks on Manhattan Island in 1633 in the third paragraph. Thus, it seems logical to consider the first paragraph, which describes today's bricks, as an introductory paragraph that does not support the main idea of the selection.

3.   **Paragraph 1.** MI   **Paragraph 4.** E

   Paragraph 2. E   **Paragraph 5.** RE

   Paragraph 3. E

The main idea of the selection is stated in the last sentence of the first paragraph: "Small businesses are presently involved in activities that help bring stability and higher productivity to the U.S. economy." Paragraph two has a stated main idea in the first sentence: "Small businesses aid the economy by playing an innovative role in the development and introduction of new goods and services in the marketplace." Paragraph three also has a stated main idea in its first sentence: "Many small businesses act as market demand 'shock absorbers.' " The main ideas of paragraphs two and three both support the main idea of the selection by giving examples of the activities of small businesses which help the U.S. economy. The stated main idea in paragraph four, which is found in the last sentence, also gives an example of an activity of small business that helps the U.S. economy: "[Therefore,] small businesses help to increase and expand the capacity of the U.S. economy by adding productive workers to the labor force." The stated main idea of paragraph five is found in the first sentence: "Thus it can be said that small businesses add much to the U.S. economy." This paragraph main idea closely resembles the stated main idea of the selection. Paragraph five can be considered a restatement of that selection main idea.

4. **IMPLIED MAIN IDEA:** This selection tells about the use of footings to support buildings.

> Paragraph 1. E   Paragraph 3. E
>
> Paragraph 2. E/R   Paragraph 4. E

The implied main idea of paragraph one provides a definition of footings and describes how their size is determined for use in a building. The implied main idea of paragraph two indicates the uses of footings, giving examples of their use as well as reasons for it. The implied main idea of paragraph three indicates that it is about forming footings. The stated main idea of paragraph four is found in the first sentence and tells where footings should be placed: "Footings must rest on undisturbed earth, and steel reinforcing rods usually are placed in the footings." Thus, each of the paragraph main ideas supports the selection's implied main idea.

5.   Paragraph 1. MI/E   Paragraph 4. E

Paragraph 2. E   Paragraph 5. E

Paragraph 3. E

The selection main idea is stated in the second sentence of the first paragraph: "Several factors, [however,] have been cited as possible causes for this decline in productivity." The first cause of the decline is also included in the first paragraph: "First, in recent years the U.S. has experienced major changes in the composition of its work force." Each of the following four paragraphs has a stated main idea in its first sentence, and each of these stated main ideas is an example of a cause of the decline in U.S. productivity. The main idea in paragraph two states: "Another potential cause is recent changes in industrial composition." In paragraph three, the main idea states: "There has also been a shift in the ratio of capital input to labor output in American industry." In paragraph four, the main idea states: "Another factor that may have contributed to the decline in productivity growth is a decrease in spending for research and development." In paragraph five, the main idea states: "Finally, increased government regulation is frequently cited as a factor that has affected productivity."

Note that the author of this selection has used specific terms such as "first," "another," "also," and "finally" at the beginning of each paragraph to guide you in selecting details which support the main idea of the selection.

Now go on to Skill Development Exercise 6 on page 119, which will provide you with additional practice in identifying main ideas in selections.

Then go on to Skill Application 6 on page 125, where you will use what you have learned about forming blocks of related information with selections from your own career-related materials.

SKILL DEVELOPMENT EXERCISE 6
Identifying Main Ideas and Selecting Supporting Details in Selections

DIRECTIONS: Read each selection carefully. Use the three questions to help you to identify the main idea of the selection and the details that support the selection main idea.

1. *What is the topic of the selection?*

2. *What does the author want you to know about that topic?*

3. *What specific information in the selection supports the main idea?*

Select and indicate only details which support the main idea as example (E) or reason (R) so that you are developing blocks of related information. Do not include restatements or filler.

1. HOW TO USE A MICROPHONE WELL*

(1) Public speaking may be part of your professional responsibilities. If so, you want to get your message across to the audience as clearly as possible. However clear your message, bungling at the microphone can create a "sound barrier" between you and your audience. Here's some sound advice on using a sound system effectively to bring your ideas to the audience in a powerful, intimate way.

(2) The mike must be aimed at your mouth, about six to eight inches away from you. Adjust the microphone height to mouth level quickly, before you say a word. Then point the mike toward your mouth. Don't hunch over to reach the mouthpiece; instead, says recording engineer David Satz, "Let the microphone address you."

(3) Check out the sound system before you speak. "You have a right to have someone there who knows the system," says Satz, "and you have a right to a few moments of practice." If possible, meet with the sound operator. If a sound engineer likes you, you will sound better—he's more likely to stay around during your speech to deal with problems that arise.

(4) When you test a microphone, just talk into it normally and ask someone to listen. Never blow into it.

*Reprinted with permission from *Working Woman* Magazine. Copyright 1986 by Working Woman, Inc.

(5) Let the sound system work for you—let *it* do the broadcasting. Keep your volume, inflections, and pacing in your normal range. Listen to how well the system is working for those ahead of you and, when it's your turn, adjust your voice as necessary.

(6) When using a hand-held microphone, hold it in front of you, aimed at your mouth (not under your chin). Be careful that your handling of the microphone does not make noises—watch out for clunking finger rings.

(7) In a question-and-answer session, don't aim your microphone at the questioner. Instead, repeat the question over the sound system (following this procedure also gives you an extra moment to frame an answer).

(8) Know when not to use a sound system. If you can be heard comfortably by all the people in the room without amplification, by all means talk without a microphone. Relying on a sound system for a few dozen people, or in a room with excellent acoustics, distances you from your audience. Check your audibility by stepping away from the mike and asking listeners in the back if they can hear you. Unless you see puzzled stares, proceed on your own steam.

MAIN IDEA (IF IMPLIED): _____

_____

_____

Paragraph 1. _____   Paragraph 5. _____

Paragraph 2. _____   Paragraph 6. _____

Paragraph 3. _____   Paragraph 7. _____

Paragraph 4: _____   Paragraph 8. _____

2. THE BASIC ELEMENTS OF ACCOUNTING

(1) Financial information is commonly classified into the categories of assets, liabilities, owner's equity, revenues, expenses, and net income (or net loss). In this section of the chapter, we will concentrate first on assets, liabilities, and owner's equity.

(2) An asset is anything of value that is owned by a business. It is used in producing income for the business. Common examples of assets include cash, accounts receivable (a promise of a future cash receipt), merchandise, machinery, buildings, land, and furniture. The kinds and quantity of assets vary with the enterprise. A manufacturer may have a large building with many machines and other assets. A doctor may require only a small office with relatively few pieces of equipment or furniture.

(3) A liability is a legal obligation to pay a debt. It is what a business owes to other businesses or individuals. Any asset may be used to pay a debt, but cash is most commonly used. Accounts payable and notes payable are the most common liabilities. An account payable is an unwritten promise to pay for something at a later date. It arises when an item, such as merchandise, equipment, supplies, or services, is purchased on credit. A note payable is a written promise to pay a specified amount of money at a fixed future date. When an account payable is repaid, the creditor issues a written receipt which cancels the obligation.

(4) Owner's equity is an owner's interest in, or claim to, the assets of a business. It is the difference between the amount of assets and the amount of liabilities. Thus, assets are something owned, liabilities are something owed, and the difference is the owner's equity. Proprietorship, capital, and net worth are other terms for owner's equity.

(5) It is important to separate a company's business activities from its owner's personal activities. A business is a distinct economic unit that exists separately from its owner. This is known as the entity concept. For accounting purposes, only the assets, liabilities, and economic activities of a single economic unit are considered. Thus, if one person owns several businesses, each business is treated as a separate entity, and care must be taken to separate each one's accounting. It is also important that the owner's personal economic activities not be included in the businesses' records.

MAIN IDEA (IF IMPLIED): _____

_____

_____

Paragraph 1: _____   Paragraph 4: _____

Paragraph 2: _____   Paragraph 5: _____

Paragraph 3: _____

3. NO TITLE

(1) The United States' economy is one that increasingly takes the form of complex and interlocked networks that can have an effect on consumers. Today, more power has been put in the hands of consumers than ever before. New trends, or patterns, in purchasing goods and services are emerging in America.

(2) American households are looking for—and finding—new and different products or services as a result of two critical factors, diversity and technology. First, there is the fact that U.S. households are growing

more diverse, and second, there is the fact that technology and trade bring a greater variety of products to market at prices not significantly higher than those of "mass produced" goods. Technology also makes it possible to reach small markets efficiently.

(3) Changing incomes and income distribution have changed consumer purchasing patterns. Higher income families, for example, tend to spend a higher fraction of their incomes on recreation, education, and clothing and less on food and health. In addition, the increase in households headed by single women and inequality in the distribution of property-type income has led to greater inequality in the distribution of after-tax income among families.

(4) Direct consumer purchases of services are increasing. Much of the growth has been in the form of demand for financial services (including credit), hired substitutes for work formerly performed by unpaid household labor (like child care and care for the elderly), and increased expenditures on health care. A declining share of U.S. income has gone to purchases of food, but the share spent on food-related services (primarily in restaurants) has increased over the past 30 years.

(5) Purchases of energy and materials are declining as comparatively light, high-value products (such as personal computers) represent an increasing share of purchases. Purchases of heavy durables are leveling off.

(6) People are buying more and more products tailored to their specific needs, from magazines to insurance policies. There has always been a demand for tailored services of this kind, and new technology is now making it possible to serve specialized markets by lowering the differences in cost that have traditionally made batch production more expensive than mass production.

MAIN IDEA (IF IMPLIED): _____

_____

_____

Paragraph 1. _____   Paragraph 4. _____

Paragraph 2. _____   Paragraph 5. _____

Paragraph 3. _____   Paragraph 6. _____

4. THE ENERGY CRISIS

(1) The term energy crisis refers to the general realization that our energy resources are not limitless. This realization was first brought on by the 1973–74 Arab oil embargo. Threatened by cutbacks, much of the industrialized world scrambled for ways of conserving energy. Conser-

vation measures are widespread—for example, reduced speed limits and inducements to increase the use of insulation.

(2) Several facts have now become evident about the energy crisis of the 1970s. First, the crisis has forced business and society to rethink the current allocation of energy resources. Existing energy sources are being expanded. Traditional resources like coal are being rediscovered. New resources are being sought. Perhaps the most important fact is that attempts are being made to cut waste in energy utilization. The oil embargo of the 1970s forced the industrialized free world to take the necessary steps for self-preservation.

(3) Marketing has also been affected by the energy crisis. For example, the U.S. tire industry has had to deal with three energy-related setbacks:

1. Reduced levels of driving, causing a reduction in sales;
2. Lower new car sales, reducing the original equipment market for tires; and
3. Increased costs of petroleum-based raw materials.

Other markets have faced similar problems: The toy industry, for example, depends on a petroleum derivative—plastic. Some plastics have increased substantially in price within a very short time.

(4) As shortages began to appear in many critical industrial areas, marketers were faced with a relatively strange phenomenon. How should limited supplies be allocated to customers whose demands exceed the quantities available for distribution? Many marketers were not prepared to cope with such a situation. The energy crisis and other shortages have forced marketing to devise a fuller range of strategy alternatives.

MAIN IDEA (IF IMPLIED): _____

_____

_____

    Paragraph 1: _____   Paragraph 3: _____

    Paragraph 2: _____   Paragraph 4: _____

5. IN-HOUSE ADVERTISING AGENCIES

(1) The "full-service house agency," set up within a company and staffed to do the work of an independent full-service advertising agency, saves the company money and also centralizes all of the advertising activities in the company. Being fully self-contained means that the in-house advertising agency is capable of developing and accomplishing every type of publicity, sales promotion, and advertising required by the company.

(2) The in-house advertising agency is basically a total-capability advertising department. All aspects of advertising creativity, production, and media placement are performed in-house. Operating as a company's advertising agency, it also retains any media commission it earns.

(3) There are several reasons advertisers set up their own in-house advertising agencies. Usually the most important is the hope of realizing savings by cutting overhead expenses and saving the commissions and charges which are paid to an outside agency. Advertisers likewise feel that they can receive more attention from their agency if the company is its only client.

(4) In-house agencies can usually respond better to pressure deadlines because they can focus their full resources on the project. Although outside agencies may be able to produce just as quickly, they often have to hire freelance help, thereby incurring potentially enormous overtime charges. Likewise, house agencies tend to have a greater depth of understanding of the company's products and markets.

(5) Finally, many companies feel they have better management control of and involvement in the advertising when it is done in-house.

MAIN IDEA (IF IMPLIED): _____

_____

_____

Paragraph 1. _____   Paragraph 4. _____

Paragraph 2. _____   Paragraph 5. _____

Paragraph 3. _____

SKILL APPLICATION 6
Identifying Main Ideas and Selecting Supporting Details in Selections

DIRECTIONS: Choose two selections from materials related to your own career. Duplicate the selections and attach them to this sheet. They may/may not have a title or subtitle and should be at least three paragraphs in length. Identify the main idea and supporting details in each selection so that you develop blocks of related information. Write the selection main idea and supporting details in the same format used in this chapter. Be sure to include the source information for each selection.

SELECTION 1 SOURCE INFORMATION

Title: _____

Author: _____

Place of publication: _____

Publisher: _____

Copyright Date: _____ *Page(s):*_____

SELECTION 1:
MAIN IDEA (IF IMPLIED):

_____

_____

DETAILS: _____

_____

_____

_____

_____

SELECTION 2 SOURCE INFORMATION

Title: _____

Author: _____

Place of publication: _____

Publisher: _____

Copyright Date: _____ *Page(s):* _____

SELECTION 2:
MAIN IDEA (IF IMPLIED):

_____

_____

DETAILS: _____

_____

_____

_____

_____

Chapter Seven

Analyzing Graphics

Graphics can be a critical component in your block of related information because they help you to understand the other parts of that block. These graphics, which are actually visual presentations of information, include graphs of various types, tables, charts, maps, diagrams, and photographs. Graphics enable you to see large quantities of information at a glance. They have a visual impact which is lacking in a written presentation of the same information.

Authors use graphics in several important ways. First, graphics can be used to clarify difficult concepts by providing visual presentations of written information. Second, graphics can be used to substitute for written information; they are used in place of text. In addition, a graphic sometimes fulfills both purposes; it may clarify the information that is in the text and, at the same time, add to that information in a visual presentation.

An author decides on the kind of graphic to best represent the written information or to stand in place of it. Regardless of the kind of graphic used, graphics make it easier for you to visualize information, thus improving your ability to understand and remember it.

The value of graphics increases with your awareness of their importance and with your ability to use them. If you have any doubt as to their importance, check your daily newspaper or any periodical related to your own career and see how frequently graphics are used to clarify written text, to substitute for text, or both. Since graphics take time and skill to design and are more costly to print than written text, they must have been included in the printed material because someone thought they would be of help to the reader. Take advantage of that help by combining graphics with the written text whenever both are provided for you.

Authors use a variety of graphics in a variety of presentations depending on the information they want to convey. Regardless of the kind of graphic that is chosen by an author to clarify concepts, you can use it most effectively if you ask the following critical questions and add to what you already have in your block of related information.

1. *Does the text refer you to a graphic?*

    As you read, you may be directed to see some kind of graphic. It is usually fairly close to the written material. Find that graphic and use it as you continue with the written text. If you see a graphic on the page and are not directed to it, keep in mind that the graphic should fit in somewhere within the written information.

2. *What is the purpose of this graphic?*

    Remember that the purpose of any graphic can be to clarify written information by supplementing it, to substitute for written text, or a combination of both. If the graphic is used to supplement written information, it is crucial that you use graphics and written text together as a combined source of information. If the purpose of the graphic is to substitute for written text, you must fit it into its logical place and use it in combination with the text. With either purpose, the information provided by any kind of graphic belongs in your block of related information.

3. *What general information does this graphic provide?*

    There may be important general information about the content of the graphic presented at its top, bottom, or at the side. This information may be in the form of a brief title or may include a fairly extensive explanation of what is presented in that graphic. Read it before you examine the graphic itself.

4. *What specific information does this graphic provide?*

    Examine the graphic material very carefully. Apply what you know about individual kinds of graphics to determine exactly what the author wants you to know. Then carry out the purpose of the graphic: Use this specific information as a supplement to the written text or decide where it fits and use it in place of that text. In either case, remember to consider the text and graphic as a combined source of information.

In this chapter, the above questions are applied to graphs, tables, and some other kinds of graphics which are frequently found in career materials. Keep in mind that the same questions can also be applied to any graphic.

GRAPHS

Graphs are drawings which are used to show relationships between two or more things. There are three major kinds of graphs: line, bar, and circle graphs. Each of these graphs is described below.

Line Graphs

A line graph is drawn with two lines at right angles to each other. The vertical line, or axis, shows a measure of something and the horizontal line, or axis, shows a measure of something else. The relationship between these two measures is shown by a line which is plotted, or drawn, on the graph. Sometimes more than one relationship between measures is shown by different kinds of lines (dotted, dashed, colored, and so on) plotted on the same graph. It is often possible to make generalizations or anticipate future developments about the information on the graph by noting trends or movements of the line(s).

Line graphs are sometimes difficult to read with complete accuracy. If the author has not provided a specific scale between numbers, you must estimate measurement(s) as closely as possible. For example, if the vertical axis shows 10, 20, 30, and so on as measures and the line plotted on the graph falls between those numbers, you must estimate as accurately as possible exactly where the line does fall. In addition, you may need to use a ruler to draw a vertical or horizontal line of your own within the graph to determine exactly where the relationship occurs.

SAMPLE A: Line Graph with Text

With very few exceptions, major medical benefits are not paid until the participants have paid a deductible. The purpose of this deductible is to keep the premium cost down and discourage unnecessary use of medical services. A deductible amount of $100 has been the most common since the survey's inception in 1979, applying to nearly half of all plan participants. However, 36 percent were required to pay deductibles of $150 or more in 1986, up from 29 percent in 1985, 21 percent in 1984, and 12 percent in 1983 (chart 1). Higher deductibles were less prevalent for blue-collar workers than for white-collar workers.

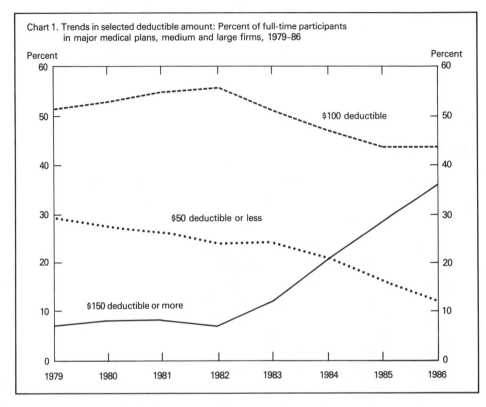

Chart 1. Trends in selected deductible amount: Percent of full-time participants in major medical plans, medium and large firms, 1979–86

1. *Does the text refer you to a graphic?*

Yes, the material directs you to Chart 1, which is a line graph.

2. *What is the purpose of this graphic?*

This line graph is used to clarify the specific information in the written text and to show additional information related to deductibles in medical plans.

3. *What general information does this graphic provide?*

According to the title, this line graph is concerned with the trends in deductible amounts selected by full-time participants in major medical plans who were employed in medium and large firms from 1979 to 1986.

   The vertical axis measures the percentage of these full-time employees and the horizontal axis denotes 1-year periods from 1979 to 1986. The relationship between the two measures is shown with three different kinds of lines: dotted to show a deductible of $50 or less, dashed to show a deductible of $100, and solid to show a deductible of $150 or more.

4. *What specific information does this graphic provide?*

The following questions and their answers show some examples of the kind of specific information that can be obtained from Sample A.

a. The text says that the $100 deductible has been the most common since 1979. In what year did the greatest percent of participants select that deductible?

   1982

b. In what year did less than 15 percent of the participants select the $50 deductible?

   1986

c. When did the $150 deductible begin to surpass the $50 deductible as second choice of participants?

   1984

d. If you follow the trend of the $150 deductible since 1982, what can you predict about the future of that deductible?

   More participants probably will select the $150 deductible.

e. If you follow the trend of the $50 deductible since 1983, what can you predict about the future of that deductible?

   Fewer participants probably will select the $50 deductible.

Bar Graphs

A bar graph is similar in concept to a line graph in that it also has a vertical axis which measures something and a horizontal axis which measures something else. The bar graph also shows the relationship between these two measures. However, a bar graph uses bars drawn to scale rather than a line, or lines, to show the relationship between the two measures. Like a line graph, a bar graph can be used to show changes over time and, thus, can serve as a basis for making generalizations or anticipating future developments regarding the information presented.

Some bar graphs use more than a single bar to show the relationship between the vertical axis and the horizontal axis. These multiple bars are differentiated from each other by the use of color, stripes, dots, and so on.

The bar(s) within a bar graph may be placed in either a vertical or horizontal position. It does not make any difference; the graph is read in exactly the same way.

As with line graphs, bar graphs are sometimes difficult to read with complete accuracy. If the author has not provided a specific scale between numbers, you must estimate measurement(s) as closely as possible. For example, if the vertical axis shows 5, 10, 20, and so on as measures and the height of a bar falls between those numbers, you must estimate as accurately as possible. You may need to use a ruler to draw a vertical or horizontal line of your own within the graph to determine exactly where the relationship occurs.

SAMPLE B: Bar Graph with Text

Both large and small businesses can be expected to continue hiring more women, and women will continue to increase their share of total employment. By the year 2000, women are expected to make up 47 percent of the total work force and more than 50 percent of the small business work force (Chart 14).

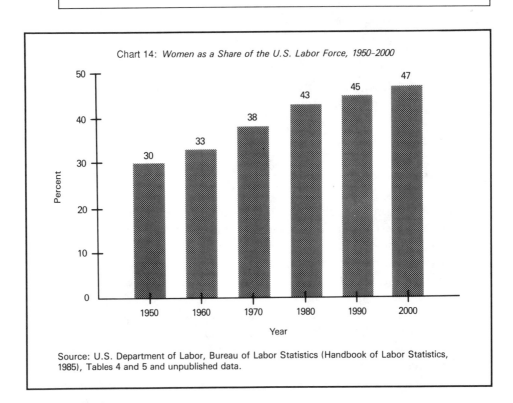

Chart 14: *Women as a Share of the U.S. Labor Force, 1950–2000*

Source: U.S. Department of Labor, Bureau of Labor Statistics (Handbook of Labor Statistics, 1985), Tables 4 and 5 and unpublished data.

1. *Does the text refer you to a graphic?*

Yes, you are directed to Chart 14.

2. *What is the purpose of this graphic?*

Since only one year is mentioned in the text, the major purpose of this bar graph is to substitute for written information.

3. *What general information does this graphic provide?*

This bar graph illustrates the percentage of women in the U.S. labor force in the past (since 1950), and in the present, and it predicts the number who will be in that labor force in the future (the year 2000).

The vertical axis measures the percentage of women who are a share of labor force, and the horizontal axis measures by ten-year periods from 1950 to 2000.

4. *What specific information does this graphic provide?*

The following questions and their answers show some examples of the kind of specific information that can be obtained from Sample B.

a. What has the designer of the graph included to make it easy for you to determine accurate percentages for each bar?

> The percent for each bar is written at the top of it; you don't even need to refer to the vertical axis for its value.

b. What information about the year 2000 is presented in the text but not represented in the graph?

> The text states that by the year 2000 women are expected to make up more than 50 percent of the small business work force. This information is not reflected in the bar graph since it includes the total U.S. work force without breaking it into categories such as small business.

c. How much gain in the percentage of women employed in the labor force was achieved from 1960 to 1980?

> 10 percent

d. How much gain in the percentage of women employed in the labor force is expected from 1950 to 2000?

> 17 percent

e. If the gain in percentage continues at the rate shown on the graph, will the percent of women in the labor force reach 50 percent by 2010? Why/why not?

> No. The gain from 1980 to 1990 was 2 percent and the gain from 1990 to 2000 was also 2 percent. If this trend in the growth of women's share of the labor force continues, the gain from 2000 to 2010 will probably be 2 percent, bringing the total for that year to 49 percent.

Circle Graphs

A circle graph (sometimes called a pie graph) shows how a whole entity has been subdivided into its parts. If the parts are measured in fractions, the whole always equals the number one. If the parts are measured in percentages, the whole always equals 100 percent.

SAMPLE C: Circle Graph without Text

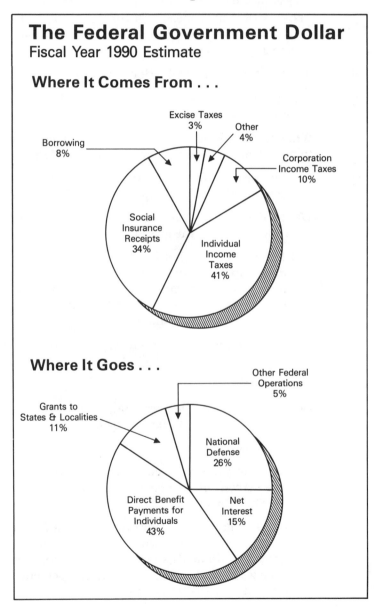

The Federal Government Dollar
Fiscal Year 1990 Estimate

Where It Comes From . . .

Excise Taxes 3%
Other 4%
Borrowing 8%
Corporation Income Taxes 10%
Social Insurance Receipts 34%
Individual Income Taxes 41%

Where It Goes . . .

Other Federal Operations 5%
Grants to States & Localities 11%
National Defense 26%
Direct Benefit Payments for Individuals 43%
Net Interest 15%

1. *Does the text refer you to a graphic?*

   No, the circle graph originally appeared without accompanying text.

2. *What is the purpose of this graphic?*

   This circle graph is used in place of written text.

3. *What general information does this graphic provide?*

   According to the title and two subtitles, the circle graph presents an estimate of where the federal government dollar comes from and where it will go in fiscal year 1990.

4. *What specific information does this graphic provide?*

   The following questions and their answers show some examples of the kind of specific information that can be obtained from Sample C.

   a. What does each circle graph represent?

      Each circle graph represents one dollar either received by the federal government or spent by that government.

   b. From which two sources does the federal government get 75 percent of each dollar it receives?

      The federal government gets 34 percent from social insurance receipts and 41 percent from individual income taxes for a total of 75 percent of each dollar received.

   c. What accounts for the other 25 percent of the federal government's dollar?

      The other 25 percent of the federal government's dollar is accounted for by the following: borrowing, 8 percent; excise taxes, 3 percent; corporation income taxes, 10 percent; and other, 4 percent.

   d. On what does the federal government estimate it will spend approximately one quarter of every dollar in 1990?

      The federal government estimates it will spend 26 percent of every dollar on national defense.

   e. On what does the federal government estimate it will spend the smallest percent of every dollar?

      The federal government estimates it will spend only 5 percent on other federal operations, meaning items not shown on the rest of the circle graph.

SAMPLE PRACTICE
Analyzing Graphs

DIRECTIONS: Read the text and carefully analyze each graph. Ask the first three questions for interpreting graphics about each of the following graphs and the text that goes with them. Then answer the fourth question by examining the graph for specific information.

LINE GRAPH

> Returns to investments in education appeared to be falling during the early 1970s, in part because of the large number of baby boomers entering the work force. Many were better educated than the people they were replacing. The declining wages paid for education led in part to speculation that Americans were "overeducated." Figure 11−10 makes it clear, however, that education has been paying increasing returns in the 1980s. An analysis of 1980 census data for white male workers seems to reveal a much stronger return to investments in education than to work experience after age 30.

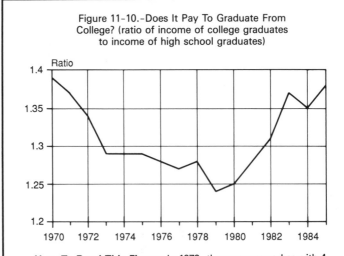

Figure 11-10.-Does It Pay To Graduate From College? (ratio of income of college graduates to income of high school graduates)

How To Read This Figure: In 1979, the average worker with 4 years of college had earned income 24% higher than the average worker with only 4 years of high school (an income ratio of 1.24). By 1985, college graduates earned an average of 38% more than high school graduates (a ratio of 1.38).

1. *Does the text refer you to a graphic?*

   _____

2. *What is the purpose of this graphic?*

   _____

   _____

3. *What general information does the graphic provide?*

   _____

   _____

   _____

4. *What specific information does the graphic provide?*

   a. What has the designer of this line graph provided to make reading
       and understanding it easier?

       _____

       _____

   b. In which year was the ratio of earned income of college graduates to
       earned income of high school graduates the highest?

       _____

   c. In which year was the ratio of earned income of college graduates to
       earned income of high school graduates the lowest?

       _____

   d. What was the percentage difference in earned income between the
       two groups in 1984?

       _____

   e. From the information presented in this line graph, what can you
       infer about college-educated workers?

       _____

       _____

       _____

BAR GRAPH

Services are often stereotyped as low-productivity, low-wage industries such as fast food and barber shops. The reality is that many of the
largest service industries involve relatively high wages and advanced technology. Although the largest single category is retail trade, education and
health care are the second and third largest employers, followed by government and the finance industry (see Figure 1-7).

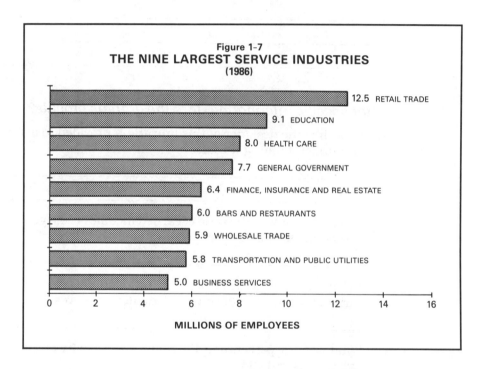

Figure 1-7
THE NINE LARGEST SERVICE INDUSTRIES
(1986)

Millions of Employees	Industry
12.5	RETAIL TRADE
9.1	EDUCATION
8.0	HEALTH CARE
7.7	GENERAL GOVERNMENT
6.4	FINANCE, INSURANCE AND REAL ESTATE
6.0	BARS AND RESTAURANTS
5.9	WHOLESALE TRADE
5.8	TRANSPORTATION AND PUBLIC UTILITIES
5.0	BUSINESS SERVICES

MILLIONS OF EMPLOYEES

1. *Does the text refer you to a graphic?*

_____

2. *What is the purpose of this graphic?*

_____

_____

3. *What general information does this graphic provide?*

_____

_____

_____

4. *What specific information does this graphic provide?*

a. The author of the bar graph has not provided you with a title for the vertical axis. Based on the text and graph, what is a logical title for that axis?

_____

b. What does the horizontal axis measure? (Be specific.)

_____

c. How has the author made it easy for you to know how many employees are in each service industry?

_____

_____

d. Which three service industries are close in the number of persons employed?

_____

_____

e. Which service industry employs the fewest number of persons?

_____

CIRCLE GRAPH

As the chart of Exhibit 3 shows, there are five reasons why workers may experience unemployment. Exhibit 4 indicates the share of unemployed workers in each of these categories in 1985. Interestingly, 12.5 percent of the unemployed workers were first-time entrants into the work force. Another 27.1 percent were reentering after exiting for additional schooling, household work, or other reasons. Thus, nearly two out of five unemployed workers were experiencing unemployment as the result of recent entry or reentry into the labor force. A little more than 10 percent of the unemployed quit their last job. People laid off and waiting to return to their previous positions contributed 13.9 percent to the total. Workers terminated from their last job accounted for 35.9 percent of the unemployed workers.

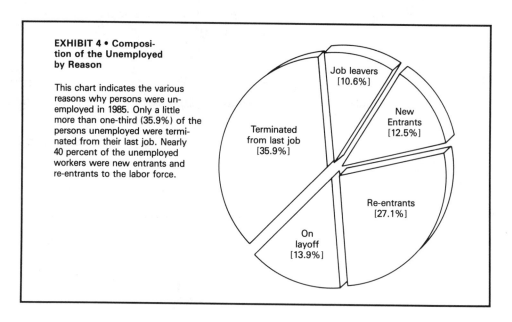

EXHIBIT 4 • Composition of the Unemployed by Reason

This chart indicates the various reasons why persons were unemployed in 1985. Only a little more than one-third (35.9%) of the persons unemployed were terminated from their last job. Nearly 40 percent of the unemployed workers were new entrants and re-entrants to the labor force.

Job leavers [10.6%]

New Entrants [12.5%]

Terminated from last job [35.9%]

Re-entrants [27.1%]

On layoff [13.9%]

1. *Does the text refer you to a graphic?*

_____

2. *What is the purpose of the graphic?*

_____

_____

3. *What general information does this graphic provide?*

_____

_____

_____

4. *What specific information does this graphic provide?*

   a. When added together, what do the five parts of this circle graph equal?

     _____

   b. What was the reason given for the fewest number of unemployed?

     _____

     _____

     _____

   c. What percentage were apparently unemployed because of some kind of job-related unhappiness?

     _____

   d. What percentage were unemployed for reasons which probably were beyond their personal control?

     _____

   e. In your opinion, what is one generalization you can make based on the information in this circle graph?

     _____

     _____

     _____

Check your answers below. Carefully analyze any given answers that do not match yours.

Sample Practice Answers

LINE GRAPH

1. *Does the text refer you to a graphic?*

Yes, you are referred to Figure 11-10.

2. *What is the purpose of this graphic?*

This line graph substitutes for written text since the ratios shown on the graph are not mentioned in that text.

3. *What general information does the graphic provide?*

According to the title, the line graph responds to the question, "Does It Pay to Graduate from College?" by comparing a ratio of income of college graduates to income of high school graduates.

4. *What specific information does the graphic provide?*

a. The designer has provided you with directions on how to read the graph directly below it.

b. The ratio of earned income of college graduates to earned income of high school graduates was the highest in 1970—with a ratio of 1.39 or 39 percent.

c. The ratio of earned income of college graduates to earned income of high school graduates was the lowest in 1979—with a ratio of 1.24 or 24 percent.

d. The percentage difference in earned income between the two groups in 1984 was 35 percent.

e. It pays to graduate from college. From 1970 to 1985 the income of college graduates has been higher than that of high school graduates. Since the low point in 1979, the percentage of difference has increased from 24 percent to 38 percent.

BAR GRAPH

1. *Does the text refer you to the graphic?*

Yes, you are told to see Figure 1-7.

2. *What is the purpose of this graphic?*

The bar graph substitutes for written text since the actual numbers of employees in the service industries and the categories below finance are not mentioned in the text.

3. *What general information does this graphic provide?*

According to the title, this bar graph is concerned with the nine largest service industries in 1986.

4. *What specific information does this graphic provide?*

    a. A logical title for the vertical axis would be "categories of Service Industries." (You may have worded this answer slightly differently. Be sure you have the same concept as the title given here.)

    b. The horizontal axis measures the number of employees in the nine largest service industries in terms of millions.

    c. The actual number of employees in the category is written to the right of each bar.

    d. The three service industries which are close in the number of persons employed are "Bars and Restaurants" (6.0 million), "Wholesale Trade" (5.9 million), and "Transportation and Public Utilities" (5.8 million).

    e. The "Business Services" industry employs the fewest number of people (5.0 million).

CIRCLE GRAPH

1. *Does the text refer you to a graphic?*

Yes, the text refers you to Exhibit 4, the circle graph.

2. *What is the purpose of the graphic?*

This circle graph clarifies written text since it presents the same information but in a different form. Note that some of the same information also appears at the side of the circle graph.

3. *What general information does this graphic provide?*

According to the title, this circle graph shows the composition of the unemployed by reason.

4. *What specific information does this graphic provide?*

    a. The five parts of the circle graph equal 100 percent.

    b. The smallest number of unemployed were job leavers (10.6 percent).

    c. The number of people who were unemployed because they left or quit their last job was 10.6 percent.

    d. The number of people who were unemployed due to reasons which may have been beyond their control was 49.8 percent (35.9 percent terminated, 13.9 percent on layoff).

e. Any of the following generalizations will answer this question. (Your answer to this question may vary slightly from the ones given below.)

1. It may not be easy to become employed if you are a new entrant or a reentrant. In 1985, 40.6 percent of the unemployed were in that category.

2. You may not have a great deal of control over your own job. In 1985, almost half of the unemployed were in that position because of situations beyond their control; 35.9 percent were terminated and 13.9 percent were laid off.

3. Most employed persons were satisfied to some extent with their last jobs. The fewest number of unemployed were job leavers who may have left by choice (10.6 percent).

Now go on to Skill Development Exercise 7–1 on page 145, where you will be provided with additional practice analyzing graphs.

SKILL DEVELOPMENT EXERCISE 7–1
Analyzing Graphs

DIRECTIONS: Read the text carefully. Ask the first three questions about each of the following graphs and the text that goes with it. Then answer the fourth question by analyzing the graph for specific information.

LINE GRAPH

> Women in the 45–54 age group led the influx into the labor force in the post-World War II period. Labor force participation for this older group soared from just over 30 percent in 1946 to 50 percent in 1960. (See Chart 2.) In contrast, rates rose more moderately for the 35- to 44-year-olds and hardly increased at all for 25- to 34-year-olds. These were the postwar baby boom years and most married women remained outside the labor force because of their child and family responsibilities. The different timing of labor force increases by age mirrored public attitudes about women working outside the home. Attitudes shifted first for older women, who generally did not have young children at home.
>
> In the early 1960s, however, women of childbearing age began to enter the labor market in large numbers. The rate of increase picked up in the mid-1960s and accelerated even more during the 1970s. (See Chart 2.) A very sharp decline in the birth rate in the 1960s was a major contributing factor. At the same time, total employment was rising strongly, with much of the growth occurring in services and the public sector (especially education), where large numbers of women are employed. Increasing levels of education and rapidly changing views about the home and work roles were also factors in the tremendous jump in women's labor market activities during the 1960s and 1970s.

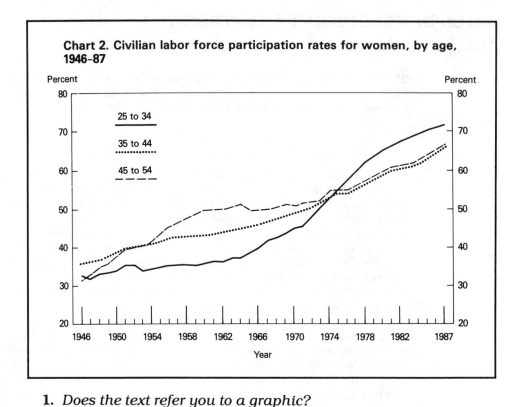

Chart 2. Civilian labor force participation rates for women, by age, 1946–87

1. *Does the text refer you to a graphic?*

   _____

2. *What is the purpose of this graphic?*

   _____

   _____

   _____

3. *What general information does this graphic provide?*

   _____

   _____

   _____

   _____

4. *What specific information does this graphic provide?*

   a. What do the short vertical lines on the horizontal axis represent?

   _____

b. Why does this line graph begin with 1946?

_____

c. In which year was the same percentage of women from all three age groups participating in the civilian labor force?

_____

d. In which years was the percentage of women ages 35—44 the same as the percentage of women in the 25—34 age group?

_____

e. Of the three age groups of women participating in the civilian labor force, which group had the largest percentage by 1987?

_____

BAR GRAPH

> Although the majority of the increase in net foreign claims on the United States has been in financial assets, foreign direct investment in the United States has also increased in the 1980s. Chart 3—6 breaks down the foreign direct investment position in the United States since 1982 by nationality. Direct investment by the United Kingdom represents the largest component of foreign ownership in the United States, averaging 25 percent of total foreign direct investment since 1982. The Netherlands, at 20 percent, is the next largest single investor. Other European direct investment averaged 22 percent. Japanese direct investment constituted 11 percent, growing from 8 percent in 1982 to 13 percent in 1987. Canadian and other direct investment make up the remainder.

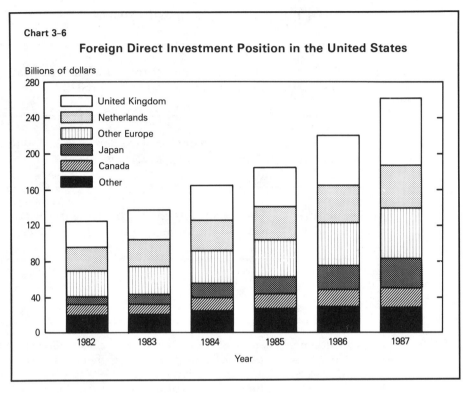

Chart 3-6

Foreign Direct Investment Position in the United States

Legend:
- United Kingdom
- Netherlands
- Other Europe
- Japan
- Canada
- Other

Billions of dollars (vertical axis: 0, 40, 80, 120, 160, 200, 240, 280)

Year (horizontal axis: 1982, 1983, 1984, 1985, 1986, 1987)

1. *Does the text refer you to a graphic?*

   _____

2. *What is the purpose of this graphic?*

   _____

   _____

3. *What general information does this graphic provide?*

   _____

   _____

4. *What specific information does this graphic provide?*

   a. What does the vertical axis measure? (Be specific.)

   _____

   b. Which country's direct investments in the United States have grown
      from $40 billion in 1982 to $80 billion in 1987?

   _____

c. What is the difference between the two labels "Other Europe" and "Other?"

_____

d. Which country's direct investments in the United States have grown from under $40 billion in 1982 to almost $60 billion in 1987?

_____

e. Who has shown the smallest growth in direct investments in the United States from 1982 to 1987?

_____

CIRCLE GRAPH

In addition to the falling dollar, the nation's persistent trade deficit* was once again a major story in U.S. international economic relations in 1987. Although the deficit decreased by 5 percent in constant dollars, in nominal terms it set a new high in 1987 for the fifth consecutive year at $171.2 billion, up from $156.2 billion in 1986. Significant deficits were registered against Japan, $59.8 billion; the so-called Four Tigers (Singapore, Hong Kong, South Korea, and Taiwan), $37.7 billion; Western Europe, $30.2 billion; the Latin American Free Trade Association countries, $14.9 billion; and Canada, $11.7 billion. West Germany ($16.3 billion) accounted for over half of the U.S. deficit with Western Europe, while Mexico and Brazil accounted for $10.3 billion of the deficit with the Latin American Free Trade Association countries. The deficits recorded with the Four Tigers individually were: Singapore, $2.3 billion; Hong Kong, $6.5 billion; South Korea, $9.9 billion; and Taiwan, $19 billion. Chart 3 shows the relative shares of the U.S. trade deficit by region.

* The trade deficit discussed here is the result of the United States' buying more from other countries than it sells to them.

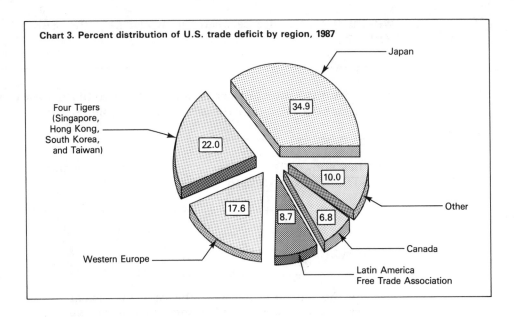

Chart 3. Percent distribution of U.S. trade deficit by region, 1987

1. *Does the text refer you to a graphic?*

_____

2. *What is the purpose of this graphic?*

_____

_____

3. *What general information does this graphic provide?*

_____

_____

_____

4. *What specific information does this graphic provide?*

   a. How has the author of this material made it easier for you to understand the huge amounts of money described in the text?

   _____

   _____

b. In which region does the U.S. show the largest trade deficit?

_____

c. How much difference is there between the trade deficit with Japan and the trade deficit with the Four Tigers?

_____

d. In which region does the U.S. show the smallest trade deficit?

_____

e. Considering the information presented on the circle graph, what can you generalize about the U.S. trade deficit as related to Asia?

_____

_____

TABLES

Authors use tables to show a great deal of information in a simple, organized form. Tables may consist of all numbers, all words, or a combination of the two. A table may clarify complex material in the written text and, therefore, should be read along with the text. On the other hand, a table may be used as a substitute for lengthy text material, in which case the author may simply refer you to that table.

SAMPLE D: Table with Text

The European Community (EC) received 39 percent of total U.S. exports of medical and dental instruments and supplies in 1986 and supplied about 52 percent of U.S. imports of such goods.

**Table 2: U.S. Trade in Medical and Dental
Instruments and Supplies in 1986**
(in millions of U.S. dollars)

Exports		Imports	
DESTINATION		SOURCE	
Total, all destinations	2,760.0	Total, all destinations	2,148.6
Canada	366.1	West Germany	636.6
Japan	363.0	Japan	545.9
West Germany	263.3	United Kingdom	141.7
United Kingdom	191.5	France	108.1
Netherlands	168.2	Netherlands	97.9

1. *Does the text refer you to a graphic?*

   No. The table simply appears below the text which mentions the same kind of information.

2. *What is the purpose of this graphic?*

   This table substitutes for information about the U.S. export and import of medical and dental instruments and supplies not found in the written text.

3. *What general information does this graphic provide?*

   Table 2 shows the countries to which the U.S. exported medical and dental instruments and supplies in 1986 and the countries from which such items were imported during the same year.

4. *What specific information does this graphic provide?*

The following questions show some examples of the kind of specific information that can be obtained from Sample D.

a. How is the dollar amount of U.S. trade in medical and dental supplies expressed in this table?

> The amount of U.S. trade in medical and dental supplies is expressed in millions of dollars.

b. What do the terms "Destination" and "Source" indicate in the table?

> "Destination" refers to countries who bought and received the medical and dental instruments and supplies, and "Source" refers to the countries from whom the U.S. obtained such goods.

c. Which country bought medical and dental instruments from the U.S. but did not sell any to it?

> Canada bought medical and dental instruments from the U.S. but did not sell any to it.

d. Which country sold these goods to the U.S. but did not purchase any in 1986?

> France sold these goods to the U.S. but did not purchase any.

e. The text refers to the export and import of these goods to the European Community. Does the table actually go with that written text? Why/why not?

> No. The written text refers to the European Community while the table goes beyond that group to include non-European countries such as Canada and Japan.

FLOWCHARTS

Authors may use flowcharts to illustrate various kinds of information such as the way a company is organized, the stages of a process, or a set of instructions. The resulting graphic makes it easy for you to understand and follow the information through a series of steps or levels. Sometimes the author may provide you with arrows or numbers to assist you in seeing the relationships between items of information and to guide you in the right direction through the flowchart.

SAMPLE E: Flowchart and Text

Organization of a Typical Police Agency

Organization is the bringing together of people to perform specific tasks and dividing the total workload into individual units for assignment to individual people. Organization by itself will not complete any task. A typical organizational chart for a community of 23,000 is shown in Figure 7–2, and a chart for a large police agency is offered in Figure 7–3.

Figure 7-2. Typical organization chart for a community of 23,000 people.

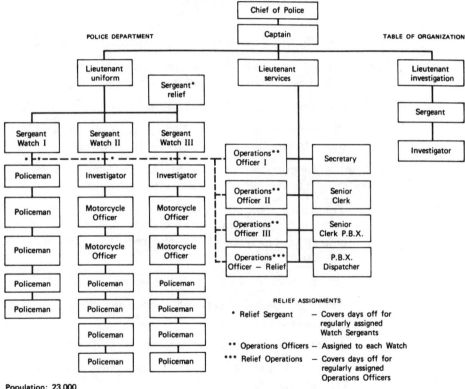

1. *Does the text refer you to a graphic?*

In the text, you are directed to two graphics, Figure 7–2 and Figure 7–3. However, only the flowchart, Figure 7–2, is presented and examined here.

2. *What is the purpose of this graphic?*

The purpose of this flowchart is to substitute for information that is not included in the text. The text only directs you to the flowchart.

3. *What general information does this graphic provide?*

The flowchart provides an organizational chart of a typical policy agency for a community of 23,000.

4. *What specific information does this graphic provide?*

The following questions show some examples of the kind of specific information that can be obtained from Sample E.

a. Who answers directly to the Captain?

The Lieutenant/uniform, Lieutenant/services, and Lieutenant/investigation answer directly to the Captain.

b. What is the purpose of the dashed lines under each Sergeant of the Watch and to the left of the Operations Officers?

The three Operations Officers work under the Lieutenant/services but are assigned to each Watch. The Relief Operations Officer covers days off for the regularly assigned Operations Officers.

c. How many relief persons are shown on the flowchart?

There are two relief persons, the Sergeant/relief and Operations Officer/relief.

d. What is the job of these relief persons?

They cover days off for regularly assigned Watch Sergeants and Operations Officers.

e. Which two kinds of personnel do not work in Watch I but do work in the other two Watches?

The Investigator and Motorcycle Officer work only in Watches II and III.

DIAGRAMS

The types of diagrams, or drawings, used by authors are extremely varied. For example, authors may use diagrams to illustrate parts of machinery or equipment, steps in a process, parts of the human body, directions to follow, or cartoons drawn to emphasize a point. Maps can also be included as diagrams since they are often drawn illustrations.

SAMPLE F: Diagram without Text

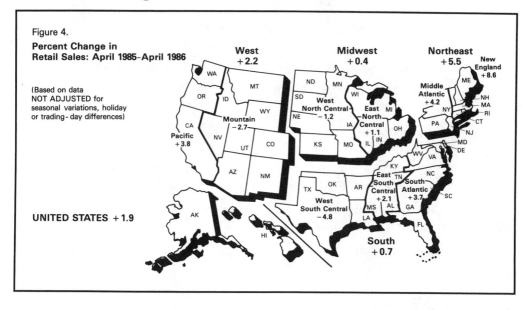

Figure 4.

Percent Change in Retail Sales: April 1985–April 1986

(Based on data NOT ADJUSTED for seasonal variations, holiday or trading-day differences)

UNITED STATES +1.9

West +2.2
Pacific +3.8
Mountain −2.7

Midwest +0.4
West North Central −1.2
East North Central +1.1

Northeast +5.5
New England +8.6
Middle Atlantic +4.2

East South Central +2.1
South Atlantic +3.7
West South Central −4.8

South +0.7

1. *Does the text refer you to a graphic?*

   No. This map appeared in a government report without any accompanying text. It is used as a sample in this chapter to make you aware that this situation does occur and how to react to it.

2. *What is the purpose of this graphic?*

   Obviously, this map takes the place of written text.

3. *What general information does this graphic provide?*

   According to its title, this map of the United States provides information pertaining to changes in the percentage of retail sales from April 1985 to April 1986.

4. *What specific information does this graphic provide?*

The following questions show some examples of the kind of specific information that can be obtained from Sample F.

a. How has the author of this map made it easier for you to determine the changes in retail sales in different parts of the country?

   On this map, the United States has been divided into regions and subregions.

b. What is the percentage change in retail sales for the entire country from April 1985 to April 1986?

   The percentage change in retail sales for the United States is +1.9.

c. Which region shows the largest percentage gain in retail sales?

   The Northeast shows the largest percentage gain (+5.5 percent).

d. The region labeled "South" is subdivided into how many sub-regions?

   There are three subregions within the "South": West South Central, East South Central, and South Atlantic.

e. Which subregion within a region shows the largest percentage of loss in retail sales?

   The West South Central region shows the largest percentage of loss (−4.8 percent).

SAMPLE PRACTICE
Analyzing Tables, Flowcharts, and Diagrams

DIRECTIONS: Read the text that accompanies each graphic carefully. Ask the first three questions about each of the following graphics and the text that goes with them. Then answer the fourth question by examining the graphic for specific information.

TABLE

Components of Compensation Costs

In March 1988, employer costs for employee compensation in private industry averaged $13.79 per hour worked. Benefits made up 27.3 percent of compensation costs. That figure compares with 26.8 percent in March 1987. Text table 4 compares the distribution of costs among major components in 1987 and 1988.

Definitions of Compensation Components

Wages and salaries—the straight-time hourly wage rate or, for workers not paid on an hourly basis, straight-time earnings divided by corresponding hours. Straight-time wage and salary rates are based on total earnings before payroll deductions, excluding premium pay for overtime and for work on weekends and holidays, shift differentials, and nonproduction bonuses such as lump-sum payments provided in lieu of wage increases. Production bonuses, incentive earnings, commission payments and cost-of-living adjustments are included in straight-time wage and salary rates.

Benefits covered by the survey are: *Paid leave*—vacations, holidays, sick leave, and other paid leave.

Supplemental pay—premium pay for overtime and work on weekends and holidays, shift differentials, and nonproduction bonuses such as lump-sum payments provided in lieu of wage increases.

Insurance benefits—health, life, and sickness and accident insurance.

Retirement and savings benefits—pension and other retirement plans, and savings and thrift plans.

Legally required benefits—Social Security, railroad retirement and supplemental retirement, railroad unemployment insurance, federal and state unemployment insurance, workers' compensation, and other benefits required by law such as state disability insurance.

Other benefits—severance pay, supplemental unemployment insurance, and merchandise discounts in department stores.

Text table 4. Percent distribution of components of compensation costs, private industry, March 1987 and March 1988

Compensation component	March 1987	March 1988
Total compensation	100.0	100.0
Wages and salaries	73.2	72.7
Total benefit costs	26.8	27.3
Paid leave	6.9	7.0
Supplemental pay	2.4	2.4
Insurance	5.4	5.6
Retirement and savings	3.6	3.3
Legally required benefits	8.4	8.8
Other benefits	0.1	0.2

1. *Does the text refer you to a graphic?*

   _____

2. *What is the purpose of this graphic?*

   _____

   _____

3. *What general information does this graphic provide?*

   _____

   _____

   _____

4. *What specific information does this graphic provide?*

   a. Into what two major categories is the total compensation divided?

   _____

   b. Which of these two categories accounts for less of a percentage of the total compensation in 1988 than it did in 1987?

   _____

   c. Which benefit cost has remained the same for both years?

   _____

   d. Which benefit cost accounts for less of a percentage of the total benefit costs in 1988 than it did in 1987?

   _____

   e. What are "other benefits?"

   _____

FLOWCHART

Buying or Contracting by Negotiation—Request for Proposal

A. Solicitation process

1. When formal advertising is not suitable or possible due to the nature of the product or service sought, the government will negotiate for the product or service. Small purchases are most often made through special expedited negotiation procedures. Purchases under $10,000 are "set aside" for small businesses if the Contracting Officer determines that (a) there is a reasonable expectation that offers will be obtained from at least two responsible small business concerns and (b) awards will be made at reasonable prices.

2. Requests for Proposals (RFP) are issued to potential contractors whose names are on the agency bidders list. RFPs are also sent upon the request of any prospective contractor.

3. Public announcements are also made, such as those in the *Commerce Business Daily.*

B. Proposal requirement

The Request for Proposals (RFP) describes the product or service desired, delivery time, and other terms of the contract. The Request for Quotations (Standard Form 18, see Appendix 1) is usually used to submit quotations for small purchases but may also be used for large purchases. Proposals submitted are generally expected to contain:

1. pricing information,
2. a description of products or services offered.

C. Contract award

1. The contract award is made through evaluations and negotiations after proposals have been received and reviewed.

2. Award is made to the offeror whose final offer is most advantageous to the government, not necessarily to the company offering the lowest price.

D. Time span for negotiated contracts: the time involved varies in accordance with the contract type and complexity of the requirement.

Figure 4 indicates the key or significant events in the negotiation process.

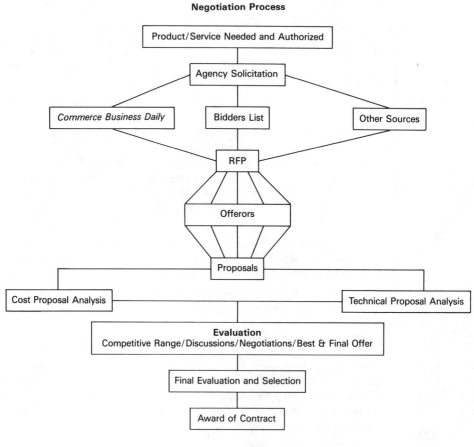

Figure 4

1. *Does the text refer you to a graphic?*

_____

2. *What is the purpose of this graphic?*

_____

_____

3. *What general information does this graphic provide?*

_____

_____

_____

4. *What specific information does this graphic provide?*

a. According to the text, what does Figure 4 indicate?

_____

b. What is the RFP?

_____

_____

c. According to the flowchart and the text, how does an agency
    publicize the RFP?

_____

d. What is the first thing that happens to a proposal after it is
    submitted?

_____

_____

e. How many evaluations does a proposal go through before the
    contract is awarded?

_____

DIAGRAM

Burns Burns to the eyes can be caused by chemicals, heat, or light.

Chemical Burns. Turn the patient's head to the side so that you can flush the eyes with a steady stream of water. The pour should be from the medial (nasal) corner across the globe to the lateral corner. Use sterile water if it is available; otherwise, use tap water. For patients wearing contact lenses, remove the lenses while washing the eyes (see p. 297). Some EMS* Systems are very specific on the time of the wash. If the chemical is known to be an acid, continue the wash for at *least* 5 minutes. If you know the chemical was an alkali, flush with water for at least 15 minutes. Alkaline substances will continue to burn and damage tissues even when diluted. If the chemical is unknown, wash for 20 minutes. The safest policy to follow is to wash the eyes for 20 minutes or until transfer is made at the medical facility.

For most chemical burns, it is best to start the wash as soon as possible and continue to irrigate the patient's eyes during transport to the medical facility. This will prevent transport delay and allow the patient to receive specialized care much sooner. If the ambulance does not carry equipment for eye irrigation, use the rubber bulb syringe in the obstetric kit. When this bulb is used, control the flow so that it gently washes the eye. After washing, close the eyelid and apply a loose sterile dressing.

Heat Burns. In many cases, only the eyelids will be burned. *Do not* attempt to inspect the eyes if the eyelids are burned. With the patient's eyelids closed, apply a loose, moist dressing.

Light Burns. Light injuries can be caused by a strong source of light or an ultraviolet light source. Light burns commonly occur from the flash of an arc welder or by the extreme brightness of the sun as it is reflected off sand or snow. These burns are generally very painful, with many patients saying that it feels as if there is sand in the eyes. The onset is usually slow, often taking several hours after exposure before symptoms develop. In order to make the patient more comfortable, close his eyelids and apply dark patches over both eyes. If you do not have dark patches, apply a pad of dressings followed with a layer of opaque (light-blocking) material such as dark plastic. Instruct the patient not to rub his eyes.

* Emergency Medical Services

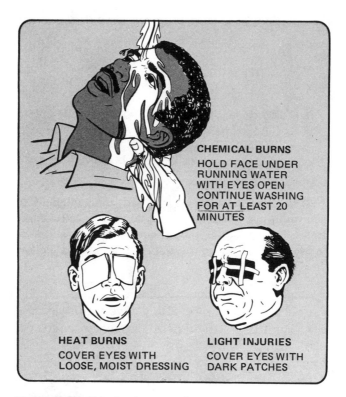

CHEMICAL BURNS
HOLD FACE UNDER
RUNNING WATER
WITH EYES OPEN
CONTINUE WASHING
FOR AT LEAST 20
MINUTES

HEAT BURNS
COVER EYES WITH
LOOSE, MOIST DRESSING

LIGHT INJURIES
COVER EYES WITH
DARK PATCHES

Figure 12–12. Treating burns to the eyes.

1. *Does the text refer you to a graphic?*

_____

2. *What is the purpose of this graphic?*

_____

_____

3. *What general information does this graphic provide?*

_____

_____

_____

4. *What specific information does this graphic provide?*

    a. What two things has the author of this diagram done to make it easier for you to learn how to treat burns to the eyes?

    _____

    b. What three things can cause burns to the eye?

    _____

    c. How do you treat chemical burns to the eye?

    _____

    d. How do you treat heat burns to the eye?

    _____

    e. How do you treat light burns to the eye?

    _____

Check your answers. If any of your answers do not match those given below, examine the differences. You may need to go back to the graphic and analyze it again.

Sample Practice Answers

TABLE

1. *Does the text refer you to a graphic?*

Yes, you are told what Text table 4 will show you.

2. *What is the purpose of this graphic?*

Table 4 clarifies the information in the written text, and it also substitutes for a more lengthy description of the compensation components.

3. *What general information does this graphic provide?*

According to the title, this table presents information about the "percent distribution of components of compensation costs, private industry, March 1987 and March 1988."

4. *What specific information does this graphic provide?*

    a. Total compensation is divided into "Wages and salaries" and "Total benefit costs."

    b. "Wages and salaries" has gone down from 73.2 percent of the total compensation package in 1987 to 72.7 percent in 1988.

    c. "Supplemental pay" has remained the same at 2.4 percent of the total benefits costs for both years.

    d. "Retirement and savings" has gone down from 3.6 percent of the total benefits package in 1987 to 3.3 percent in 1988.

    e. "Other benefits" include severance pay, supplemental unemployment insurance, and merchandise discounts in department stores. (See the text following the table.)

FLOWCHART

1. *Does the text refer you to a graphic?*

Yes, you are directed to Figure 4.

2. *What is the purpose of this graphic?*

The flowchart substitutes for information in the written text.

3. *What general information does this graphic provide?*

This flowchart indicates the steps to follow in the negotiation process. According to the written text, "Figure 4 indicates the key or significant events in the negotiation process."

4. *What specific information does this graphic provide?*

    a. The negotiation process begins when a product/service is needed and authorized.

    b. The RFP is a "Request For Proposals."

    c. An agency publicizes the RFP by sending it to potential contractors on the bidder's list. An RFP is also sent upon request to any prospective contractors. Finally, the agency places a public announcement in publications such as the *Commerce Business Daily.*

    d. After a proposal is submitted, it undergoes two analyses, a "Cost Proposal Analysis" and a "Technical Proposal Analysis."

    e. A proposal goes through two evaluations before a contract is awarded.

DIAGRAM

1. *Does the text refer you to a graphic?*

    No.

2. *What is the purpose of this graphic?*

    This diagram clarifies the information found in the written text.

3. *What general information does this graphic provide?*

    According to the title, this diagram shows ways of treating burns to the eyes.

4. *What specific information does this graphic provide?*

    a. The author of the diagram has made it easier for you to learn how to treat burns to the eyes by reducing the written text and showing how the eyes are to be treated in case of burns.

    b. Chemicals, heat, and light injuries can cause burns to the eye.

    c. To treat chemical burns, hold the face under running water with eyes open and continue washing for at least 20 minutes.

    d. To treat heat burns, cover the eyes with a loose, moist dressing.

    e. To treat light burns, cover the eyes with dark patches.

Now go on to Skill Development Exercise 7–2 on page 169, where you will be provided with additional practice in analyzing a table, a flowchart, and a diagram.

Then go to Skill Application 7 on page 177. Here you will apply what you have learned about analyzing graphics to your own career material.

SKILL DEVELOPMENT EXERCISE 7–2
Analyzing a Table, Flowchart, and Diagram

DIRECTIONS: Ask the first three questions about each of the following graphics and the text that goes with them. Then answer the fourth question by examining the graphic for specific information.

TABLE

Many people are primarily interested in the projected change in employment in particular occupations. People also have great interest in knowing which occupations are growing most rapidly, are adding the most jobs, or are declining the most. The accompanying tables give this information. The occupations are drawn from the total of more than 500 occupations for which projections are made and therefore differ from lists that would be drawn from the 225 occupations in "The 1988–89 Job Outlook in Brief."

Occupations With the Largest Job Growth, 1986–2000

[Numbers in thousands] Occupation	Employment Projected 1986	Employment Projected 2000	Change in employment, 1986–2000 Number	Change in employment, 1986–2000 Percent	Percent of projected job growth, 1986–2000
Salespersons, retail	3,579	4,780	1,201	33.5	5.6
Waiters and waitresses	1,702	2,454	752	44.2	3.5
Registered nurses	1,406	2,018	612	43.6	2.9
Janitors and cleaners	2,676	3,280	604	22.6	2.8
General managers and top executives	2,383	2,965	582	24.2	2.7
Cashiers	2,165	2,740	575	26.5	2.7
Truckdrivers	2,211	2,736	525	23.8	2.5
General office clerks	2,361	2,824	462	19.6	2.2
Food counter and related workers	1,500	1,949	449	29.9	2.1
Nursing aides, orderlies, and attendants	1,224	1,658	433	35.4	2.0
Secretaries	3,234	3,658	424	13.1	2.0
Guards	794	1,177	383	48.3	1.8
Accountants and auditors	945	1,322	376	39.8	1.8
Computer programmers	479	813	335	69.9	1.6
Food preparation workers	949	1,273	324	34.2	1.5
Teachers, kindergarten and elementary	1,527	1,826	299	19.6	1.4

Occupations With the Largest Job Growth, 1986–2000 (*cont.*)

[Numbers in thousands] Occupation	Employment		Change in employment, 1986–2000		Percent of projected job growth, 1986–2000
	Projected				
	1986	2000	Number	Percent	
Receptionists and information clerks	682	964	282	41.4	1.3
Computer systems analysts	331	582	251	75.6	1.2
Cooks, restaurant	520	759	240	46.2	1.1
Licensed practical nurses	631	869	238	37.7	1.1
Gardeners and groundskeepers	767	1,005	238	31.1	1.1
Maintenance repairers	1,039	1,270	232	22.3	1.1
Stock clerks	1,087	1,312	225	20.7	1.0
First-line clerical supervisors and managers	956	1,161	205	21.4	1.0
Dining room and cafeteria attendants	433	631	197	45.6	.9
Electrical and electronics engineers	401	592	192	47.8	.9
Lawyers	527	718	191	36.3	.9

1. *Does the text refer you to a graphic?*

_____

2. *What is the purpose of this graphic?*

_____

_____

3. *What general information does this graphic provide?*

_____

_____

_____

4. *What specific information does this graphic provide:*

   a. What does "Numbers in thousands" mean?

   _____

   b. Using the table as a guide, which three occupations would you be most likely to avoid as future career choices?

   _____

c. Which occupation has the highest percent of projected job growth from the years 1986 to 2000?

_____

d. Which occupation shows the smallest change in numbers employed from the years 1986 to 2000?

_____

e. Which occupation shows the greatest percent change in employment from the years 1986 to 2000?

_____

FLOWCHART

> ***Location within the organization.*** A data processing department can be positioned in one of three ways within the organization it serves. First, it can be linked to the larger organizational unit that contains its primary user. For example, if accounting is the most important customer, then data processing personnel would report to the Finance Department, of which accounting is a part. This alternative, sometimes known as *operational location*, gives each major group its own independent data processing activities; other groups with only minimal data processing requirements may purchase services from one of these independent data processing departments or from outside as needed. This allows computer time to be "dedicated" or reserved for certain priority activities. (See Figure 14–2.)

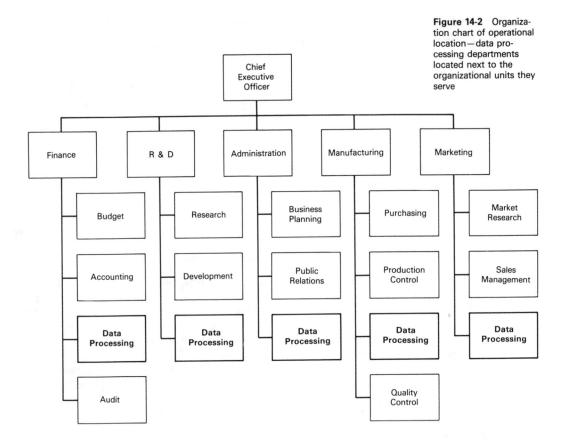

1. *Does the text refer you to a graphic?*

   _____

2. *What is the purpose of this graphic?*

   _____

   _____

3. *What general information does this graphic provide?*

   _____

   _____

   _____

4. *What specific information does this graphic provide?*

    a. According to the text, how many ways can a data processing department be positioned within the organization it serves?

_____

    b. How many of these ways are shown in Figure 14–2?

_____

    c. What is "operational location"?

_____

    d. How does Figure 14–2 indicate that this organization uses "operational location" for its data processing activities?

_____

    e. As illustrated in the flowchart, who are the primary users of the data processing activities?

_____

DIAGRAM

Maintaining a Balance

A truly complex challenge to management is to achieve and maintain a balance and consistency among the strategy, structure, and processes of the organization. This design challenge is analogous to the task confronting the three "people" in Figure 11–6. They seek to preserve the water in the bucket while the ground beneath them is shifting in diverse and unanticipated ways. Each supporting element—strategy, structure, and processes—must adapt to the others to be successful in maintaining the balance.

    When consistency among the three factors is achieved, design changes will still be needed because with the passage of time, to sustain the balance, the premises on which the original design was based will have changed. The changing values, expectations, and skills of employees warrant accommodation through changes in strategy, structure, processes, or all three. For example, changes in the laws and institutions in society may dictate corresponding modifications of strategy and human resource needs and development. Changes in technology and resource availability will affect any or all of the design factors. The challenge is to anticipate and detect the need for redesign, and to invent and create alternative combinations of the three components of design. The need for redesign is vividly illustrated by some general patterns of organization change that have been observed historically—a topic we will consider next.

FIGURE 11–6 Organizational Design: Key Elements Underlying Effectiveness

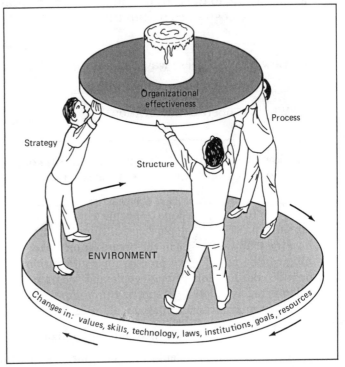

1. *Does the text refer you to a graphic?*

   _____

2. *What is the purpose of this graphic?*

   _____

   _____

3. *What general information does this graphic provide?*

   _____

   _____

   _____

4. *What specific information does this graphic provide?*

   a. What do the three people in Figure 11–6 represent?

   _____

   b. What are the three people attempting to do with the water in the bucket?

   _____

   c. What does the water in the bucket represent in the diagram?

   _____

   d. Why is the environment in the diagram shown to be moving?

   _____

   e. What changes might occur in the environment?

   _____

SKILL APPLICATION 7
Analyzing Graphics

DIRECTIONS: Choose two different kinds of graphics with their accompanying text from your own career materials. Duplicate them and attach one to each side of this sheet. Then answer the questions below the source information.

GRAPHIC 1 SOURCE INFORMATION

Title: _____

Author: _____

Place of publication: _____

Publisher: _____

Copyright Date: _____ *Page(s):* _____

ANSWER THESE QUESTIONS:

1. *Does the text refer you to a graphic?*

   _____

2. *What is the purpose of this graphic?*

   _____

   _____

3. *What general information does this graphic provide?*

   _____

   _____

   _____

4. *What three specific things did you learn from this graphic?*

   _____

   _____

   _____

GRAPHIC 2 SOURCE INFORMATION

Title: _____

Author: _____

Place of publication: _____

Publisher: _____

Copyright Date: _____ *Page(s):* _____

ANSWER THESE QUESTIONS:

1. *Does the text refer you to a graphic?*

   _____

2. *What is the purpose of this graphic?*

   _____

   _____

3. *What general information does this graphic provide?*

   _____

   _____

   _____

4. *What three specific things did you learn from this graphic?*

   _____

   _____

   _____

Chapter Eight

Mapping

Have you ever read a paragraph, a page, a chapter in a textbook, or an article in a professional magazine and been more confused than enlightened? Did you then ask yourself, "What is all that about?" If you are lucky, the author of the material has provided one or more graphics to clarify the information and thus enable you to comprehend it. If, however, the text is unaccompanied by a graphic, you probably can't answer this question, and your reaction will be to return to the material only to read it again without much improvement in comprehension. One of the basic reasons for this kind of difficulty is that the material may include a number of major and minor details. The result is that you are unable to organize what you read, cannot develop a block of related information, and therefore have difficulty understanding and retaining information.

Mapping is a technique you can use to simplify written material by graphically illustrating main ideas, major details, and minor details. A major detail is a detail which directly supports a main idea by providing information about it. A minor detail, in turn, provides information which supports a major detail. To clarify this concept of the relationship between main idea, major detail, and minor detail, examine the following example.

MAIN IDEA: Williamson Electronics has increased its volume of business over 60 percent in the past two years.

MAJOR DETAIL: During this time, Williamson Electronics opened 27 new retail outlets, adding to the 56 already in operation. (This detail directly supports the main idea since it is a reason why the company has increased its volume of business.)

MINOR DETAIL: Of the 27 new retail outlets, 16 were opened in California and 11 in Florida. (This minor detail supports the major detail by adding information about the 27 new retail outlets. In this case, the minor detail provides examples of where the new retail outlets are located.)

When you read material that you feel is difficult to understand, ask yourself this question: **Does the information include a number of major and minor details?** If the answer is yes, mapping is an appropriate technique to apply to that material. When mapping, you will produce a graphic, for one of the same reasons that authors include graphics when they wish to provide help for the reader—because graphics clarify written material.

To a great extent, the ease with which you can map depends upon your skill in identifying main ideas and selecting supporting details as you develop blocks of related information. A key action in mapping is to exclude any information that is not pertinent to the main idea of the material you are working with. If, however, you have mastered the skills required for developing blocks of related information, you will find mapping to be a logical followup.

Mapping of information can be applied to material of any length from a single paragraph to an entire book. Using this technique, any material can be reduced to main ideas and supporting details in a diagram that is easy to read at a glance.

Mapping is a personal technique. Like the Professional Vocabulary System, which you used when deciding about which terms to include in your personal career-related dictionary, you have complete control of what you do with this skill. You decide when material needs to be simplified by mapping and how much information you want to include in your map.

As you become aware of the value of mapping, you will begin to accumulate a number of maps. Keep track of them so that you can find and use your maps when you need them. Map on standard notebook paper and label the maps as to source, including page numbers, so you can refer to the original material if necessary. File your maps in a separate binder, or file them with class lecture notes and other related study materials, or use any other filing system that makes it easy for you to find specific maps when you need them.

In this chapter, mapping is applied only to paragraphs and selections. Keep in mind, however, that this technique is just as appropriate for use with longer materials. Once you have developed skill in mapping, you should be able to apply it to any materials as needed.

MAPPING A PARAGRAPH

When you decide that mapping a paragraph will clarify the information presented, follow these basic steps.

1. Identify the stated or implied main idea of the paragraph and write it at the top of your map.

2. Identify major details which directly support the main idea and place them beneath the main idea. Show major details of equal value coming from the main idea by placing them next to each other.

3. Identify minor details which provide additional related information about the major details and write them beneath the major details. Show minor details of equal value coming from the same detail by placing them next to each other.

4. If there are additional minor details which support the minor details identified in step 3, place them beneath those minor details.

5. Reduce all of the information in steps 2, 3, and 4 to words and/or short phrases. Use signs, symbols, or abbreviations that are appropriate. You want to keep your map as easy to read at a glance as possible.

6. Draw lines to connect the main idea and levels of supporting details.

7. Enclose information in boxes as shown in Sample A on page 000 so that it becomes easier to differentiate the different levels of major and minor details. (For increased clarity, you may want to use different geometric shapes for each level. For example, major details can be placed within ovals, the first level of minor details in rectangles, and the next level of minor details in circles.) Note that all maps presented in this book have major details placed in orals.

Since information is presented in a multitude of ways, there isn't any one universal format for mapping a paragraph. The number of major details varies, as does the number of minor details and levels of information. Mapping is most effective when you let the information in the paragraph guide you.

Examine Sample A and relate it to the steps described above. This sample illustrates the positions of the main idea, major details, and minor details in any map. For demonstration purposes, the material hypothetically includes three major details.

SAMPLE A: Placement in a Paragraph Map

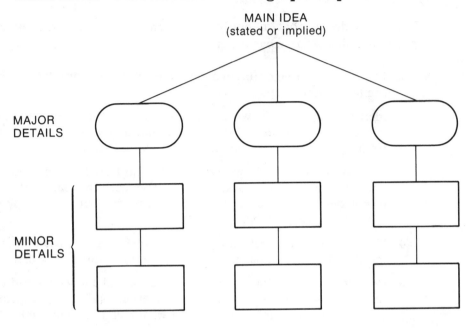

Sample B presents a paragraph which includes levels of information. Read the paragraph carefully and then examine how it has been mapped.

SAMPLE B: Paragraph Map

In general, manufacturers of fashion goods can be divided into three groups. One group is made up of firms that produce innovative, high-fashion apparel. This group is usually identified as the "better market." A second group of firms sometimes produces originals. But it usually turns out adaptations of styles that have survived the introduction stage and are in the rise state of their fashion life cycle. This group of firms is usually identified as the "moderate-priced market." A third group of manufacturers makes no attempt to offer new or unusual styling. Rather, these firms mass-produce close copies or adaptations of styles that have proved their acceptance in higher-priced markets. This group is usually identified as the "budget market."

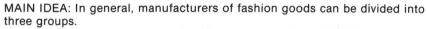

MAIN IDEA: In general, manufacturers of fashion goods can be divided into three groups.

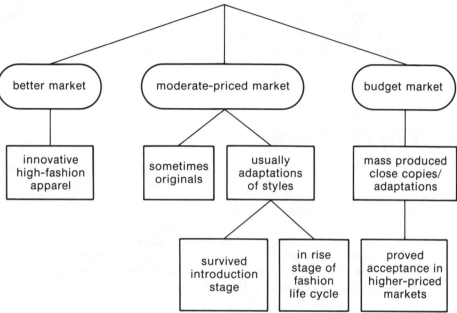

Note that, with the exception of the main idea, all of the information in the map has been reduced to words or phrases. Also note that the three major details, "better market," "moderate-priced market," and "budget market," are three examples of groups of manufacturers of fashion goods (the stated main idea of the paragraph). The minor details, where they are present, are either examples of or reasons for the major details. Under "usually adaptations of styles," both minor details are examples of styles: styles that have survived the introduction stage and styles that are in the rise stage of the fashion life cycle. Under "mass-produced close copies/adaptations," the minor detail is a reason; it tells why these copies are made for the budget market. Since I've reduced this information using my own words, your map of the same material might have included the same concepts but with slightly different wording.

You can easily check the accuracy of your map. Make sure that each level, beginning with the main idea, is appropriately supported by the information that is connected to it in the level below. That support is in the form of example or reason details.

The map in Sample B includes one major detail level and two minor detail levels. As you draw maps of your own materials, you can decide just how detailed you want these maps to be. As you increase the number of levels of minor details, the information becomes more and more specific. You may decide that you don't need all of that additional information. You may elect to include only major details and only one level of minor details. That's fine. Tailor your maps to meet your individual needs.

SAMPLE PRACTICE
Mapping Paragraphs

DIRECTIONS: Use the basic steps for drawing a paragraph map presented on page 181 to help you become accustomed to this technique. For these paragraphs, map to as many levels as the material allows. You have been provided with space for each of your maps.

1. Products may be classified as consumer or industrial goods. Consumer goods are those products and services purchased by the ultimate consumer for personal use. Industrial goods are those products purchased to be used, either directly or indirectly, in the production of other goods for resale. Most of the products you buy—books, clothes, tacos—are consumer goods. Raw cotton is an industrial good for Burlington Industries, rubber is a raw material for B. F. Goodrich Company.

2.   The conscious patient with a complete airway obstruction will try to speak, but he will not be able to do so, nor will he be able to cough. Usually he will display the distress signal for choking by clutching the neck between thumb and fingers. It will soon become apparent that he cannot breathe. The unconscious patient with a complete airway obstruction exhibits none of the usual signs of breathing, namely rhythmic chest movements and air exchange at the nose and mouth. The typical signs of shock can be seen in unconscious patients with full airway obstruction.

3.   Marketing is the combination of all those business activities that are concerned with understanding and satisfying consumer needs and wants. Marketing includes product planning and development activities that bring about new products and improve existing products, promotional activities that communicate information about products and services to consumers, distribution activities that deliver products to places where consumers can see and acquire them easily, and finally, pricing and packaging activities that make the product appealing in the marketplace.

Compare your three maps with those on the following two pages. If your maps do not resemble those given, reread the paragraphs and analyze the differences.

Sample Practice Answers

Note that the information on each map is reduced to its barest essentials without losing the sense of the material. Remember that your wording within the map may differ slightly from that presented below. That is all right as long as concepts remain similar. If your basic concepts and placement of information don't match those presented, analyze how they are different.

Notice that in all of the maps, each level of information is supported by an example(s) or reason(s) below it. Be sure to read the explanation below each map.

1. MAIN IDEA: Products may be classified as consumer or industrial goods.

The main idea of this paragraph is stated in the first sentence. Note that the two major details, consumer goods and industrial goods, are examples of the main idea. The first level of minor details are examples of each kind of goods. The next level of minor details gives specific examples of each kind of goods.

2. MAIN IDEA: Patients show signs of complete airway obstruction.

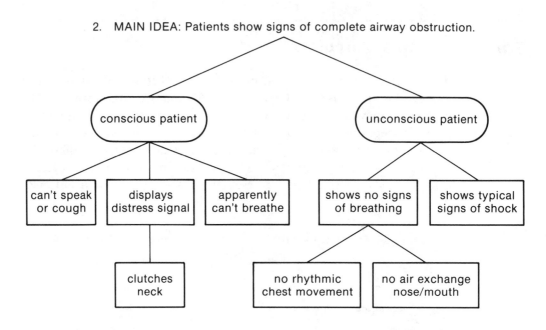

The implied main idea of the paragraph has been used as its title. There are two examples of patients with complete airway obstruction, conscious and unconscious patients, which are major details. The first level of minor details represents examples of the signs of complete airway obstruction in both kinds of patients. The second level of minor details gives more specific indications for two of the signs.

3. MAIN IDEA: Marketing is the combination of all those business activities that are concerned with understanding and satisfying consumer needs and wants.

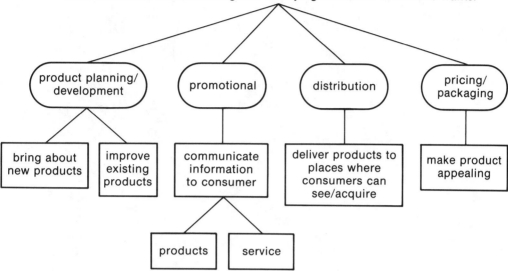

The main idea of the paragraph, which is stated in the first sentence, has been written at the top of the map. The four major details are examples of business activities which are concerned with understanding and satisfying consumer needs and wants. The first level of minor details gives reasons for each of these activities. The single minor level, communicate information to consumer, has two examples of communicating. Note that information at each level of the map is supported by information below it.

Now go on to Skill Development Exercise 8–1 on page 191 for additional practice in mapping paragraphs.

SKILL DEVELOPMENT EXERCISE 8–1
Mapping Paragraphs

DIRECTIONS: Map each of the following paragraphs. Refer to the steps for mapping a paragraph on page 181 if you need help. Let the information within the paragraph guide you as to the number of levels of minor details to include. You have been provided with space to map below each paragraph.

1.   Accounting is a measurement and communication process designed to provide useful and timely financial information. This process includes identifying, recording, classifying, summarizing, and interpreting business transactions. The first step is the identification of those events that are financial in nature and should be recorded. Recording may be done by hand, or with the help of typewriters, bookkeeping machines, word processors, and machines for encoding information on magnetic tape, paper tape, or cards. Computers are also used for recording transactions. Classifying is the grouping of similar items together in order to make the recording of many different events and transactions more efficient. Summarizing is the stating of groups of data in concise form. Interpretation provides explanations and develops relationships that give meaning to the information.

2.   The division of labor separates production tasks into a series of related operations. Each worker performs a single task, only one of perhaps hundreds of tasks necessary to produce a commodity. There are several reasons why the division of labor often leads to enormous gains in output per worker. First, specialization permits individuals to take advantage of their existing abilities and skills. Productive assignments can be undertaken by those individuals who are able to accomplish them most efficiently. Second, a worker who specializes in just one task (or one narrow area) becomes more experienced and more skilled in that task with the passage of time. Finally, and most importantly, the division of labor lets us adopt complex, large-scale production techniques unthinkable for an individual household.

3.   The basic functions of social work—restoration, provision of resources, and prevention—are intertwined and interdependent. Restoration of impaired social functioning may be subdivided into curative and rehabilitative aspects. Its curative aspects are to eliminate factors that have caused breakdown of functioning, and its rehabilitative aspects, to reorganize and rebuild interactional patterns. Illustrations of restoration would include assistance in obtaining a hearing aid for a partially deaf child or helping a rejected lonely child to be placed in a foster home. The rehabilitative aspect might be helping the one child to psychologically accept and live with the hearing aid and supporting the other child as he or she adjusts to the new foster home.

4.   The bulk of financing for noncommercial radio stations comes from the budgets of the educational institutions which own the stations. Indirectly this is frequently tax money, since taxes form the basis for the income of public schools.Other forms of financing are endowments, grants, and public donations. Endowments sometimes come from alummi of a university donating a substantial sum of money with the stipulation that the interest earned from the money be used to operate a radio station. Special grants from individuals, companies, or government agencies, including the Corporation for Public Broadcasting, are usually used for specific purposes, such as buying new equipment or producing a series of programs. Some stations, mainly those owned by private groups, attempt to subsist on donations from listeners and the limited funds they bring in by selling ads in a program guide.

5.   When considering the use of job sharing,* some potential disadvantages should be considered. First, the awkward divisions of responsibility created through the sharing of one job often lead to an increase in delays. For example, completion of a report by one sharer may be delayed until that same individual returns to work. These delays can result from poor managerial planning, improper administration, or faulty selection of personnel. Second, more time may be needed to allow for communication from supervisors and managers to job sharers, and for some overlap between the two sharers. Efficient time management is essential in order to overcome this problem. Finally, additional costs (such as insurance payments) may be incurred and could negate potential benefits.

*Job sharing is a situation in which two part-time employees share one full-time job.

MAPPING A SELECTION

Mapping a selection begins with the same question you asked about a paragraph that appeared to be complex: **Does the information include a number of major and minor details?** Again, if the answer is yes, mapping is the technique to use for simplifying the information in the selection. Your map will be a graphic representation of the information in that selection.

With a few modifications, mapping a selection is accomplished in the same way as mapping a paragraph. A very obvious difference between paragraph and selection maps is, of course, that you must deal with much more information in a selection. Since you are the one who decides such matters, you must choose how much information you want to include in your map.

The following basic steps can be very helpful to you in mapping any selection. Notice how similar they are to the steps for mapping a single paragraph.

1. Identify the stated or implied main idea of the selection.

2. Identify the stated or implied main idea of each paragraph in the selection. These main ideas are now the details that support the selection main idea as examples of it or reason for it. Call these **major details.**

3. Identify any additional related information about the major details (paragraph main ideas) that you think should be included in the map. These will be examples of the major details or reasons for them. Call these details **minor details.**

4. Reduce all information in steps 2 and 3 to words and/or short phrases.

5. When you write your reduced information on your map, use signs, symbols, or abbreviations that are appropriate. You want to keep your map as easy to read at a glance as is possible.

6. Write the main idea of the selection at the top of the map. Write major details that support this main idea below it. Draw lines to connect the main idea and its supporting major details.

7. Write minor details that support major details below them. Draw lines to connect major details and the minor details that support them.

8. Repeat step 7 for additional levels of minor details.

9. In steps 7 and 8, show minor details of equal value coming from the same detail by placing them next to each other.

10. Use boxes or other geometric figures to delineate levels of information as you did in paragraph maps.

Since there is a great variation in the way information is presented in a selection, there isn't any one format for mapping selections. The number of major details varies, as does the number of minor details and levels of information. As you found in mapping paragraphs, the only way to do this effectively is to let the information in the material guide you. Be alert for the author's use of boldface print or italics. These changes in print can help you identify main ideas and major details, and thus make it easier for you to map the selection.

Examine Sample C and relate it to the ten steps for mapping selections as described above. This sample illustrates the positions of the main idea, major details, and minor details in a selection map. For demonstration purposes, the selection hypothetically includes two major details.

SAMPLE C: Placement in a Selection Map

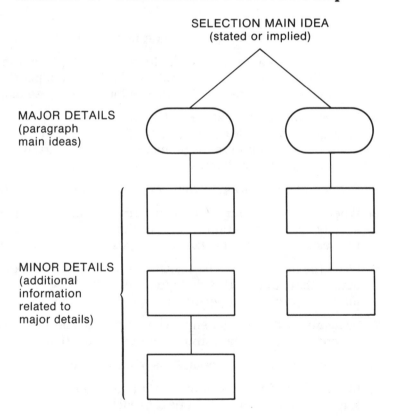

Read the selection in Sample D and then examine how this information has been mapped.

SAMPLE D: Selection Map

STRESS IN THE WORKPLACE

(1) Employers pay attention when problems in the workplace begin to affect the company's profits. A serious problem which results in both human and financial losses is stress in the workplace. While stress is probably present in any job situation, it can be lessened by programs planned and initiated to alleviate some of that stress. Today, an increasing number of companies in a wide variety of industries are making major efforts to reduce workplace stress.

(2) Company physical fitness programs are far and away the most popular method utilized to deal with stress in the workplace. These programs may take varied forms ranging from company-sponsored walking and jogging groups, aerobics, or exercise classes. Workers are also encouraged to use community or in-house fitness facilities where specialized equipment is available.

(3) Another approach to stress in the workplace is the attempt to reduce psychosocial stress through available benefits. Many companies are offering benefits such as counseling (both personal and family), programs for weight reduction, cigarette smoking, alcohol and substance abuse. The increasing use of flextime, in which personnel have more flexibility in determining working hours, is another type of stress reduction benefit.

MAIN IDEA: Today, an increasing number of companies in a wide variety of industries are making major efforts to reduce workplace stress.

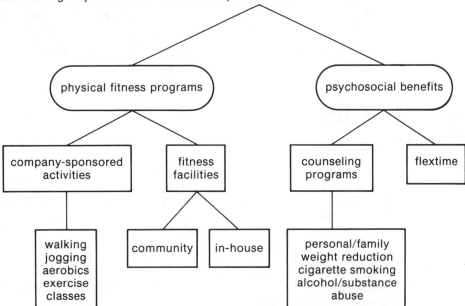

The main idea of the selection, which is stated in the last sentence of paragraph one, has been written at the top of the map. The two major details, "physical fitness programs" and "psychosocial benefits," represent the stated main ideas of paragraphs two and three. They support the main idea as examples of company efforts to reduce stress in the workplace.

The minor details, "company-sponsored activities" and "fitness facilities," support the first major detail because they are examples of physical fitness programs. The minor details, "counseling programs" and "flextime," support the second major detail because they are examples of psychosocial benefits.

The map has been taken to one more level of minor details to demonstrate how the text in the selection can guide you in this technique. In each case, the information supports the first minor detail above it by presenting examples. Thus, walking, jogging, aerobic dancing, and exercise classes are all examples of company-sponsored activities; "community" and "in-house" are examples of fitness facilities; "personal/family," "weight reduction," "cigarette smoking," and "alcohol/substance abuse" are all examples of counseling programs. Note that there aren't any examples of flextime; nor does the selection mention any reasons for it as a psychosocial benefit.

Notice how the material below the main idea has been reduced to the briefest form possible without losing the sense of the information. If you had mapped this particular selection, you probably would have come up with slightly different wording, a perfectly normal occurrence when reducing information.

You can check the accuracy of your selection maps in exactly the same way you checked your paragraph maps. Simply check each level of information to see if it supports the level above it by being an example of it or a reason for it.

SAMPLE PRACTICE
Mapping Selections

DIRECTIONS: Map the two sample selections below. Use the ten steps for drawing a selection map on page 197 as a guide through the process. Let the material guide you as to the number of levels you will use in your map. Space for your map has been provided under each selection.

1. UNTITLED

Corporations have four general characteristics, including continual life, centralized management, limited personal liability, and easy transferability of interests.

Continual Life. Corporations only "die" when they are disbanded intentionally, are absorbed into another company by merger, or become bankrupt. Otherwise, they function perpetually with new managers replacing those who retire.

Centralized Management. Large corporations can afford to attract talented professional people. A corporation's functional design lends itself to centalized management, in which trained and experienced teams are directed by, and held accountable to, a board of directors.

Limited Personal Liability. One of the most important characteristics of a corporation is its ability to shield a stockholder's personal estate from the debts of the corporation. Unlike a general partnership, in which each participant is personally responsible for his or her proportional share of a venture's liabilities, corporate stockholders' risks are limited to the extent of their investment in the company. In the event of a bankruptcy, other personal assets of the stock owners are not subject to attachment for any of the corporation debts.

Easily Transferable Interests. Because of the efficiency of the organized public stock exchanges, corporate stock ownership is relatively easy to transfer.

2. MANAGEMENT ACCOUNTING

An accountant who is employed by a business is said to be in management accounting. A small business may have only one or a few people doing this work, though a medium-sized or large company may have hundreds of accountants working under a chief accounting officer called a controller, treasurer, chief accountant, or financial vice president. There are a number of other positions that may be held by accountants at lower managerial levels.

Because of their broad and intimate view of all aspects of a company's operations, management accountants often have an important effect on management decision making. According to most recent surveys, more top-level business executives have backgrounds in accounting and finance than in any other field. Just a few of the well-known companies whose presidents or chairmen of the board are (or have been) accountants are American Airlines, General Foods, and International Business Machines.

The main task of management accountants is to give management the information it needs to make wise decisions. Management accountants also set up a system of internal control to increase efficiency and prevent fraud in their companies. They aid in profit planning, budgeting, and cost control. It is their duty to see that a company has good records, prepares proper financial reports, and complies with tax laws and government regulations.

Management accountants may certify their professional competence and training by qualifying for the status of Certified Management Accountants (CMA), which is awarded by the Institute of Certified Management Accountants of the National Association of Accountants. Under the CMA program, candidates must pass a number of examinations and meet educational and professional standards.

Compare your maps with those that follow. Analyze any differences between your maps and those presented.

Sample Practice Answers

1. MAIN IDEA: Corporations have four general characteristics . . .

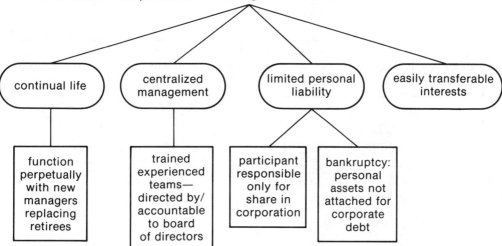

The main idea of the selection, which is stated in the first paragraph, has been reduced since the same information is presented as four major details. Three dots have been used to indicate this reduction. The four major details are examples of the characteristics of corporations. Note that these characteristics appeared in boldface print in the original selection, making it easy to determine that they are representing the stated main idea of each paragraph and that they are major details.

Each of the minor details below the first three characteristics supports that major detail by giving an example of it. These minor details can also be just as correct if the reader considered them to be reasons for the major details above it.

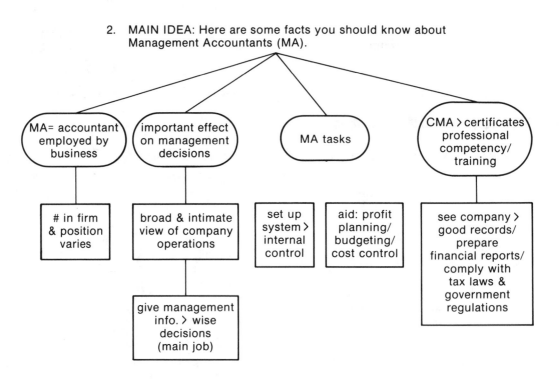

2. MAIN IDEA: Here are some facts you should know about Management Accountants (MA).

- MA= accountant employed by business
- important effect on management decisions
- MA tasks
- CMA > certificates professional competency/ training

- # in firm & position varies
- broad & intimate view of company operations
- set up system > internal control
- aid: profit planning/ budgeting/ cost control
- see company > good records/ prepare financial reports/ comply with tax laws & government regulations

- give management info. > wise decisions (main job)

This selection represents a case in which the information is so varied in each of the paragraphs that there isn't a single common thread throughout except that the selection provides information about management accountants. This is reflected in the selection implied main idea at the top of the map. The implied main idea could also be: This selection presents information about management accounting.

The main ideas of paragraphs 1, 2, and 4, which are stated in the first sentence in each of these paragraphs, are major details. Paragraph 3 has an implied main idea that is represented as "MA tasks" and is also a major detail. (To keep the information at this level brief, the main ideas have been reduced.)

Notice the use of symbols and abbreviations to reduce the wording in this map. You may have chosen to use words instead of these symbols, used other symbols, or abbreviated in a different way. That is fine as long as you can easily read your map and you haven't changed any of the concepts presented in the original material.

Now go on to Skill Development Exercise 8–2 on page 207, where you will be provided with additional practice in mapping selections.

In Skill Application 8 on page 217 you will be asked to apply your skill in mapping to your own career materials.

SKILL DEVELOPMENT EXERCISE 8–2
Mapping Selections

DIRECTIONS: Draw a map for each of the following selections. Use the steps described on page 197 to help you as needed. Let the selection material guide you in identifying the main idea, major details, and minor details. Space has been provided for your map below each selection.

1. LOCATION FACTORS

When you plan to open a retail business, first, study the industry in the area where you plan to locate the business. Payrolls create buying power for your potential customers. If the area doesn't have permanent industry, making a big investment there is probably unwise. If, to the contrary, the area is booming with permanent industry, this is a good location for your retail business.

Second, study the population growth trend of the area. Declining, stationary, or small populations will not support your retail business over the years. Instead, select an area that has a growing and wealthy population which will desire your goods or services. The reason for this is simple: These people will assure that your retail business will be a great success.

Next, study the potential market in terms of the needs and desires of the people you want to serve. For example, look at how they live, the age and the general characteristics of the population in the area where you want to open your business.

In addition, study the competition in advance. Instead of waiting until you have selected a location for your retail business, look through the area for competitors before you decide on the spot to open. Although competition is to be expected and a healthy sign of a good location, you don't want to find yourself surrounded by established stores offering the same goods or services that you plan to offer.

Also, it is a good idea to check with the Chamber of Commerce, trade associations, city or county planning departments and existing competition to find out as much as you can about the retail location that interests you. Play detective—you'll be amazed at how much you can learn that can be of value to you.

Finally, consider the city or town facilities. Is public transportation available near you if you hope to draw customers from all over the location area? Are there special problems in receiving merchandise or supplies in that area? Are there banks and post offices nearby? Furthermore, is the local government helpful to new businesses or does it make existence difficult for those who want to open retail operations in the area?

2. LEGAL IMPLICATIONS IN SPECIAL PATIENT SITUATIONS

The Emergency Medical Technician (EMT) must know how to handle special patients and special care situations which have legal implications. Some of these are described below.

Mentally Disturbed Patients. Care is usually provided under the laws of implied consent. If the patient is violent and likely to hurt himself or others, then restraint may be necessary. The law does not expect an EMT to risk his or her own safety to care for any patient. Typically, local laws will not allow an EMT to apply restraints unless ordered to do so by a physician or by the police. In some cases, a court order may be required.

Alcohol and Substance Abuse Patients. You must, when possible, carry out a complete patient assessment and provide needed care for patients who are under the influence of alcohol or drugs or have been injured while under such influence. Since medical practice views both alcohol and drug abuse as illnesses and not crimes, you should know if your state requires you to report cases of alcohol and drug abuse to legal authorities.

Attempted Suicide Patients. You are not required to endanger yourself to reach and care for patients attempting suicide (unless your agency spells out such responsibility). If you believe an injury or poisoning is due to an attempted suicide, your state may require you to report your suspicions to the emergency department staff or the police.

Felony-related Cases. If you have any reason to believe that the patient is the victim of a crime or was injured while committing a crime, then you may be required to report this suspicion to the police. This will hold true for possible cases of assault, rape, child abuse or neglect, gunshot wounds, knife wounds, and any other suspicious wound or injury. Your best course of action is to report to the emergency department staff and/or the police any cases in which you believe a possible crime is related to the patient's problem.

Animal Bite Patients. Such cases are usually required to be reported to the hospital personnel or to the police. If the animal is dead, you should protect the carcass so that it can be examined by medical authorities. If the animal is at the scene, you should protect yourself first, then the patient and bystanders. Do *not* try to capture the animal unless you are specifically trained do so and such action is part of your duties.

3. COMMUNICATION BARRIERS

Communication barriers are often mentioned by managers as being critical and persistent. There are three critical barriers to communication: semantic, technical, and perceptual. Better communication comes about when people are aware of these barriers.

The semantic barrier is a barrier of words. Communication can be difficult because words or symbols can have different meanings. For example, the word *fire* can mean either a flame or to discharge an employee.

The way people use words can build semantic barriers. For example, the use of technical language, or "jargon," simplifies in-group communication (such as in a group of CPAs). But if the CPAs use the technical words when communicating with others who do not understand the language, real barriers to understanding are erected.

Technical problems can prevent a message from conveying the intended meaning. If you were in a room talking with friends and a rock band was playing loudly, you might not accurately hear what was said. Likewise, any message can be interrupted by noises before it reaches the receiver. Both noise and physical barriers can be technical problems in oral communication. You cannot always assume that messages sent will be received as intended.

Lack of effective listening habits is a technical barrier that does lie with the receiver. People talk past each other for several reasons. Often they do not listen but simply wait for their turn to speak. Or they seek only the information that is consistent with what they want to hear—a result of perceptual barriers.

Perceptual problems occur because people have different mental frameworks. If Maria attempts to tell Paul about a dog, Paul conjures a visual image of a dog. Maria may be talking about a chihuahua, while Paul may be thinking about a German shepherd.

Emotion can set up perceptual barriers. The stronger the feelings, the less likely people are to communicate clearly. If a supervisor is appraising an employee's performance, at the end of which time she will (or will not) recommend a salary increase, the employee will probably become defensive at any suggestion of inadequate performance. The employee is less likely to hear suggestions for improvement because of greater interest in the salary adjustment recommendation.

4. FACTORS IN SETTING BAIL

Several elements are generally considered in determining whether a felony defendant should be entitled to a low bail or release on non-monetary conditions.

Nature of the Charge. A serious offense carrying a heavy penalty is frequently viewed as one justifying substantial bail. The idea is that the lengthy sentence which can attend conviction in a serious case may inspire the accused to flee after pretrial release, and flight is probable unless the accused is anchored by the prospect of significant property loss.

Employment History and Family Ties. Defendant's roots in the community are relevant factors, and where he has a favorable employment record with a local company and dependents in the locale, the prospect of flight is diminished. Accordingly, these factors militate [operate] in the direction of low bail or nonmonetary release when they appear in a given case. Still, if the offense is an aggravated one and there is a good possibility of protracted imprisonment, the "roots" consideration mentioned above may be outweighed.

Prior Criminal Record. This factor cuts two ways. If the defendant has a criminal record which includes bail jumping, escape from prison, or violation of probation or parole, the risk of flight is enhanced. Also relevant are consecutive convictions of specified felonies which may potentially subject the defendant to increased punishment under habitual offender laws if convicted again. But prior convictions are a two-edged sword. If the record shows that the defendant was freed before trial several times in prior years in connection with other arrests or offenses, and the record further shows that he dutifully appeared as required in each instance, this could work to his advantage.

Mental Condition. Active narcotics addicts, except those making an effort to break the habit, may be untrustworthy and high-risk cases if released before trial. Other factors are also relevant, including prior escapes of the defendant from a mental institution, present mental illness, or the fact that the offense with which the defendant is presently charged was the product of a mental disorder. These factors may be indicators in a given case that the defendant has a diminished understanding of his obligation to appear in court pursuant to [in accordance with] judicial order, or an inability to comply.

These are some of the significant considerations which may be relevant in any bail decision. Others may be important depending upon the particular facts of each case. In reviewing all the criteria, however, one guiding principle controls. Bail should be fixed in an amount or with conditions adequate to deter flight and insure a defendant's appearance in court. Bail set at a higher figure simply to insure defendant's incarceration before trial may be open to attack as "excessive" under the United States Constitution.

DIRECTIONS: Map the following selection, "Careers of the Future." Include only the title of the map, one major detail and one minor detail. Space for your map is provided below the selection.

5. CAREERS OF THE FUTURE

From Geography to Ethics, New Jobs Are Opening Up For Those Who Know Where to Look

by John Naisbitt

Remember when geography was a subject you took in elementary school and a geographer was someone who knew things like the length of the Amazon River, the height of Mount McKinley, and the depth of the Pacific Ocean?

Today, for a growing number of urban geographers, it is far more than that. In recent years there has been a career boom in such information-intensive areas as finance, education, and health, but many job opportunities are opening up in several lesser-known fields as well. In addition to geography, these include technology assessment, knowledge engineering, data security, telecommunications management, and ethics. Here is a rundown:

Urban Geography. "When I tell people I'm a geographer, they're fascinated, but they also aren't sure what to think," says Jeanette Rice, who is currently employed by Embrey Investments Inc., a San Antonio real estate development company. Rice is one of a new breed of geographers whose business cards are likely to read "director of market research" and whose jobs involve examining demographic patterns to determine the market potential for particular businesses.

Technology Assessment. By reading technical magazines and tapping outside resources, a technology assessor insures that his company keeps abreast of new technological developments. The job requires creative, intelligent thinkers with broad technical backgrounds and business know-how. Technology assessment will become increasingly crucial as high-tech companies struggle to keep up with the competition. Leading corporations that already employ technology assessors are General Electric, Allied-Signal, and Exxon.

Knowledge Engineering. Look for this still-small job category to explode with the growth of the artificial-intelligence industry. Knowledge engineers interview experts to study the thought processes they use in decision making, and then construct computer programs that mimic their thinking. "You need people who can learn fast and become instant 'mini-experts,'" says William Turpin, manager of knowledge-systems engineering for Texas Instruments Data Systems Group in Austin, Tex. "That doesn't mean they need an extensive background in

John Naisbitt is the author of the best-sellers Megatrends *and* Reinventing the Corporation. *This column for* SUCCESS *was co-authored by Jerry Kline, managing editor of* John Naisbitt's Trend Letter.

computer science. We've had music majors who turn out to be excellent knowledge engineers. The person just has to be a good interviewer who knows how to listen."

Data Security. It is the responsibility of data-security managers to make sure that corporate information is not misused—that, for instance, computerized information on business orders and clients is kept from competitors and doesn't fall into the wrong hands. According to Robert D. McCrie, editor of the trade journal *Security Letter*, there is a "dearth of management talent" in this industry. A few universities have responded by offering courses in data security, including St. John's University and John Jay College of Criminal Justice, both in New York.

Telecommunications Management. These managers develop office communications budgets, buy equipment, and focus on improving the flow of information. The job calls for both the installation capabilities of an experienced technician and the strong management skills of an executive.

Ethics. Of 279 U.S. corporations surveyed last year by the Bentley College Center for Business Ethics in Waltham, Mass., 208 had written codes of conduct, 40 had ethics committees, and 17 had ethics ombudsmen. Cummins Engine Co. in Columbus, Ind., for example, had a full-time ethicist, with the title of corporate responsibility director, who advised managers and staff members on how to deal with sticky ethical decisions and evaluate the ramifications of major policy decisions. With growing publicity about corporate wrongdoing, this is an area that executives are finding difficult to ignore.

SKILL APPLICATION 8
Mapping

DIRECTIONS: *Map one paragraph and one selection from your own career materials such as textbooks, manuals, class notes, or professional magazines. Duplicate these materials and attach them to this sheet. The selection may/may not have a title or subtitle and should be at least three paragraphs in length. Be sure to include the source information.*

PARAGRAPH SOURCE INFORMATION

Title: _____

Author: _____

Place of publication: _____

Publisher: _____

Copyright Date: _____ *Page(s):* _____

SELECTION SOURCE INFORMATION

Title: _____

Author: _____

Place of publication: _____

Publisher: _____

Copyright Date: _____   *Page(s):* _____

Chapter Nine

Charting

Charting is a second technique which enables you to simplify material by analyzing and organizing it into a graphic presentation. The material thus becomes easier for you to understand and remember.

Sometimes materials are complex because the author expects you to understand and remember a number of things about a number of items. For example, you might be expected to learn and remember the description, advantages, and disadvantages of three different kinds of businesses: single proprietorship, partnership, and corporation. How do you keep all of this information straight? One way is to graphically present the information in a chart which clearly shows each kind of business and what you must know about it. All of the facts can now be seen at a glance.

When you encounter that kind of material—information which seems to have an overwhelming number of facts—ask yourself this question: **Is the author presenting the same kind of information about a number of major details?** If the answer is yes, charting is an appropriate way to organize this material.

Charting is similar to mapping in several ways. Charting is also dependent to a great extent on your skill in identifying main ideas and selecting supporting details as you develop blocks of related information. In addition, a key action in charting, as in mapping, is to exclude any information that is not pertinent to the main idea of the material.

Also like mapping, charting can be applied to material of any length from a single paragraph to an entire book. Using this technique, any material can be reduced to main ideas and supporting details in a graphic that is easy to read at a glance.

In addition, charting is also a personal technique. As such, you decide when a chart is needed, what information is to be included, and, to some extent, where that information is to be placed on the chart. When charting, however, always let the material guide you in chart material.

At times, you may find that some materials lend themselves to either mapping or charting. In such cases, it is up to you to decide which technique you feel is most appropriate to apply. Certain materials, however, can only be presented in a chart because of the way they are written and the kinds of information they include. For example, information concerned with comparison or contrast of two or more things, people, or events produces very good charts. The description, advantages, disadvantages, and results of any group of things or actions also produces very usable charts. As you work in this chapter, be aware of the kind of information that is clarified by charting. With practice, you will soon be surprised at your skill in spotting potential charts as you work with your own textbooks and career materials.

The purpose of charting is to make it easy for you to see a large quantity of information at a glance. This information is reduced and written into boxes which separate important concepts. To make it easier to read your charts and master the information in them, keep in mind that this is one time when neatness counts. A chart which isn't clear and easy to read is of no use to you. Use a pen rather than a pencil for a sharper and more lasting image, and always use a ruler to draw definite boxes.

As you become convinced of the value of charting, you will begin to accumulate a number of charts. Keep track of them in the same way that was suggested to you regarding maps in Chapter Eight. Design your charts on standard notebook paper. Label them as to source, including page numbers, so that you can refer to the information in its original form if necessary. Either keep all of your charts together in a binder or file them where they fit with class lecture notes and other study materials. Use any filing system you prefer. The key point is that your charts should be ready for retrieval as you need them.

Although this chapter emphasizes charting complex paragraphs and selections, your skill in using this technique can be applied to material of any length from a single paragraph to an entire book. The following chart, designed by a student, is a good example of how extensive material can be reorganized, reduced, and thus, clarified. This particular chart represents critical information from twelve pages of a data processing textbook.

MAIN IDEA: There are differences in high-level programming languages.

LANGUAGE	KEY FEATURES	LIMITATIONS
BASIC	—simplified naming of variables —optional formatting —conversational programming mode —good diagnostics	—not designed to facilitate structured programs —needs substantial modifications to run on another program
COBOL	—machine independence —self-documentation —four distinct divisions • identification • environment • data • procedure —input/output orientation	—programs lengthy —large & sophisticated language translator needed —difficult to implement on many small computers —not suitable: scientific/ engineering applications
FORTRAN	—fast program execution —accuracy	—weak in structured programming —difficult follow logic of programs —inferior to COBOL
Pascal	—easy to learn structured orientation —memory efficiency	—marginal input/output —not suitable for data processing applications

As you can see when you examine it, this well-designed chart consists of a box of related information which includes a main idea used as the title, four major details which support that main idea, and two categories of information about the major details.

CHARTING A PARAGRAPH

When you have answered yes to the question **Is the author presenting information related to a number of major details?** and have made the decision to chart a paragraph, the technique will be easier to do if you follow these eight specific steps:

1. Identify the implied or stated main idea of the paragraph. It will become the title of your chart.

2. Identify the major details. They will provide direct information about the main idea. They will be examples or reasons that support the main idea of the paragraph. (Look for clues to major details; they are sometimes written in boldface print or italics.)

3. Write these major details in a vertical column down the left-hand side of what will be your chart, leaving space between details.*

4. Decide what categories of information you have been given about these major details. The categories of information will generally apply to all or most of the major details.

5. Write the categories of information across what will be top of your chart, leaving space between details.*

6. Use a ruler to draw boxes.

7. Write the appropriate information in each box. This material will represent information about the major details on the left-hand side of the chart. (Every box may not be filled, but you know that you are dealing with appropriate major details and categories of information if most of the boxes are filled. It is a good idea to mark the empty boxes in some way so that you know, if you use the chart at a later date, that the empty spaces represent lack of information and not careless charting.)

8. Condense all the information written in boxes into its briefest possible form. Pretend that you are sending this information in a telegram in which each word costs money. Include only enough essential words to make the entry understandable. Don't hesitate to use signs, symbols, or abbreviations in your chart. They can be used in place of words or phrases or to increase the readability of the information in the boxes, especially when more than one point is made.

*When charting, you may decide that you prefer to place the major details across the top of the chart and the categories of information in a column down the left-hand side of the chart. That is perfectly all right and does not change the information selected and written into the boxes in the chart. Use whichever format feels most comfortable to you.

Examine the placement of information in a chart as presented in Sample A. Relate the first seven steps described above to the sample.

SAMPLE A: Placement of Information in a Chart

TITLE

MAJOR DETAILS	CATEGORY OF INFORMATION	CATEGORY OF INFORMATION	CATEGORY OF INFORMATION	CATEGORY OF INFORMATION

Read the paragraph in Sample B. It is very long and contains so many details that it will not be surprising if you have difficulty understanding and retaining all of the important information. Remember that the purpose of charting is to simplify such complex material, and this is the kind of information that is clarified by charting. It is essential for your comprehension that you identify the important concepts presented in this kind of paragraph and arrange them in an organized form so they can easily be seen.

When you have finished reading the paragraph, examine the chart based on the material. Pay particular attention to the placement of major details and categories of information in the chart.

SAMPLE B: A Paragraph Chart

The total number of offenses by juveniles in any given period of time is impossible to ascertain. Although the Federal Bureau of Investigation records and statistically analyzes the number of juvenile arrests for various offenses each year, the illegal behavior by juveniles that is not detected or reported to the police is not accounted for in any statistical report. **Information about the amount and nature of juvenile misbehavior comes from three major sources.** First, official statistical information is provided by the police departments to the FBI, and reports by other agencies that deal with juvenile offenders are summarized by the Department of Justice. A second way of obtaining information about delinquency is through surveys that ask juveniles whether they have committed acts that resulted in or could have resulted in arrest or referral to the juvenile court. The findings of such surveys are called "self-reported delinquency" data. Research of this type has certain shortcomings, including the difficulty of knowing whether youths are overreporting or underreporting the amount and types of behavior in which they have engaged. Some self-reported delinquency studies have sought to verify the data collected by comparing them with juvenile court records for the same sample of youths. This technique is also limiting, however, because it does not allow the anonymity that respondents need if they are to reply truthfully, without fear of punishment. Crime victimization surveys provide a third source of information about offenses committed by juveniles. These surveys, usually conducted by telephone, solicit information from a random sample of people about their experiences as victims of crime. Those surveyed are asked to provide information on the types and number of offenses committed against them and to estimate the ages of the offenders. Again, the possibility of ascertaining the actual amount and nature of juvenile illegal activity is limited, since the victim must be willing to discuss the crime and must have seen the perpetrator in order to make an age estimate.

MAIN IDEA: Information about the amount and nature of juvenile misbehavior comes from three major sources.

SOURCE	HOW OBTAINED	LIMITATIONS
Official statistical information	Dept. Justice summaries	Doesn't account for undetected/unreported illegal juvenile behavior
Self-reported delinquency data	Surveys of juveniles: acts committed (ones possibly result in referral to juvenile court)	1. Possible over/ under reporting (amount and types behaviors) 2. Can't verify data 3. Doesn't allow for anonymity
Crime victimization surveys	Telephone surveys: random sample of crime victims	Victim must: 1. be willing discuss crime 2. have seen perpetrator & be able to estimate age

Look at how the related information in the paragraph has been organized into a chart. Note that the main idea in the original paragraph has been put into boldface print for you. That main idea becomes the title of the chart. The three major sources of information are mentioned—"official statistical information," "self-reported delinquency data," and "crime victimization surveys"—and these become your major details, which are placed in a vertical column at the left side of the chart. You are then given the categories of information about the major details: (1) how the information in the source was obtained and (2) the limitations of each of the sources. These two kinds of categories are written across the top of the chart. The information that pertains to each major detail is written in the appropriate boxes. Notice how briefly the paraphrased information can be written in each box without losing your sense of the original material. When you chart your own material, feel free to use signs, signals, or abbreviations—with one caution. To avoid confusion, always use the same sign, signal, or abbreviation to denote the same term.

When you construct your own charts in this chapter, they may differ slightly from the ones I've done. First, you may decide to place the major details across the top of the chart and the minor details in the column at the left-hand side of the chart. Second, the information in the boxes will reflect your way of condensing it. Both of these personal decisions are fine as long as they do not change the essential concepts which you select and write on the chart.

SAMPLE PRACTICE
Charting Paragraphs

DIRECTIONS: Use the eight steps for charting on page 222 to help you chart the following paragraphs. Let the material guide you in selecting main ideas, major details, and categories of information. Space has been provided for your charts below each paragraph.

You have already mapped paragraph one in Chapter Eight. It is included here as an example of information which can either be mapped or charted.

1. Products may be classified as consumer or industrial goods. Consumer goods are those products and services purchased by the ultimate consumer for personal use. Industrial goods are those products purchased to be used, either directly or indirectly, in the production of other goods for resale. Most of the products you buy—books, clothes, tacos—are consumer goods. Raw cotton is an industrial good for Burlington Industries, rubber is a raw material for B. F. Goodrich Company.

2.   There are two major branches of pathology: anatomical and clinical. The anatomical pathologist has been trained to deal with the examination of tissues and organs at autopsies or from surgical procedures. He or she will make diagnoses to identify and recognize disease and injury patterns with the naked eye or the microscope. The clinical pathologist handles the rest of laboratory medicine—performs examinations, supervises, and teaches people to do other tests done in a hospital laboratory. These people are trained to deal with natural disease.

3.   The economic system of the United States is known as market
capitalism. It has two principal characteristics: (1) Most businesses are
owned by private individuals and (2) Most economic interactions occur
in markets where resources, goods, and services are bought and sold.
But there are other types of economic systems. The system in the Soviet
Union is planned socialism. In this type of system, most resources are
owned and their use is controlled by the government. Viewed as a
whole, economic interactions constitute an economic system or the way
society is organized to address the economic problem of scarcity.

Compare your charts with those provided below. If your charts are very different from those presented, analyze these differences. Be sure to read the explanations below each chart. Remember that wording and the placement of major details and categories of information may differ. However, the essential information from the original material must be represented on your chart.

Sample Practice Answers

1. MAIN IDEA: Products may be classified as consumer or industrial goods.

KINDS OF GOODS	DEFINITION	EXAMPLES
Consumer goods	products/services purchased by ultimate consumer > personal use	books, clothes, tacos
Industrial goods	products purchased for direct/indirect use in production other goods > resale	1. raw cotton (Burlington Industries) 2. rubber (B. F. Goodrich)

The paragraph upon which this chart is based has a stated main idea in its first sentence. That main idea serves as the title of the chart. The paragraph is concerned with two kinds of goods, consumer and industrial, and these two are the major details. They are examples of the main idea. (Note that the main idea and major details are the same as those identified when you mapped this paragraph.) In discussing the two kinds of goods, two categories of information are included: definitions and examples of both kinds of goods. These are labeled and written across the top of the chart. The material written in the boxes supplies information about the major details.

    2. MAIN IDEA: There are two major branches of pathology— anatomical and clinical.

PATHOLOGIST	TRAINING	RESPONSIBILITIES
Anatomical	Deals with exam of tissues and organs 1. autopsies 2. surgical procedures	Makes diagnoses: identify/recognize disease & injury—use naked eye/microscope
Clinical	Deals with natural disease	Rest of lab medicine 1. performs exams 2. supervise/teach others to do tests: hospital lab

In this paragraph, the main idea, which is stated in the first sentence, is the title of the chart. You are introduced to the two major branches of pathology through a description of the persons who work in the two branches: the anatomical pathologist and the clinical pathologist. These are the major details and are written down the left-hand side of the chart. Two categories of information are presented and discussed: the training of each kind of pathologist and the responsibilities of each. These categories are written across the top of the chart. The material written in the boxes represents information about the two major details.

3. MAIN IDEA: There are differences between the economic systems of the United States and the Soviet Union.

ECONOMIC SYSTEM	EXAMPLE	CHARACTERISTICS
Market capitalism	United States	1. Most resources owned > private individuals 2. Interactions in markets: resources/goods/services bought & sold
Planned socialism	Soviet Union	Most resources: 1. owned by gov't 2. gov't control of use

The main idea of the paragraph is implied. It has been written at the top of the chart to serve as the title. Two types of economic systems, identified and discussed as market capitalism and planned socialism, are major details. The categories of information, the places where these two economic systems occur and the characteristics of each, are written at the top of the chart. The material written in the boxes provides information about the major details.

Be aware that the information in the last sentence of the paragraph was not included in the chart since it is not directly related to differences between the two economic systems.

Now go on to Skill Development Exercise 9–1 on page 231 where you will have additional practice in charting paragraphs.

SKILL DEVELOPMENT EXERCISE 9–1
Charting Paragraphs

DIRECTIONS: Chart the following paragraphs. Use the eight steps on page 222 to help you. Let the material guide you in charting. Space has been provided for your charts below each paragraph.

The first paragraph may be familiar to you; its main idea was identified in Chapter Three.

1.   The Wool Products Labeling Act of 1939 (requiring that the kind and percentage of wool in a product be identified), the Fur Products Labeling Act of 1951 (requiring identification of the animal from which the fur was derived), and the Flammable Fabrics Act of 1953 (prohibiting the interstate sale of flammable fabrics) formed the original legislation in this area. A more recent law—the Fair Packaging and Labeling Act, passed in 1967—requires the disclosure of product identity, the name and address of the manufacturer or distributor, and information concerning the quality of its contents. In 1971, the Public Health Cigarette Smoking Act prohibited tobacco advertising on radio and television. Thus, rules governing advertising and labeling constitute a sphere of marketing's legal environment.

2.   Most married women did not work outside the home in the post-World War II years. In 1957, for example, only about 33 percent of married women 25 to 54 years of age were in the labor force, compared with approximately 80 percent of single women and 65 percent of widowed, divorced, and separated women combined. These differences shrank dramatically in the following three decades. Between 1957 and 1987, married women entered the labor market in record numbers and their participation rate more than doubled—to 68 percent, while the rate for single women remained around 80 percent, and that for widowed, divorced, or separated women rose to 79 percent.

3.   The ownership of land that borders on a river or stream carries with it the right to use that water in common with the other landowners whose lands border the same watercourse. This is known as a **riparian right.** The landowner does not have absolute ownership of the water that flows past his land but may use it in a reasonable manner. In some states, riparian rights have been modified by the **doctrine of prior appropriation:** the first owner to divert water for his own use may continue to do so, even though it is not equitable to the other landowners along the watercourse. Where land borders on a lake or sea, it is said to carry **littoral rights** rather than riparian rights. Littoral rights allow a landowner to use and enjoy the water touching his land provided he does not alter the water's position by artificial means. A lakefront lot owner would be an example of this.

4.　　　For an act or its omission to be a crime, not only must there be criminal intent, but the behavior must be in violation of the criminal law. Criminal law, as opposed to noncriminal or civil law, is that branch of law that deals with offenses committed against the safety and order of the state. As such, criminal law relates to actions that are considered so dangerous, or potentially so, that they threaten the welfare of the society as a whole. And it is for this reason that in criminal cases the government brings the action against the accused. Civil law, by contrast, is the body of principles that determines private rights and liabilities. In these cases, one individual brings an action against another individual—a plaintiff versus a defendant—as opposed to the state versus an accused as in criminal cases. More specifically, civil law is structured to regulate the rights between individuals or organizations; it involves such areas as divorce, child support, contracts, and property rights. Civil law also includes torts, civil wrongs for which the law gives compensation.

5.   RNs are graduates of approved schools of nursing and have passed a state licensure examination. Nursing programs may be in two-year junior colleges, three-year diploma schools, or in four-year baccalaureate institutions. Three groups of nurses, nurse anesthetists, nurse midwives, and nurse practitioners, have special training in addition to a nursing degree. The *nurse anesthetist* has special training in anesthesia to assist the anesthesiologist (a physician who specializes in anesthesiology) and to administer anesthesia without direct supervision in certain defined situations. The *nurse midwife* specializes in obstetrical care and has sufficient training to manage routine pregnancies and deliveries. The *nurse practitioner*'s role is similar to that of the physician's assistant. Because of the nurse practitioner's training and background in nursing skills, however, the nurse practitioner's approach to patient care is believed to be more comprehensive than that of the physician's assistant. Nurse practitioners may also work more independently of physicians than physician's assistants.

CHARTING A SELECTION

When charting a selection, you are, of course, faced with a much greater amount of information to analyze and organize. However, with slight modification you can chart a selection in much the same way you did a paragraph.

Once again, your decision to chart any selection is a result of answering yes to the question **Is the author presenting the same kind of information about a number of major details**? The following modified steps can help you create a well-designed selection chart.

1. Identify the overall stated or implied main idea of the selection. It will become the title of your chart.

2. Identify the main idea of each paragraph in the selection: These are the items being discussed in each paragraph; and they are the major details. They will provide direct information about the selection's main idea. They will be examples or reasons that support the main idea of the paragraph. (Look for clues to major details; they are sometimes written in boldface print or italics.)

3. Write these major details in a vertical column down the left-hand side of what will be your chart, leaving space between details.*

4. Decide what categories of information you have been given about these major details. The categories of information will generally apply to all or most of the major details.

5. Write the categories of information across what will be the top of your chart, leaving space between details.*

6. Use a ruler to draw boxes.

7. Write the appropriate information in each box. This material will represent information about the major details on the left-hand side of the chart. (Every box may not be filled, but you know that you are dealing with appropriate major details and categories of information if most of the boxes are filled. It is a good idea to mark the empty boxes in some way so that you know, if you use the chart at a later date, that the empty spaces represent lack of information and are not caused by careless charting.)

8. Condense all information written in boxes in the briefest possible form. Pretend that you are sending this information in a telegram in which each word costs money. Include only enough essential words to make

---

* Remember that you can reverse the position of the major and minor details in the chart, if you so desire.

the entry understandable. Don't hesitate to use signs, symbols, or abbreviations in your chart. They can be used in place of words or phrases or to increase the readability of the information in the boxes, especially when more than one point is made. Again, be consistent in your use of such sign, symbols, or abbreviations.

The following sample selection and the chart that represents its essential information demonstrate how the above eight steps are applied. Read the selection and then carefully examine the chart based on that information. Notice, particularly, how the information in the boxes has been reduced.

SAMPLE C: Charting a Selection

CATEGORIES OF INFORMATION

There are three categories of information related to managerial levels and the decisions managers make. The first level is strategic information, which relates to long-range planning policies that are of direct interest to upper management. Information such as population growth, trends in financial investment, and human resources changes would be of interest to top company officials who are responsible for developing policies and determining long-range goals. This type of information is achieved with the aid of decision support systems (DSS) on a computer.

The second level of information is managerial information. It is of direct use to middle management and department heads for implementation and control. Examples are sales analysis, cash flow projections, and annual financial statements. This information is of use in short- and intermediate-range planning—that is, months rather than years. It is maintained with the aid of management information systems (MIS) on a computer.

The third information level is operational information, which is short-term, daily information used to operate departments and enforce the day-to-day rules and regulations of the business. Examples are daily employee absence sheets, overdue purchase orders, and current stocks available for sale. Operational information is established by data processing systems (DPS).

MAIN IDEA: There are three categories of information related to
managerial levels and the decisions managers make.

LEVEL	USED BY	USED FOR	EXAMPLE OF INFO.	COMPUTER SYSTEMS
Strategic information	Top officials responsible: developing policies & long-range goals	Long-range planning	1. Population growth 2. Trends in financial investment 3. Human resources changes	Decision support systems (DSS)
Managerial information	Middle management & dept. heads	Implementation & control of short- & intermediate-range planning, financial statements	1. Sales analysis 2. Cash flow projections 3. Annual financial statements	Management information system (MIS)
Operational information	?	1. Dept. operation 2. Enforcing day-to-day rules & regulations 3. Short-term daily info.	1. Employee absence sheets 2. Overdue purchase orders 3. Current stocks available for sale	Data processing systems (DPS)

Notice how this chart follows the eight steps for charting selections
which appear on pages 237 and 238. The stated main idea of the selection,
which is found in the first sentence of the selection, is used as the title of the
chart. The three major details—"strategic information," "managerial information," and "operational information"—are actually main ideas of the
three paragraphs. They have been reduced to phrases in order to limit the
words in each box. They have been placed in the column down the left-hand
side of the chart. The headings for four categories of information have been
written across the top of the chart. The material in the boxes represents
information about the headings written across the top of the chart. Be aware

of the great reduction in the wording of the information in the boxes. Also note that one box contains only a question mark. There isn't any information available in the selection for this box. I have placed the question mark in it to denote that there is a lack of information rather than an omission of information that appeared in the original selection.

SAMPLE PRACTICE
Charting Selections

DIRECTIONS: Chart the following selections. Use the eight steps for charting found on pages 237 and 238 to help you. Be sure to let the material guide you. Space has been provided for your charts below each selection.

1. CLEANING

There are several methods of cleaning masonry structures. The first consists of spraying a *water mist.* A water mist will remove a gypsum crust which forms on limestone and marble, removing the gypsum along with the imbedded dirt. The problems with this method include potential freeze/thaw damage, or entrapment of moisture in deteriorating masonry or in loose mortar joints. Another problem is the evacuation of what may be significant amounts of water from the site.

The second method is *chemical cleaning* with proprietary chemical cleaners. The efficiency of these cleaning agents has been greatly increased. Care must be taken and tests made of a particular masonry surface. Not all proprietary products work equally well on all types of masonry.

The third cleaning method is the use of *muriatic acid and water.* The mix can be varied to fit the project. While this method may be cheaper than the use of proprietary cleaning chemicals, the dangers of etching the surface of the masonry, changing the color, and bleaching are greater.

The fourth method is *abrasive cleaning.* Sand blasting is the prime example of this type of cleaning. During the manufacturing process, construction materials acquire a finish surface or crust. The firing of brick gives a hard crust. The quarrying and finishing of granite develops a similar surface. Sandblasting tends to destroy this natural protective finish; it breaks the crust on brick, terra cotta, granite, limestone, and marble, exposing a porous surface that is susceptible to freeze/thaw or wet/dry damages. This causes the building to soil quicker and to change color. High pressure blasting, even blasting with glass beads, pulverized walnut shells or corn cobs, may do irreparable damage to masonry surfaces.

2. ANCIENT BEGINNINGS

Although we think of public relations as a twentieth-century phenomenon, its roots are ancient. Leaders in virtually every great society throughout history understood the importance of influencing public opinion through persuasion. For example, the Iraqis of 1800 B.C. hammered out their messages on stone tablets so that farmers could learn the latest techniques of harvesting, sowing, and irrigation. The more food the farmers grew, the better the citizenry ate and the wealthier the country became: a good example of planned persuasion to reach a specific public for a particular purpose—in other words, public relations.

Later on, the Greeks put a high premium on communication skills. The best speakers, in fact, were generally elected to leadership positions. Occasionally, aspiring Greek politicians enlisted the aid of Sophists (individuals renowned for both their reasoning and rhetoric) to help fight verbal battles. Sophists would gather in the amphitheaters of the day and extol the virtues of particular political candidates. Often, their arguments convinced the voters and elected their employer. Thus, the Sophists set the stage for today's lobbyists, who attempt to influence legislation through effective communication techniques.

The Romans, particularly Julius Caesar, were also masters of persuasive techniques. Faced with an upcoming battle, Caesar would rally public support through assorted publications and staged events. Similarly, during World War I, a special U.S. Public Information Committee, the Creel Committee, was formed to channel the patriotic sentiments of Americans in support of the U.S. role in the war. Stealing a page from Caesar, the committee's massive verbal and written communications effort was successful in marshalling national pride behind the war effort. Said a young member of the Creel Committee, Edward L. Bernays (later considered by many as the "father of public relations"), "This was the first time in our history that information was used as a weapon of war."

Compare your charts with those shown below and analyze any differences. Be sure to read the explanation below each chart.

Sample Practice Answers

1. MAIN IDEA: There are several methods of cleaning masonry structures.

CLEANING LEVEL	METHOD/USE	PROBLEMS
Water mist	Removes gypsum & dirt which forms on limestone & marble	1. Freeze/thaw damage 2. Entrapment of moisture > deteriorated/loose mortar joints 3. Getting rid of water
Chemical cleaning	Uses proprietary chemicals—need check on small area first	Not all proprietary = good cleaning on all types masonry
Muriatic acid and water	Mix varies with project	Dangers: 1. etching surface of masonry 2. changing color 3. bleaching
Abrasive cleaners	Blasting: sand, water (high pressure), glass beads, nut shells, corn cobs	1. Breaks protective cover/crust: terra cotta, brick, granite, limestone, marble 2. Exposes porous surfaces to freeze/thaw & wet/dry damage 3. Soils quicker 4. Color changes

In the above selection, the main idea is found in the first sentence and becomes the title of the chart. The main idea tells you that there are several methods of cleaning. There are actually four methods, and they are the major details written in the left-hand column of the chart. Two categories of information are included in the selection: the methods and/or use of cleaning masonry structures and the problems encountered when each of these methods is applied. The minor details are written in the boxes and support the four major details.

Notice how similar the designing of a selection chart is to the designing of a paragraph chart. Both result in graphic presentations of the material.

2. MAIN IDEA: Leaders in virtually every great society throughout history understood the importance of influencing public opinion through persuasion.

SOCIETY	EARLY APPLICATION OF PR	LATER USE OF TECHNIQUE
Iraqis	Influence public opinion through persuasion	PR as planned persuasion > reach specific public for particular purpose = public relations
Greeks	Premium on communication skills - - - - - - - - Ex: Sophists: speakers to convince voters to elect political candidates	Lobbyists > attempt to influence legislation > communication techniques
Romans	Masters of persuasive techniques to rally support - - - - - - - - Ex: Julius Caesar > public support for battles	World War I—U.S. Public Information Committee (Creel Committee) > gain support for U.S. role in war

The stated main idea of this second selection is the title of the chart rather than the subtitle of the selection, "Ancient Beginnings." Three early societies are the major details. The categories of information provided for each major detail are "early applications of PR techniques" and "later use of these same techniques." Examples of early applications of PR are included for the Greeks and Romans. If you so desire, these examples could be reflected in an additional column rather than presented as they are above. In such a case, a question mark would appear in the top box since there was no example given for the Iraqis.

In this chart, I used a number of symbols to replace words. That is perfectly all right. When you chart, be sure to assign a meaning to each symbol so that it can be read as easily as a word. Such symbols do help to reduce the number of words and the space needed for information in a box.

Now go on to Skill Development Exercise 9–2 on page 247. You will be provided with additional practice in charting selections.

In Skill Application 9 on page 259, you will be asked to chart a paragraph and a selection from your own career materials.

SKILL DEVELOPMENT EXERCISE 9–2
Charting Selections

DIRECTIONS: Chart each of the following selections using the eight steps on pages 237 and 238. Remember to let the material guide you. Space has been provided for your charts following the selections.

1. CARPETING

Six basic types of carpet are now produced: Axminister, Wilton, velvet, tufted, knitted, and shag.

Axminister comes closest to hand weaving. Tufts are inserted separately to make the most intricate patterns with more than six colors. The pile is cut to an even level to make a plush surface.

Wilton uses only five or six yarn colors that are pulled to the surface to create unique designs. The pile can be cut to form an embossed or sculptured surface.

Velvet carpets are the simplest weave of all. The yarn is looped over steel wires which are withdrawn as each row is finished. This carpet is usually in a single color or a tweed having a smooth-cut pile called a plush.

Tufted carpets are made by punching thousands of needles through a prewoven backing. A latex coat of foam, jute, high-density vinyl, or rubber is then applied. Many textures in solids or multicolor patterns may be produced by this method.

Knitted carpets are produced by a method similar to hand knitting. Backing, pile, and stitching are looped together. This carpeting has a low looped appearance. Backing can be applied for indoor or outdoor usage.

Shag carpets are similar to the Axminister carpets except the piles are not trimmed.

2. REAL ESTATE AUCTIONS

To take advantage of real estate auction opportunities, it is imperative that both buyers and sellers are aware of the methods of offering properties at auction. Each of the following techniques has distinct characteristics that impact on both buyer and seller.

Single-product/single-owner auctions are those in which only a single building or residential development is offered. This type of auction offers a major advantage to the seller in that it can be held at any time or place.

Multiple-product/single-owner auctions are those in which one owner offers several properties or a number of residential units in a given subdivision or condominium project. With this type of auction, the seller can avoid the tedious piecemeal disposal of an entire portfolio.

Scattered-site housing auctions are conducted to sell numerous single-family residences differing widely in size and quality and located over a large area (e.g., 50 square miles). This method generally benefits buyers by offering a wide variety of residential properties from which to choose.

Multiple-product/multiple-owner auctions combine dissimilar properties owned by different parties. Thus, residential, investment, commercial, industrial, and office properties may be marketed simultaneously to reduce advertising costs. In addition, larger, investment-grade properties from different geographic areas may be promoted in one event, giving the auction a national or international scope.

3. TYPES OF RADIATION

Radiation is a general term that applies to the transmission of energy. When we speak of radiation accidents, we are referring to **ionizing radiation.** This radiation is from an atomic source and is used to generate electricity, provide isotopes for medicine and industry, and make nuclear weapons. The three major types of ionizing radiation include alpha particles, beta particles, and gamma rays.

Alpha particles do little damage since they can be absorbed (stopped) by a layer of clothing, a few inches of air, paper, or the outer layer of skin. This is a low-energy source of radiation.

Beta particles are higher in energy level but can be stopped by heavy clothing. This is not to say that the danger of exposure to alpha and beta radiation can be taken lightly. Irradiated dust particles and smoke can be inhaled into the lungs, particles can contaminate open wounds, and irradiated foodstuffs can be ingested. Once inside the body, they continue to cause cell damage until they are removed or until they decay.

Gamma rays and x-rays can be considered the same thing. Gamma radiation is extremely dangerous, carrying high levels of energy able to penetrate thick shielding. The rays easily pass through clothing and the entire body, inflicting extensive cell damage.

4. REPRODUCTION OF DRAWINGS

The majority of all architectural working drawings are made on either tracing paper, vellum, or film, for the sole purpose of making economical reproductions. Drawings have little value unless they can be satisfactorily reproduced. Sets of the "prints," often referred to as "blueprints," must be furnished to contract bidders, estimators, subcontractors, workmen, and others who are concerned with the construction of the proposed building; the original drawings are retained by the architectural or engineering office. Several types of reproduction equipment are in use for making prints; each type requires the original tracing to have opaque and distinct linework and lettering in order to produce legible copies. Some architectural offices have their own print-making equipment; others send their tracings to local blueprint companies which charge a nominal square-foot fee for the service.

Ozalid Prints. These are prints produced on paper coated on one side with light-sensitive diazo chemicals. The sensitive paper, with the tracing above it in direct contact, is fed into an Ozalid machine and exposed to ultraviolet light for a controlled amount of time. The pencil or ink lines of the tracing prevent exposure of the chemical directly below; while the translucent areas are completely exposed. After the exposure, the sensitized paper only is fed again into a dry developer, utilizing ammonia vapors, which turns the background of the print white and the lines either blue, black, or sepia, depending upon which type of paper has been selected. Dry development does not shrink the paper and change the scale of the drawing. The white background of Ozalid prints also allows changes or notes to be added, if necessary, directly on the page with ordinary pencils.

Blueprints. This process has been used extensively for many years as the conventional method of producing prints of all types of technical drawings. The blue nature of the prints has given rise to the common term "blueprints." These prints are made by exposing sensitized paper and tracing paper, in direct contact, in a blueprint machine. They are exposed to ultraviolet light similar to that of the Ozalid machine for a controlled amount of time (the sun could also be used as a light source). The exposure is followed by a fixing bath of potassium bichromate and water, followed by a bath of clear water, which turns the background of the sensitized paper dark blue and the linework white. After the baths, the print must be dried. If a reverse color print is desired, a "Vandyke" paper can be used as an intermediate print. The Vandyke then serves as a negative; it is made from the original tracing and appears dark brown. This negative can be used to make positive, white-background-and-blue-line prints. Both blueprints and Ozalid prints will gradually deteriorate in color if continually left in open sunlight.

Photostat Reproductions. If it becomes necessary to change the size of a drawing, enlargements or reductions can be made photographically. A large, specially designed camera is used to change the size of drawings made on either tracing paper or regular paper. The direct print has white lines and black background. The process is more expensive than Ozalid or blueprint methods, but the prints are more permanent in nature.

Photocopy Prints. A number of manufacturers have photocopy equipment on the market for duplicating drawings. Light-sensitive paper of limited sizes produces prints of high contrast; however, various pencil tones are not clearly defined.

5. THE VITAL FEW

and Other Great Management Ideas

by Auren Uris

Are you stymied in your competition with a co-worker? A concept termed "the winning edge" may be the key to victory. Do you need to get a clear idea of where your sales force should concentrate its efforts? The Pareto Principle may shed some light. These are two of the insights that, in the author's words, have "helped transform management from a seat-of-the-pants activity to a profession on which progress, and indeed our civilization, depend."

ZEIGARNIK EFFECT

Concept: Industrial psychologists have studied the need for closure, an individual's wish to finish a task once started. This urge to complete is called the "Zeigarnik Effect" after its major investigator, whose finding explains why people tend to resist interruption.

Action Opportunities: The Zeigarnik phenomenon clarifies unexpected work-scene behavior, such as:

- Why people don't like to "change horses in midstream."

- Why some employees will work after hours to wrap up a project.

Examples: Executive Elsie Moore tells the office manager: "We've got to get that special mailing out before the end of the day. If my arithmetic is correct, you'll need extra help to make the deadline."

The office manager, an old hand, says, "My group will do the job." She knows her group, reinforced by the need for closure, will put out a bit extra to make the deadline.

How To Use:

- *Build a tradition of flexibility.* One manager says, "From the first minute a new employee comes aboard, I make it clear that our schedules are subject to change without notice. They understand that the customers come first.

- *Be creative about deadlines:* "I try to have time goals coincide with regular breaks—lunchtime, quitting time, end of the week, and so on," says a drafting supervisor. "Somehow, the deadline becomes a more tangible—and reachable—target." Stopping a job at a regular work break makes for a smooth halt and an easier start-up.

- *Explain the change.* A phrase, a sentence of explanation as to why tasks are to be reshuffled, will water down the Zeigarnik reaction. There are few employees who don't understand the practical necessity described by the phrase, "A top customer wants us to. . . ."

MINIMAX TECHNIQUE

Concept: In economics, "minimax" refers to an action aimed at minimizing the maximum loss in an undertaking. But the term also suits a strategy that psychologist Kurt Lewin recommends in dealing with resistance to change. Lewin shows how the resistance is best overcome by minimizing the forces that oppose the change, and simultaneously maximizing the favorable forces; hence, "minimax."

Example: Bob Brell and his partner Tony Lewis own a suburban sanitation service. Brell tells Lewis, "We must raise our charges by 10 percent. The accountant says if we don't, we'll soon be operating at a loss." Lewis says, "Our customers don't like us and if we boost the fees, many will go back to dumping their garbage in the woods." Lewis is right about the community attitude. An irate customer once described their building and surroundings as a "smelly eyesore." The partners work out a program to improve community relations. The approach consists of minimizing the company's unpopularity, maximizing the favorable points:

- Building a high, opaque fence around the parking lot where the garbage trucks are stored.
- Putting $500 into plantings, flower boxes, and paint.
- Buying spray equipment that provides a high-power stream of water plus deodorant for the trucks. Each one is now cleaned every third day of use, alongside the building, in full public view.

The next step was to maximize the partners' participation in community activities. Brell gave talks to the Parent-Teacher's Association on protecting the environment and planning for future waste disposal. Lewis and his wife organized a social-activities program in the local senior citizens' center. The press gave them coverage.

Some time later, the firm announced a rate increase for the new year. Only four customers canceled, but new ones signed up at a steady rate.

How To Use: *Plan and apply a program of weakening the negative factors and strengthening the positive ones for the strongest possible total effect.*

THE PARETO PRINCIPLE

Concept: Vilfredo Pareto, a 19th-century Italian economist, analyzed the distribution of wealth in his time. He discovered that most of it was in the hands of a small number of people, whom he called "the vital few," while the rest existed in poverty. These he called "the trivial many." Pareto's idea is sometimes called the "80-20 rule," meaning that 20 percent of the known variables will produce 80 percent of the results. This simple but revealing fact is relevant to important executive concerns. It suggests that analyzing a cause-effect situation makes it possible to isolate key factors, either positive or negative, for remedial action. Either the vital few or the trivial many may hold the secret of improvement.

Action Opportunities: Pareto's principle can be used where managers seek to improve an operation or performance area such as costs, sales, customer evaluation, quality control, accident reduction, employee productivity.

Examples: Paul Greene, head of production in a furniture factory, sees that absenteeism is rising. Analysis shows that about 10 percent of the roster causes 75 percent of the absenteeism. The findings were spelled out to the department heads and a program developed by which each manager would work closely with the vital few, the individuals who were a major cause of the problem. As a result, the reasons for their staying away from work were pinpointed—they ranged from travel difficulties to need for infant day care—and minimized. Attendance soon improved.

How To Use: The Pareto Principle can be applied to any management problem that has a clear cause-effect core. Five simple steps lead to its application:

- Record the factors involved in the matter being investigated.
- Arrange the items in order of importance relative to the problem— largest first, smallest last.
- Identify the vital few.
- Identify the trivial many.
- Act on the findings. In some cases your remedy will focus on the vital few, in others on the trivial many.

QUANTIFICATION

Concept: Roger Bacon said that knowledge was not scientific unless it used numbers. Sir Francis Galton, who launched the modern theory of statistics, suggested, "Whenever you can, count." Numbers are an important tool in problem solving. Matters that seem vague and unmanageable come into focus whenever you can count and compare.

Action Opportunities: For some problems quantification is built in; for example, "In order to break even, we have to produce and sell 1,000 widgets a week." For others, efforts must be made to put factors into numbers or other systems of quantification. The more successful the effort, the better your chances of dealing with the situation.

Example: A group of executives are assessing the three finalists for a vice-presidential job. Credentials and experience have been noted, and each has interviewed the candidates. But the discussion of comparative merits gets out of hand. Finally the president says, "We must simplify matters. Let's agree on the five key qualifications for this job and rate each of the candidates on a scale of 0 to 10." Now they can clarify the murk of abstractions and generalities.

How To Use: *Pinpoint the factors.* You must be clear on exactly what you are assigning values to. "Let's say that Tom represents a 6 in dependability, and Sandra a 10" sets a standard.

Assign values. There can be a complication in numerical rating. The factors may be unequal when compared to each other. This may be overcome by "weighting." For instance, you want to evaluate the performance of an employee whose job involves three elements of differing importance. You assign 50 percent to Factor A; B and C are given 25 percent each. Now as you rate performance in each area, the weighting makes your total more meaningful.

THE WINNING EDGE

Concept: A simple statement of the winning-edge idea: "All you need to win, either over a single competitor or a field of them, is a *slight advantage.*" You can see this principle at work at the racetrack when a horse wins by a nose. A basketball team may defeat its opponent by a single point, but the feat goes into the win column as solidly as if it had been by 20 or 30 points.

An early propounder of this idea was Professor Aaron Levenstein of City College of New York, who has helped prepare a generation of would-be managers for their profession. His familiarity with business practicalities led him to identify the concept as a guide for managers, who traditionally operate in competitive situations.

Action Opportunities: The slight edge can shape your thinking in large, small, or medium strivings, and in setting personal, departmental, or company goals. The recommendation isn't that you set objectives at a minimum, but that you view competition realistically. The margin of victory may be tiny, the fruits of victory huge.

How To Use: The principle of the winning edge holds promise, but the important element is implementation—that is, how cannily it is used.

- *Focus on your adversary.* The better you understand where your competition is, and the strengths and weaknesses you are up against, the more effectively you can make your next step.

- *Decide on the edge to strive for.* For example, in a face-off with a competitor for an important customer, you may have to explore factors other than price, such as assured delivery, early delivery, or a special benefit you can offer because of advanced equipment or specially trained personnel.

- *Use your advantage.* This is the implementation step. Exactly how you make your moves can be a decisive factor in the victory.

- *Push for the payoff.* This story may be apocryphal but it makes a point: Ed gets a red-hot tip on a horse; it wins by a nose and he runs about shouting, "I won, I won." Then he tears up his winning ticket and goes home.

This final step is the wrap-up. Make sure you get the "prize money." Winning gives you a victory. Exploiting the victory gives you the benefits.

SKILL APPLICATION 9
Charting

DIRECTIONS: *Chart one paragraph and one selection from any of your own career materials. Duplicate these materials and attach them to this sheet. The selection may/may not have a title or subtitle and should be at least three paragraphs in length. Be sure to include the source information.*

PARAGRAPH SOURCE INFORMATION

Title: _____

Author: _____

Place of publication: _____

Publisher: _____

Copyright Date: _____   *Page(s):* _____

SELECTION SOURCE INFORMATION

Title: _____

Author: _____

Place of publication: _____

Publisher: _____

Copyright Date: _____   *Page(s):* _____

Chapter Ten

Summarizing

Summarizing, like mapping and charting, serves to simplify material of any length by drastically reducing its content. Ask yourself this question: **Do I need only the main points of a written piece of material?** In other words, do you need the material reduced to its most essential information in order to master it more easily, to write essay exam answers, or to briefly report on the information in a class or in the workplace? If the answer is yes, summarizing is the technique to apply.

Like mapping and charting, summarizing requires you to apply what you know about main ideas and related details and then to use your own words. Also like mapping and charting, summarizing is a personal technique; you decide what to summarize, how much to include in the summary, and then how to write that summary in your own words. As with any technique which involves using your own words, your summaries will probably differ somewhat in their wording from those presented as samples in this chapter. That is all right as long as the ideas in the summaries are similar to those given as samples or suggested answers.

When mapping and charting, you learned to use only main ideas and supporting details. Just as there isn't any place for restatement or filler in a map or chart, the same holds true for summaries. A summary of any material never includes restatement or filler. However, summarizing is unlike drawing maps or designing charts in several important ways. First, summaries are not graphic representations. Rather, they present essential information in well-written sentences and, when summarizing longer materials, in well-constructed brief paragraphs. Second, maps and charts are reserved for complex materials, but summarizing is a technique which can be used for both simple and complex material. When material is very complex, however, it often makes sense to map or chart it first for clarity before trying to summarize it.

In this chapter you will write summaries only for paragraphs and selections. However, as you become proficient in summarizing materials of limited length, you can easily extend the same skills to summarizing longer materials such as chapters in a textbook or articles in professional journals.

SUMMARIZING A PARAGRAPH

When you answer yes to the question **"Do I need only the main points of a written piece of material?"** and the material is a single paragraph, the following steps should help you in summarizing that paragraph.

1. Read the paragraph carefully, making sure that you thoroughly understand what the author is saying.

2. Identify the stated or implied main idea of the paragraph and the details which support that main idea.

3. Write the main idea and supporting details in your own words. Do not take sentences from the original material, since your summaries should be written in your own words and not the author's. Eliminate all unnecessary words or ideas so that only essential information remains. (In cases where you need only the very briefest summary, you might want to use the reworded main idea to represent the entire paragraph.)

4. Rewrite these essentials in clear, well-written sentences.

5. If your summary includes more than one sentence, be sure to write them in the same order followed by the author of the original material.

6. Reread your summary and compare it to the original paragraph to make sure that you haven't lost or misstated the author's message.

Read the paragraph in Sample A and then examine how this paragraph has been summarized into a single sentence.

SAMPLE A: Simple Paragraph Summary

Without realizing it, you have probably participated in some accounting transaction today. If you bought a meal on the way to class or purchased a newspaper, you were involved in an accounting transaction. Broadly speaking, the purpose of accounting is to provide useful and timely information about the financial activities of an individual, a business, or another organization. This accounting information, stated in terms of dollars, is used by a variety of people in making a wide range of personal and/or business decisions.

SUMMARY: Accounting provides useful and timely financial information about individuals or groups, is stated in dollars, and is used to make a wide range of personal and/or business decisions.

This summary consists of a reworded stated main idea, which is found in the middle of the paragraph, and some information from the supporting detail which follows it. Note that the first two sentences do not support the main idea and, therefore, are not included in the summary.

Sometimes you will find that it is easier to summarize a paragraph if you first organize and reduce the material into a map or chart. Since maps and charts consist of only main ideas and supporting details, you then need only to rewrite this information into good sentences to have a summary of the original material. The complex paragraph in Sample B illustrates this kind of situation. Read the paragraph, observe how it has been mapped, and then note how the paragraph summary has been written in two sentences without losing the essence of the information.

SAMPLE B: Complex Paragraph Summary

The trial judge in an American jury case serves only as a sort of umpire. He applies the procedural rules to the lawyers and explains the substantive principles of law to the jurors, but generally the jurors, and they alone, decide what facts have been established beyond a reasonable doubt by the evidence. In other words, the judge is the arbiter of the law; the jurors are the arbiters of the facts. The jurors, in reaching their verdict, apply to the facts, as found by them, the law as it is explained to them by the judge in his instructions (sometimes called the judge's "charge" to the jury). Of course, if trial by jury has been waived, the trial judge himself will find the facts and apply the law to them in what is referred to as a bench trial.

SAMPLE B MAP

MAIN IDEA (implied): The American judge and jury play different roles in a trial.

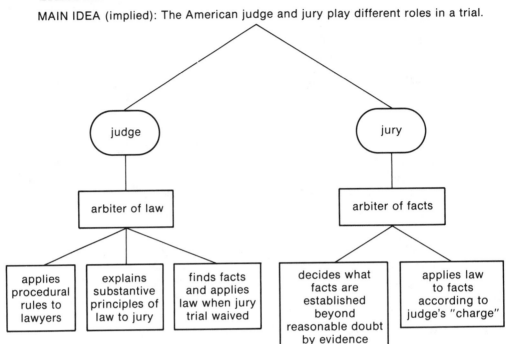

SUMMARY: In an American trial, the judge's role as arbiter of law is to apply procedural rules to lawyers, explain principles of law to the jury, and find facts and apply law when a jury trial has been waived, while the jury's role as arbiter of facts is to decide on facts that have been proven with evidence and apply the law to the facts according to the judge's "charge."

Note how easy it is to summarize that complex paragraph after the information has been analyzed and organized into a chart. It is now a fairly simple task to compose a single sentence to explain the roles of the judge and the jury.

SAMPLE PRACTICE
Summarizing Paragraphs

DIRECTIONS: Read each paragraph carefully and then summarize its content. Map or chart on a separate sheet of paper if you feel it is necessary to do so. Keep your summaries as brief as possible. Use the six steps for summarizing on page 262 to help you. Space has been provided below each paragraph for your summary.

1.   Metallurgical engineering may be divided into two branches. One branch deals with the location and evaluation of deposits of ore, the best way of mining and concentrating the ore, and the proper method of refining the ore into basic metals. The other branch deals with the fabrication of the refined metal or metal alloy into various machines or metal products.

2.   It is impossible to determine when surveying was first used, but in its simplest form it is surely as old as recorded civilization. As long as there has been property ownership, there have been means of measuring the property or distinguishing one person's land from another. Even in the Old Testament, there are frequent references to property ownership, property corners, and property transfer. For instance, Proverbs 22:28: "Remove not the ancient landmark, which thy fathers have set." The Babylonians surely practiced some type of surveying as early as 2500 B.C. because archaeologists have found Babylonian maps on tablets of that estimated age.

3.   While no one is perfect, we can do our very best at all times. This means being honest, truthful, trustworthy, and responsible. It also means upholding the professional ethics of the field of medicine in dealing with patients, families, and other members of the health profession. Unethical people are a threat and a danger to the patients served and to the medical profession and must not be tolerated. Legal actions involving lawsuits, fines, and sometimes imprisonment are frequently the results of unethical practices.

4.   Conventional supermarkets and traditional shoe stores such as Thom McAn are examples of retailers that define their target markets* in very broad terms. These stores have several different product lines and stock many kinds of items at a variety of prices. On the other hand, the small boutique or a fruit or vegetable store exemplifies the retailer who selects a well-defined and narrow consumer group. Both of these outlets have a narrow product assortment and pricing scheme because they attract a certain type of customer, not everyone. Most department stores seek multiple market segments. These stores cater to several different groups of consumers and provide unique products and services for each group. For example, women's clothing may be subdivided into several distinctive boutiques scattered throughout a department store. Large retail chains frequently have divisions that appeal to different market segments. Associated Dry Good operates the fashion-oriented Lord & Taylor as well as the discount-oriented Caldor.

**Definition of "target market":* consumer group the retailer tries to satisfy.

5.　　　One of the most unlikely kinds of office work to be done at home is professional work that involves only one person's creative activity (programming, writing reports) or contacts usually carried out by telephone (sales, brokering*). A second kind is clerical activities that are unitized, repetitive, and routine. For example, data entry and word processing can be monitored and measured electronically, computer checked for errors, and paid as piecework. Raw data and finished work can be physically transported between office and home in batches, or can be sent by telephone. Whether professional or clerical, work at home is the kind that does not require much face-to-face supervision or collaboration between co-workers.

*acting as an agent in making contracts or selling stocks.

Check your summaries of the above five paragraphs. Since summarizing is a personal skill, my summaries will probably not exactly match yours word for word. In fact, it would be surprising if they did, since summaries are written in your own words. However, the following summaries do include the content that is important in the original material, and your summaries should match in content.

Note that each of the following summaries includes the main idea, stated or implied, and selected supporting details presented in the original material. Check your summaries carefully to be sure that they contain only important information.

Sample Practice Answers

1. There are two branches of metallurgical engineering; each is involved in different aspects of dealing with ore—from its location to its fabrication into metal products.

2. Evidence of surveying can be found in the Old Testament and Babylonian tablets, thus reinforcing the idea that ways to measure property and determine ownership have existed as long as poeple have owned property.

3. Unethical medical personnel must not be tolerated since they are dangerous to patients and to the profession and can cause legal actions.

4. This paragraph is easier to summarize if you first chart it.

MAIN IDEA: Retail operations define and meet the needs of their target markets in different ways.

TYPE OF OPERATION	TARGET MARKET DEFINED	HOW OPERATE
1. Conventional supermarket 2. Traditional shoe stores	Broad terms	1. Different product lines 2. Stock many items 3. Variety of prices
1. Small boutiques 2. Fruit/vegetable stores	Well-defined narrow consumer group	Narrow product assortment & pricing scheme
Most department stores	Multiple market segments	Provide unique products & services for each group
Large retail chains	Divisions that appeal to different markets	?

SUMMARY: Retailers define and meet the needs of their target markets in different ways. While supermarkets and shoe stores have broad markets that are to be provided with a wide variety of items and prices, small boutiques and fruit/vegetable stores have narrow, well-defined consumers and a narrow assortment of goods and prices. Most department stores have a multiple-segmented market that is to be provided with unique products and services, while large retail chains operate within divisions that appeal to different markets.

5. This paragraph is easier to summarize if you first map it.

MAIN IDEA (implied): There are different kinds of work which can be done at home.

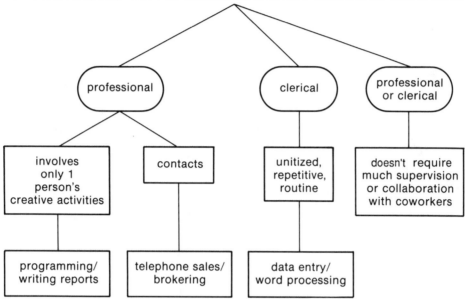

SUMMARY: Professional and clerical work can be done at home. Such professional work includes tasks that require individual creative activities and telephone contacts, while clerical activities include those that are unitized, repetitive or routine. Both kinds of work must be such that they do not require much supervision or collaboration with co-workers.

Now go on to Skill Development Exercise 10–1 on page 271 for additional practice in summarizing paragraphs.

SKILL DEVELOPMENT EXERCISE 10–1
Summarizing Paragraphs

DIRECTIONS: Write a summary of each of the following paragraphs. Keep your summaries as brief as possible. Map or chart on a separate sheet of paper prior to writing the summary if you so desire. Use the six steps for writing a paragraph summary on page 262 to help you as needed. Space has been provided for your summary below each paragraph.

1. The theory of self-fulfilling prophecy asserts that what you expect of others will determine their reactions. If you expect low achievement, your employees will produce little. In some organizational settings, people become "X-minded" because they are treated as inferior, lazy, materialistic, dependent, and irresponsible. In other organizational settings, employees become "Y-minded" when they are treated as responsible, independent, understanding, goal-achieving, growing, and creative people.

2. The ability to visualize or think in three dimensions is one of the most important requisites of the successful engineer or scientist. In practice, this means the ability to study the views of an object and to form a mental picture of it—to visualize its three-dimensional shape. To the designer, it means the ability to synthesize and form a mental picture before the object even exists and the ability to express this image in terms of views. The engineer is the master planner in the construction of new machines, structures, or processes. The ability to visualize and to use the language of drawing as a means of communication or recording of mental images is indispensable.

3.   Although most would-be business owners are certain the one ingredient they need for success is money, Dun and Bradstreet, Inc., the oldest (1841) and probably the most prestigious of the business information service companies, says nearly 93 percent of business failures are due—not to lack of financing—but to managerial inexperience and incompetence. When one considers that about 1,000 small business firms fail each day, and that over half of those which close their doors each year are less than 5 years old, the importance of good business management cannot be overemphasized.

4.   People have lived with the same complex carbohydrate plants for thousands of years. In fact, no important new plants of any kind (except tomatoes and coffee) have been domesticated in the last 2,000 years. Thai farmers were cultivating rice 12,000 years ago; North American natives ate beans and squash at least 9,000 years ago; wheat and barley were under cultivation 7,000 years before the Christian era began. In contrast, the purification of simple carbohydrate into table sugar is a process only 100 years old. We have not had time to adapt to it.

5.　　Any expenditure of time, effort, and money is wasted unless records can be produced when they are required. Consequently, records must be arranged systematically, according to some storage plan and procedures that will make it possible to find them immediately upon request. Such a plan is called a **filing method, and the steps to be followed in using that method are called filing and finding procedures.** Together, they represent one of the most important phases of office work. Frequently, however, executives give this phase of office operation little attention until the loss of a valuable paper emphasizes the need for a more effective system of records storage and control or for better-trained files supervisors and operators. One record lost, mislaid, or delayed can inconvenience a dozen or more people in their work.

SUMMARIZING A SELECTION

If you answer yes to the question **"Do you need only the main points of a written piece of material?"** when dealing with a selection, you can apply your skill in summarizing paragraphs to reduce the selection to its most essential information. In a selection, of course, you do have much more material to reduce. With some modification, however, a selection summary can be written in the same way as the summary of a single paragraph.

A comparatively simple selection summary is written as briefly as possible based on the material as presented by an author, while a more complex selection is probably easier to work with if you first map or chart it. No doubt, you will find yourself adding one of these extra steps more frequently in working with a selection than with a typical paragraph. The extra step of drawing a map or designing a chart is time well spent since it greatly simplifies your summarizing of a selection.

The following steps should help you to write a summary for a selection. Notice how similar these steps are to those given for writing a summary of information in a paragraph.

1. Read the selection carefully, making sure that you thoroughly understand what the author is saying.

2. Identify the overall stated or implied main idea of the selection. Then identify the main idea of each paragraph and the details which support it.

3. Using the method you adopted in Chapter 6 of this textbook, let the main ideas of individual paragraphs represent major details that support the selection main idea.

4. Write the main idea of the selection and the individual paragraph main ideas in your own words. Do not take sentences from the original material, since your summaries should be written in your own words, not the author's. You may want to include some supporting (minor) details from paragraphs if you think they contain very important information. (Of course, the main ideas of paragraphs which do not support the selection main idea do not belong in a summary.)

5. Write this essential information from the selection in clear, well-written sentences within a paragraph.

6. Be sure to write the sentences in your summary in the same order as followed by the author of the original material.

7. Reread your summary and compare it to the original material to make sure that you haven't lost or misstated the author's message.

Your summaries of selections will not exactly match those presented in this chapter since they are written in your own words. Remember, however, that the content included in your summary should be the same as mine.

Sample C presents a selection you have seen earlier in this textbook—as a sample in Chapter Six. Reread the selection and examine the brief summary based on this material. The main idea of the selection is underlined for you and the main ideas of the paragraphs are in boldface print.

SAMPLE C: Summary of a Selection

1. BUSINESS COMMUNICATIONS IN YOUR FUTURE

(1) *There are many reasons why you should know how to write effective business communications, regardless of the type of equipment to which you have access.* **In the first place, your value to the organization you work for will be greatly enhanced, which often means more rapid progress up the promotion ladder.** Competent writers are not as plentiful as you might imagine, and those who write well stand out like a beacon.

(2) **Second, those who can compose effective business letters make new friends and keep old ones for the organization, thereby increasing sales and profits, which all businesses need to survive.**

(3) **Third, good writers can save a great deal of time, effort, and money for an organization.** Millions of dollars are wasted each year by people who write windy and garbled messages that exhaust and befuddle their readers.

(4) **Finally, your rating as an employee—which hinges greatly on your skill in working harmoniously with the people around you—shoots up dramatically when you master the art of writing sensible, tactful, and finely honed memorandums.**

SUMMARY: Writing effective business communications is important for a number of reasons, including, for example, the fact that such communications will increase your value to the organization and may help you go up the promotion ladder quickly. Also, your effective business letters can increase the organization's sales and profits. In addition, you can save time, effort, and money for the organization if you are a good writer. Finally, when you write sensible, tactful, and finely honed memorandums, you will increase your rating as an employee because you can work well with others.

The summary based on this selection consists of four sentences which present its essential content. Notice that the reworded stated main idea of the selection has been used to begin the summary. The main idea of the rest of the first paragraph has been included in the same sentence. The main ideas of the other paragraphs are reworded in additional sentences. The information in the summary has been written in the same order as it appeared in the original selection. As you may recall, the title is too broad to actually reflect the content of the selection. Therefore, it has not been included in the summary.

At times, a selection may appear to be too complex to be summarized without first being mapped or charted. Mapping or charting a selection allows you to see major and minor details and then to decide exactly how much you want to include in your summary.

Sample D presents a selection you have read before; it was mapped in Chapter 8. Reread the selection and examine the map again before you read the summary of the material.

SAMPLE D: Summary of a Mapped Selection

STRESS IN THE WORKPLACE

Employers pay attention when problems in the workplace begin to affect the company's profits. A serious problem which results in both human and financial losses is stress in the workplace. While stress is probably present in any job situation, it can be lessened by programs planned and initiated to alleviate some of that stress. Today, there are an increasing number of companies in a wide variety of industries that are making major efforts to reduce workplace-induced stress.

Company physical fitness programs are far and away the most popular method utilized to deal with stress in the workplace. These programs may take varied forms ranging from company sponsored walking and jogging groups, aerobic dance, or exercise classes. Workers are also encouraged to use community or in-house fitness facilities where specialized equipment is available.

Another approach to stress in the workplace is the attempt to reduce psychosocial stress through available benefits. Many companies are offering benefits such as counseling (both personal and family), programs for weight reduction, cigarette smoking, alcohol and substance abuse. The increasing use of flextime, in which personnel have more flexibility in determining working hours, is another type of stress reduction benefit.

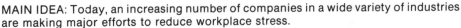

MAIN IDEA: Today, an increasing number of companies in a wide variety of industries are making major efforts to reduce workplace stress.

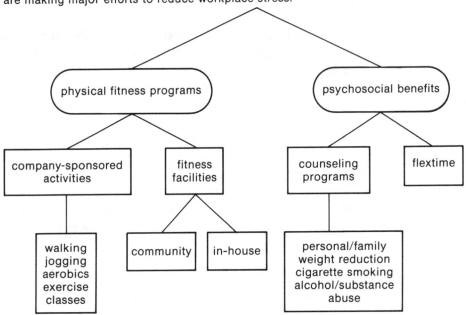

SUMMARY: The increasing major efforts made by a wide variety of companies to reduce stress in the workplace include two approaches. First, and most popular, companies are sponsoring fitness programs. Second, a variety of psychosocial benefits, including counseling programs and flextime work schedules, are being made available to employees.

Note how easy it becomes to summarize a selection when it has first been mapped. All of the information in the above summary comes from the main idea and two major details on the map. Since summarizing is a personal skill, you decide how much information you want to include in a summary. In this case, I chose not to include minor supporting details.

At times, you may choose to summarize material that is most appropriately charted for clarity before an attempt is made to summarize it. Sample E presents a selection you have read already; it was charted before in Chapter Nine. Reread the selection, examine the chart again, and then read the summary of the material.

SAMPLE E: Summary of a Charted Selection

CATEGORIES OF INFORMATION

There are three categories of information related to managerial levels and the decisions managers make. The first level is strategic information, which relates to long-range planning policies that are of direct interest to upper management. Information such as population growth, trends in financial investment, and human resources changes would be of interest to top company officials who are responsible for developing policies and determining long range goals. This type of information is achieved with the aid of decision support systems (DSS).

The second level of information is managerial information. It is of direct use to middle management and department heads for implementation and control. Examples are sales analysis, cash flow projections, and annual financial statements. This information is of use in short- and intermediate-range planning—that is, months rather than years. It is maintained with the aid of management information systems (MIS).

The third information level is operational information, which is short-term, daily information used to operate departments and enforce the day-to-day rules and regulations of the business. Examples are daily employee absence sheets, overdue purchase orders, and current stocks available for sale. Operational information is established by data processing systems (DPS).

MAIN IDEA: There are three categories of information related to managerial levels and the decisions managers make.

LEVEL	USED BY	USED FOR	EXAMPLE OF INFO.	COMPUTER SYST.
Strategic information	Top officials responsible: developing policies & long-range goals	Long-range planning	1. Population growth 2. Trends in financial investment 3. Human resources changes	Decision support systems (DSS)
Managerial information	Middle management & dept. heads	Implementa- tion & control of short- & intermediate- range planning, financial statements	1. Sales analysis 2. Cash flow projections 3. Annual financial statements	Manage- ment information system (MIS)
Operational information	?	1. Dept. operation 2. Enforcing day-to-day rules & regulations 3. Short-term daily info.	1. Employee absence sheets 2. Overdue purchase orders 3. Current stocks available for sale	Data processing systems (DPS)

SUMMARY: There are three levels of information related to the deci- sions that managers make. The first level, strategic information, which is related to long-range planning by upper management, is supported by the decision support system (DSS). The second information level, managerial information, which is used by middle management and department heads for short- and intermediate-range planning, is main- tained by the management information system (MIS). The third infor- mation level, operational, is short-term, is used to operate departments and to enforce daily rules and regulations, and is established by data processing systems (DPS).

Note how easy it becomes when a selection is first charted and then summarized. In this sample, the title, which reflects the main idea, becomes the first sentence in the summary. Information about each of the three major details is obtained by simply going across the rows and selecting what you feel is appropriate for inclusion in the summary.

SAMPLE PRACTICE
Summarizing Selections

DIRECTIONS: Summarize each of the following sample selections. Use the seven steps for summarizing a selection on page 275 to help you. Keep your summaries as brief as possible. Space has been provided below each paragraph for your summary.

You have already mapped the following selection in Chapter Eight and may want to refer to your map as an aid to writing the summary.

1. COMMUNICATION BARRIERS

Communication barriers are often mentioned by managers as being critical and persistent. There are three critical barriers to communication: semantic, technical, and perceptual. Better communication comes about when people are aware of these barriers. The semantic barrier is a barrier of words. Communication can be difficult because words or symbols can have different meanings. For example, the word *fire* can mean either a flame or to discharge an employee.

The way people use words can build semantic barriers. For example, the use of technical language, or "jargon," simplifies in-group communication (such as in a group of CPAs). But if the CPAs use the technical words when communicating with others who do not understand the language, real barriers to understanding are erected.

Technical problems can prevent a message from conveying the intended meaning. If you were in a room talking with friends and a rock band was playing loudly, you might not accurately hear what was said. Likewise, any message can be interrupted by noises before it reaches the receiver. Both noise and physical barriers can be technical problems in oral communication. You cannot always assume that messages sent will be received as intended.

Lack of effective listening habits is a technical barrier that does lie with the receiver. People talk past each other for several reasons. Often they do not listen but simply wait for their turn to speak. Or they seek only the information that is consistent with what they want to hear—a result of perceptual barriers.

Perceptual problems occur because people have different mental frameworks. If Maria attempts to tell Paul about a dog, Paul conjures a visual image of a dog. Maria may be talking about a chihuahua, while Paul may be thinking about a German shepherd.

Emotion can set up perceptual barriers. The stronger the feelings, the less likely people are to communicate clearly. If a supervisor is appraising an employee's performance, at the end of which she will (or will not) recommend a salary increase, the employee will probably become defensive at any suggestion of inadequate performance. The employee is less likely to hear suggestions for improvement because of greater interest in the salary adjustment recommendation.

DIRECTIONS: You have already charted the following selection on page 242 and you may want to refer to your chart now.

2. ANCIENT BEGINNINGS

Although we think of public relations as a twentieth-century phenomenon, its roots are ancient. Leaders in virtually every great society throughout history understood the importance of influencing public opinion through persuasion. For example, the Iraqis of 1800 B.C. hammered out their messages on stone tablets so that farmers could learn the latest techniques of harvesting, sowing, and irrigation. The more food the farmers grew, the better the citizenry ate and the wealthier the country became: a good example of planned persuasion to reach a specific public for a particular purpose—in other words, public relations.

Later on, the Greeks put a high premium on communication skills. The best speakers, in fact, were generally elected to leadership positions. Occasionally, aspiring Greek politicians enlisted the aid of Sophists (individuals renowned for both their reasoning and rhetoric) to help fight verbal battles. Sophists would gather in the amphitheaters of the day and extol the virtues of particular political candidates. Often, their arguments convinced the voters and elected their employer. Thus, the Sophists set the stage for today's lobbyists, who attempt to influence legislation through effective communication techniques.

The Romans, particularly Julius Caesar, were also masters of persuasive techniques. Faced with an upcoming battle, Caesar would rally public support through assorted publications and staged events. Similarly, during World War I, a special U.S. Public Information Committee, the Creel Committee, was formed to channel the patriotic sentiments of Americans in support of the U.S. role in the war. Stealing a page from Caesar, the committee's massive verbal and written communications effort was successful in marshalling national pride behind the war effort. Said a young member of the Creel Committee, Edward L. Bernays (later considered by many as the "father of public relations"), "This was the first time in our history that information was used as a weapon of war."

DIRECTIONS: You have worked with this selection before in Chapter Six. You may want to check the main ideas and supporting details you identified there.

3. BRICK

Building bricks are solid masonry units composed of inorganic nonmetallic materials hardened or burned by heat or chemical action. Building brick may be solid or it may have cored openings not to exceed 25 percent of its volume. Bricks are produced in a wide variety of colors, shapes, and textures.

Recent excavations in Egypt have shown that the ancient Egyptians used sun-dried and kiln-burned bricks for houses and palaces of nobility. In the Babylonian civilization (4000 B.C.), which developed in the valley of the Tigris and Euphrates Rivers, the thick mud and clay laid down by these rivers was well suited for brick, which thus became the usual building material for this civilization. Palaces and temples were constructed of sun-dried brick, faced with brilliant kiln-burned glazed brick.

The Romans also made wide use of brick in conjunction with a very efficient mortar. The Roman bricks were comparatively thin for their length. They were laid in thick beds of mortar in several patterns. After the fall of the Roman Empire, the art of brickmaking was lost throughout Europe until the beginning of the fourteenth century. The first brick buildings on the North American continent were erected in 1633 on Manhattan Island with bricks imported from Holland and England.

Check your selection summaries. Remember that your summaries should include the same content as the summaries presented below, but they will not be written in the same words. Note that the summaries presented below represent the main ideas of the selections and the main ideas of the individual paragraphs which support those main ideas as major details.

Sample Practice Answers

1.   There are three kinds of barriers that affect communication. First, semantic barriers involve words and the way we use them. Second, technical barriers affect the sending and receiving of messages. Finally, perceptual barriers, which can be caused by emotion, involve differing mental and emotional frameworks.

2.   Some early applications of Public Relations (PR) techniques were also used in later years. For example, the ancient Iraqis influenced public opinion through planned persuasion, a technique that defines PR itself. The ancient Greek emphasis on communication skills laid the foundation for today's lobbyists, while the Roman use of persuasive techniques to rally public support was a forerunner of the use of such techniques as those used to gain support for the U.S. role in World War I.

3.   Building bricks have been used for a very long time. The ancient Egyptians and the Babylonians used brick in the construction of buildings such as houses, palaces, and temples. The Romans also used brick. Later, in the seventeenth century, brick was used for buildings in North America.

Now go on to Skill Development Exercise 10–2 on page 285, which will provide you with additional practice in summarizing selections.

Then go to Skill Application 10 on page 291, where you will apply what you know about summarizing paragraphs and selections to your own career materials.

SKILL DEVELOPMENT EXERCISE 10–2
Summarizing Selections

*DIRECTIONS: Summarize each of the following selections. Keep your sum-
maries as brief as possible. Map or chart a selection on a separate sheet of
paper before summarizing it if you so desire. Use the seven steps for summarizing a selection on page 275 to help you as needed. Space has been provided for your summary below each selection.*

You have worked with selection one in Chapter Six.

1. CHOOSING A BUSINESS

If you are serious about becoming a small business owner, the very
first thing you should do is to engage in a period of investigation. Once
you have generally defined the kind of business you would like to own,
you need to examine what is involved in such a venture. The investigation will help you to determine if this is the kind of business in which
you want to invest your time, energy, and money. The time spent
investigating a potential kind of business can help you to avoid later
disappointments and problems.

Begin your investigation by getting all the facts which are readily
available about the kind of business of your choice. Find out where the
trade association is, what it publishes, and what assistance it offers.
Look at all the magazines, newspapers, and newsletters written about
that kind of business.

Clarify the business's objectives. Understand exactly what the
business is going to produce or what service it will render. Since no two
businesses, even in the same field, are alike, try to determine how yours
will be different.

Visit businesses of this type to get a firm idea of how they operate.
Talk to the owners and frankly discuss how business is and whether it
is profitable. Ask about sales volume and how long it took for the
business to become profitable. Inquire about the desirability of the
location. Include questions on what mistakes were made at the start.

Collect as much information as possible from other sources, even
the competition. Visit the Chamber of Commerce as well as state and
city development agencies. Talk with local associations and business
groups. Interview potential customers. Ask for information and opinions from persons employed in local banks.

Interpret the information with a view towards understanding the
community's composition and how the needs of your potential customers can best be served. This information should tell you where to
locate the business. It will also help you to plan on the kind of physical

plant or store you need to provide the necessary work space and/or sales area.

Finally, prepare an informal study which weighs the pros and cons from the materials you have collected during your investigation. Estimate the investment required: how much money you will need to function for one month, three months, six months, and a year. Estimate the profit possibilities: How much money can be expected from sales and how much will be left for earnings after expenses? Construct a table of income and expenses on a monthly basis for a year, determining where the break-even point is.

2. THE COMMITTEE

A committee is a group assigned to perform a specific task. The group may be permanent or temporary. Committees can be used to generate ideas or solutions; to supply information, views, and experience; to make recommendations to superiors; or to help implement policy decisions.

Committees are often formed to deal with tasks that recur on a regular basis. For example, a grievance committee handles employee grievances; an advisory committee makes recommendations in the areas of employee compensation, work practices, or company policies; a safety committee improves on-the-job safety. Committee members may be elected by co-workers or appointed by management.

When led with patience and skill, the committee has a number of advantages. It provides effective coordination, communication, and acceptance of ideas; significant motivation and involvement of members; and minimum conflict.

Making a decision by committee, however, can pose problems. Certain members may attempt to dominate the process, while others may gain acceptance of ideas by their exuberance, despite faulty reasoning. Others may form coalitions in an attempt to politicize and divide the group.

Further, timid decision making can result when committees become paralyzed by a company's bureaucratic structure. These groups make "safe" decisions to protect themselves from attack. These decisions, however, often fail to be constructive.

3. LONG-TERM PROSPECTS

The *U.S. Industrial Outlook 1988* report on the X-ray and electromedical equipment industry predicts growth for the five-year period ending in 1992. In fact, industry shipments are projected to grow at an annual rate of 7 percent during that period. The growth is anticipated in both foreign and domestic sales.

In this country, the underlying factor for growth in the X-ray and electromedical equipment industry is the increasing size of the aging population. They are the primary users of sophisticated electromedical equipment. At the same time, U.S. government efforts to limit health care costs are changing the setting of health care delivery. Diagnostic procedures, which were formerly performed only in hospitals, are now becoming commonplace in outpatient facilities. These facilities must purchase the X-ray and electromedical equipment needed to perform such procedures.

New and improved products will lead to increased sales for the industry. Increasing technological sophistication, especially in microprocessors, will spur advances in pacemakers, hearing aids, and patient-monitoring equipment. High-temperature superconductors—one of the most promising technological breakthroughs since the invention of the X-ray tube—may eventually find commercial application in magnetic resonance imaging, a diagnostic tool for examining tissue in patients.

Strong foreign demand for product lines which are developed and improved in the United States will increase exports of X-ray and electromedical equipment. The current low value of the dollar compared to other currencies will significantly benefit U.S. manufacturers in selling such products abroad.

4. THE ADVERTISING BUSINESS DEVELOPS

Mass advertising developed along with mass media. Early ad forms were handbills and printed signs. Actually, newspapers came into being as vehicles for advertising. By the early 1800s there were thousands of such publications. Most transactions were made at the local level, but as marketing techniques became more sophisticated and long-distance travel more common, many businesses wanted to expand to new markets.

To fill this need, the advertising agency was born. Volney Palmer organized the first one in the United States in 1841. Early agencies represented publishers, not products, going to potential advertisers to offer space for sale. They were given a small fee by the publishers, usually based on the total amount of revenues they brought in.

Soon, the advertising business was becoming unwieldy. Companies that advertised their products were constantly in doubt as to which publications to place their ads in and what those ads should say. Circulation figures were suspect, and advertisers had no way of knowing the real "cost per thousand" of readers reached. Into this vacuum stepped the N.W. Ayer & Son Agency. In 1875 it began offering ad counseling directly to the people with the product, advising them how to get more for their advertising dollar. The idea was a great success, and the basic strategy of advertising remains the same today.

5. CREATIVE SELLING: THE COMPETITIVE EDGE

To many customers, the salesperson is the business. Therefore, if the sales personnel are good, the business is good. But if the sales personnel are bad, then so is the firm. Although important to all businesses, effective sales personnel are especially important to small businesses. Why? Because it is difficult for a small business to compete with the big firms on things like assortment, price, and promotion. Selling effort, on the other hand, is one place where the small product or service retail business can compete with larger competitors—and win.

Effective selling doesn't happen by accident. The small entrepreneur must work to achieve a high level of sales effectiveness in his or her business. In order to work toward this goal, the businessperson should be aware of the different types of salespersons, the selling process, and the attributes of effective salespersons. Applying such knowledge to a business situation should result in the desired goal of effective sales personnel—the competitive edge.

It is important to note that retailing may involve selling services instead of products. Appliance repair, beauty shop, lawn service, and photography studio are all examples of service retailing. Even though services are intangible, personal, nonstandardized, and perishable when compared to products, they are sold by retailers either alone or in conjunction with products. The effective selling of services has the potential to give a business a competitive advantage.

There are three main types of sales personnel (Figure 1).

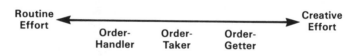

Figure 1. Types of Retail Sales Personnel (Classified by Level of Creative Effort).

Order-Handler. The ticket-taker at the concert, the checker at the food store—these salespeople are working in a routine selling environment. But due to the nature of their jobs, they will be asked numerous questions by customers as well as hear complaints about prices and service. A knowledgeable person with a pleasant personality is especially needed for this job, because this is usually the person who is dealing with the customer when the customer's money (payment) is received.

Order-Taker. More creativity is found in this job as compared to the order-handler. The counter attendant at the fast food restaurant may take the order and then suggest that the customer might also wish to buy a hot apple turnover. Pleasant personality, fast service, and suggestion selling on the part of the order-taker can result in many additional sales.

Order-Getter. For many businesses, the heart of the selling process rests with the creative selling efforts of their salespeople. Of course, one of the greatest problems is that there are numerous order-handlers and order-takers in selling positions that should have order-getters for optimum selling effectiveness. Clothing, furniture, jewelry, and appliances are just some of the many items that call for order-getters (a person who can handle a transaction, take an order, and, most importantly, get an order). As for services, the home security salesperson, for example, who calls on a prospect because it is observed that the house has no dead bolt locks, is making that special effort to be an order-getter. Even though all selling situations do not call for order-getters, all salespeople will be called upon to sell creatively from time to time. It is for this reason that all sales personnel need to have a working knowledge of the creative selling process.

SKILL APPLICATION 10
Summarizing

DIRECTIONS: *Choose one paragraph and one selection from your own career materials. Duplicate the original materials and attach them to this sheet. The selection may/may not have a title or subtitle and should be at least three paragraphs in length. Briefly summarize each of these materials. Be sure to include the source information.*

PARAGRAPH SOURCE INFORMATION

Title: _____

Author: _____

Place of publication: _____

Publisher: _____

Copyright Date: _____ *Page(s):* _____

SELECTION SOURCE INFORMATION

Title ⎯⎯⎯⎯⎯⎯⎯⎯⎯⎯⎯⎯⎯⎯⎯⎯⎯⎯⎯⎯⎯⎯⎯⎯⎯⎯⎯

Author: ⎯⎯⎯⎯⎯⎯⎯⎯⎯⎯⎯⎯⎯⎯⎯⎯⎯⎯⎯⎯⎯⎯⎯⎯

Place of publication: ⎯⎯⎯⎯⎯⎯⎯⎯⎯⎯⎯⎯⎯⎯⎯⎯⎯⎯

Publisher: ⎯⎯⎯⎯⎯⎯⎯⎯⎯⎯⎯⎯⎯⎯⎯⎯⎯⎯⎯⎯⎯⎯

Copyright Date: ⎯⎯⎯⎯⎯   *Page(s):* ⎯⎯⎯⎯⎯

Chapter Eleven

Interpreting Hidden Messages

All reading involves the sending and receiving of messages, the author being the sender and the reader serving as the receiver of these messages. Sometimes an author's message is fairly easy for the receiver to interpret; you simply have to read the words carefully. At other times, however, there may be an additional message from the author that is not obvious at all. This additional message is not reflected in the surface meaning of the words, sentences, and paragraphs that make up the material. Instead, it is implied in what the author has written. It now becomes very important that you read beyond the written words in order to interpret these not-obvious, or hidden, messages.

Accurate interpretation of a material's hidden message requires that you go beyond organizing information to translating it into terms you can understand and remember. It also includes evaluating the author's purpose in sending the message to the reader and the accuracy of that message. An author may write to inform you about something, to persuade you to accept his or her way of thinking about something, or to entertain you. The author's purpose determines whether or not written material will contain hidden messages and how they will be presented in that material. When you read beyond written words, you are able to interpret these messages.

As you read, ask yourself this question: **Does this material seem to have hidden messages?** To determine the answer, you must look for meanings beyond the written word. This chapter will make you aware of three common types of hidden messages—messages in which you must (1) separate fact from opinion, (2) detect propaganda devices, or (3) translate gobbledygook.

SEPARATING FACT FROM OPINION

It is not always easy to separate fact from opinion, especially when an author mixes the two within a single message. If, however, you keep in mind the definition of a "fact" in contrast to what constitutes an opinion, it should make it simpler for you to differentiate between them.

A fact represents something that has actually happened. Thus, the fact can be proved; it can be checked, or tested, to see if it is accurate. For example, if you say that a specific stock has gone up since you purchased it, that is a fact. You can check the accuracy of this statement by looking at the original purchase price of the stock and its current market value, and comparing the two costs of the stock.

An opinion, on the other hand, cannot be proven by any kind of test. It is usually directly related to the feelings, attitudes, values, or beliefs of the person who has expressed that opinion. For instance, if you say that Joe Smith is a tough boss to work for, that is an opinion. Joe Smith's toughness as a boss cannot be accurately measured or tested. In addition, other employees may have different opinions on the same issue of just how tough he is as a boss.

Both facts and opinions are found in written material and both are important components of that material. You, the reader, may choose material which is strictly factual, or you may select other material because you are interested in learning the author's opinions—or you may choose material that is a combination of fact and opinion. It depends upon your purpose in reading the material. It is essential, however, that you be able to differentiate between facts and opinions so that you can react to each appropriately. For example, if you are planning a business trip and want to check on the weather in a city you haven't visited before, you can check for the actual temperature on the radio or television, or by calling the local weather bureau. If you chart the temperature in that city for several days, it will aid you in packing appropriate clothing. If, on the other hand, you check weather conditions by calling a friend in that area and are told that the weather is cold, that is an opinion. "Cold weather" means different things to different people. "Cold weather" can mean you merely need a light sweater, or it can mean that you'd better bring a heavy coat, warm boots, gloves, hats, and whatever else you need to make you comfortable in such weather.

Sometimes it is difficult to separate fact from opinion when both appear in a single statement. The factual part of the statement may encourage you to accept the complete statement as fact. For example, the statement "Japan manufactures and exports the best cars in the world" is a combination of fact and opinion. Yes, it can be verified that Japan does manufacture and export cars, so that part of the statement is a fact. However, the description of these cars as the best in the world is someone's opinion. As such it is based on the feelings or values of the person who made the statement. What is the best car in the world? It depends greatly on what an individual considers important in a car. Thus, you can see how your interpretation of the complete statement would be inaccurate if you considered it to be a fact. It is easy to see how a reader can jump to conclusions which are inaccurate if he or she does not evaluate the author's message and carefully read beyond the words.

Sometimes the intermingling of facts and opinions is so subtle that you may have difficulty knowing where one begins and the other ends. You may accept opinions as facts, and this can be dangerous. Perhaps the author wants this to happen, for in this way you can be persuaded to agree with him or her. For instance, if you examine the writings of someone who you know is strongly prejudiced against a specific group of people, you will probably find that much of the material is composed of that author's opinions but that just enough facts are sprinkled in to make the whole thing appear to be factual. How important it is to read beyond the words!

SAMPLE PRACTICE
Separating Fact from Opinion

DIRECTIONS: Evaluate each of the following statements and mark them as fact (F), opinion (O), or a combination of both (FO). Keep the definitions of fact and opinion in mind as you analyze and evaluate each sample. Be able to defend your response.

1. Opening a business of your own is a frightening experience.   _____

2. This is the third year in a row that Morgan Maintenance Corporation has been listed among the Fortune 500 companies.   _____

3. The amount of bail required of defendants arrested in marijuana-related cases varies in different parts of the country. For example, the bail for a defendant arrested in Florida for conspiracy to possess marijuana was $500,000, while the bail for a defendant arrested in Vermont for the alleged sale of marijuana was $5,000.   _____

4. While manufacturing produced some 30 percent of all U.S. goods and services in 1955 and 21 percent in 1985, its share will drop to less than 17 percent by 2000.   _____

5. (1) The ABC Sprocket Company is going bankrupt because of poor management. (2) The company has had four presidents in the past 5 years, and all of them had graduate degrees in

Business Administration. (3) James Marley was the best of the four. (4) However, even Marley wasn't able to prevent the company from losing money while he was president. (5) The ABC Sprocket Company has lost over $5 million a year for the last 3 years, a sum which probably has frightened away potential purchasers of the company's stock.

1. _____   4. _____

2. _____   5. _____

3. _____

Check your responses to these statements. Be sure to read the explanations that accompany each response.

Sample Practice Answers

1. **O**—Since this statement reflects the attitude of its originator, it cannot be proven. In addition, there are any number of reactions to opening a business other than fright. For example, the new owner may feel pride, joy, relief, and so on.

2. **F**— The statement can easily be proven by checking the Fortune 500 companies for this year and the last two years.

3. **F**—Court records in Florida and Vermont can be checked.

4. **FO**—The figures for the manufacture of goods and services for 1955 and 1985 can be verified. However, you cannot prove a prediction; only events that have already occurred can be proved to be facts.

5. (1) **FO**—Statement 1 is a combination of fact and opinion. If ABC Sprocket Company has filed for bankruptcy, that part of the statement is fact. The reason for this bankruptcy may or may not be the result of poor management. There are usually a number of factors that cause a company to go bankrupt; it would be difficult, if not impossible, to measure the reasons and come up with one that is directly responsible.

   (2) **F**—Statement 2 is easily checked.

   (3) **O**—Statement 3 is an opinion since it cannot be verified. What is meant by "best?"

(4) F—Statement 4 is a fact because it can be verified by checking the financial records of the company.

(5) FO—Statement 5 is a combination of fact and opinion. The first part is fact since it can also be verified in the company's financial records. The second part of the statement is an opinion; there is no way of locating and surveying potential purchasers of stock.

Now go on to Skill Development Exercise 11–1 on page 299 for additional practice in separating facts from opinions.

In Skill Application 11–1 on page 305 you will apply what you know about separating facts from opinions to your own career materials.

SKILL DEVELOPMENT EXERCISE 11–1
Separating Fact from Opinion

A. *DIRECTIONS: Read each of the following statements carefully and mark it as fact (F), opinion (O), or both (FO).*

1. In absolute real estate auctions, the owner of the property is legally obligated to sell, even when the highest bid is far below the property's value. _____

2. Groups generally are superior to individuals in making decisions when an issue is relatively complex, since members of a group can generate more creative solutions than one person working alone. _____

3. The number of women in the labor market has increased dramatically since the end of World War II—especially for those between ages 25 and 54. _____

4. Good Samaritan laws, which provide immunity to those who try to help in emergencies, should help to lower the death toll at the scene of an accident. _____

5. The national debt of this country has increased over the past 25 years regardless of the political party represented in the White House and in control of Congress. _____

B. *DIRECTIONS: Read the following paragraphs carefully. Analyze and evaluate each sentence within the paragraph to determine if it is fact (F) or opinion (O) or both fact and opinion (FO).*

1.   (1) Cherry Hill is a prison that still stands today in Philadelphia.   (2) Cherry Hill is the notoriously famous model of the system in which prisoners were kept in separate but not solitary confinement.   (3) This Bastille-like structure of stone and iron cell-block warrens may, to some, be the most famous prison in the world—certainly not for its enlightened approach but as a monument to a social futility.

    1. _____

    2. _____

    3. _____

2.   (1) **Auditing** is the testing and checking of an organization's accounting records to see whether proper policies and practices have been followed.   (2) This is the primary activity of the **certified public**

accountant (CPA). (3) In all states, an accountant may be licensed to practice as a CPA upon fulfilling certain educational requirements, passing a rigorous uniform examination, and acquiring specified amounts of actual accounting experience. (4) Most states now require CPAs to take a certain number of hours of continuing education each year in order to renew their CPA licenses.

1. _____   3. _____

2. _____   4. _____

3. (1) Quality circles* are a Japanese invention. (2) These quality circles have been very successful for Japanese organizations as a method for achieving higher quality, improved output, increased employee involvement, greater employee satisfaction, and reduced absenteeism. (3) The cost of quality circles is relatively so low that such problem-solving committees are becoming widely accepted in industry in the United States. (4) In the United States, where the concept generally means involving workers in shop-floor decisions, company involvement success stories continue to grow. (5) According to several reports, over 1500 U.S. companies use quality circles, and reports of success number well over 1000. (6) Such reports of success are not altogether surprising.

*Quality circles are a means of attempting to increase employee involvement in decision making. They are small groups of employees who meet regularly to identify, analyze, and solve quality and related problems in their own areas of the company.

1. _____   4. _____

2. _____   5. _____

3. _____   6. _____

4. (1) During the early 1920s, radio broadcasters were not very interested in news. (2) There were no radio reporters; most news came directly from newspapers and sounded rather dull on the air. (3) Advertisers expressed little enthusiasm for sponsoring news broadcasts, preferring to back more popular entertainment and music shows. (4) Yet some news events seemed designed for radio coverage.

1. _____   3. _____

2. _____   4. _____

5. (1) People have lived with the same complex carbohydrate plants for thousands of years. (2) In fact, no important new plants of any kind (except tomatoes and coffee) have been domesticated in the last

2,000 years. (3) Thai farmers were cultivating rice 12,000 years ago; North American natives ate beans and squash at least 9,000 years ago; wheat and barley were under cultivation 7,000 years before the Christian era began. (4) In contrast, the purification of simple carbohydrate into table sugar is a process only 100 years old. (5) We have not had time to adapt to it.

1. _____   4. _____

2. _____   5. _____

3. _____

C. *DIRECTIONS: Read the article "How to Master Back-Burner Thinking" below. Then label the numbered paragraphs or sections as fact (F), opinion (O), or a combination of fact and opinion (FO) in the lines provided.*

HOW TO MASTER BACK-BURNER THINKING*

by Marilyn Harris Kriegel and Robert Kriegel

You're miles away from your desk, and the office is the farthest thing from your mind. Suddenly the solution to a problem you've been struggling with all week comes to you out of nowhere.

(1) It's a well-known quirk of creative thinking: The answers we rack our brains to find from 9 to 5 often pop up at the most unexpected times. What happens? Your conscious mind, or "front burner," lets go of the puzzle while your subconscious, intuitive mind takes over. Experts call this back-burner thinking, and it doesn't have to be left to chance.

(2) As psychologists conducting creativity seminars throughout the United States and Europe, we've helped dozens of executives achieve back-burner breakthroughs. The following strategies can help you learn to harness your subconscious creativity to get ahead on the job.

KNOWING WHEN ENOUGH IS ENOUGH

(3) Back-burner thinking doesn't mean that the answers to hard problems will simply occur to you. Researching and analying a problem increases the mental tension necessary to prompt creativity.

* Reprinted with permission from *Working Woman Magazine.* Copyright 1988 by Working Woman/McCall's Group.

But knowing when to stop fussing over something is equally important. Throwing your hands up in disgust, pounding your desk in frustration, muttering "to hell with it," all signal that enough mental steam has built up. You feel as if your mind is overloaded and you can't think straight anymore. Certainly you're not unearthing any new insights or ideas. It's time to turn your attention to something completely different that will let your mind wander.

(4) Of course, it's difficult in a high-pressure work environment to stop thinking about a problem. You've probably been taught to push harder when faced with a tough situation. But creative thinking needs the incubation period taking a break provides. Activities that don't require a great deal of mental energy set the stage best for back-burner work.

A syndicated columnist who attended one of our seminars told us, "When I get stuck writing, I've learned to stop. I may do a menial task, have a chat with someone or do some trashy reading. Anything that takes my mind off my writing.

"Invariably, either during or right after a break, I'll get a flash." says this columnist. "I don't know how else to describe it. Suddenly I'll have a new insight or perspective, and I'm excited to get back to work."

(5) During another seminar, a hospital vice president told us about a breakthrough she had when she was trying to get the community interested in a new substance-abuse program: "I tried everything, but we still weren't getting much response. Then one weekend I went to the mountains. I was tinkering with my car to adjust the carburetor's gas-and-air mix when I suddenly understood what was wrong. I had to change the marketing mix for the program just as I was changing the carburetor mix for a different altitude." She began to advertise the program on TV, and the new strategy was a huge success.

(6) Sometimes exercise is the best way to flex back-burner muscles. A recent study conducted at Purdue University proved that physical conditioning spurs the imagination.

Thomas Hoving, editor in chief of *Connoisseur* magazine, says he got some of his most creative ideas on his daily bike ride.

PROGRAMMING YOUR BACK BURNER

What if taking a break does't spur any creative flashes? In these situations you need to do things to activate and encourage your creativity.

(7) First, try thinking about the problem immediately before you pursue a relaxing activity. One executive we've worked with reviews the paperwork on tough challenges before his morning run. "Then I let my mind wander," he says. "Almost without fail I come back to the issue later in the run. I don't always get a dramatic flash that solves everything, but I do gain a new perspective or insight that can help."

Or try this process at the end of the workday. "Before I leave my office," says one manager, "I take a few minutes to go over a problem I'm stuck on. Then I write a few key words on my calendar. Even though I don't give it any more thought, the next day when I look at the calendar, I usually see things more clearly."

(8) You can also use this strategy before falling asleep. When difficulties at the office keep you up nights, put that tossing-and-turning time to good use. Take a few minutes to formulate a major question related to the problem, then write it down. Now read a magazine and forget about the problem. As you drift off or when you're asleep, your subconscious mind will reorganize information, make new connections and develop new perspectives.

In the middle of the night you may wake up with an "I've got it!" Or a dream may help you come up with an answer. Be prepared for these insights. Keep a pad and pen or mini tape recorder by your bed.

HOW TO SPARK CREATIVITY IN A CRUNCH

(9) When deadlines and other pressures make it impossible to take a creativity break, you can do mental exercises to activate your back-burner thinking. To gain a new perspective on a situation, make a list of five people you admire and imagine how each would handle the problem.

If that doesn't work, make a list of absurd solutions. Quickly jot down all the silly ideas you can think of. Read through the list and imagine the reaction to each. You may find that a modified version of one isn't so absurd after all.

Finally, look for random clues to a solution—in the next song you hear on the radio or the next article you read in the paper. Even if you don't hit on the answer right away, you'll be opening your mind to all types of solutions.

(10) Relying on your subconscious mind may seem a little disconcerting at first. If you feel uneasy, remember those times when you had a sudden breakthrough. It's easier to make time for back-burner breaks when you realize how much they can boost your performance.

So the next time you feel overloaded, relax. Take a walk, practice the piano, play soccer with your kids, fly a kite. It will do wonders for your career.

Paragraph 1. _____   **Paragraph 6.** _____

Paragraph 2. _____   **Paragraph 7.** _____

Paragraph 3. _____   **Paragraph 8.** _____

Paragraph 4. _____   **Paragraph 9.** _____

Paragraph 5. _____   **Paragraph 10.** _____

SKILL APPLICATION 11–1
Separating Fact from Opinion

DIRECTIONS: Choose and duplicate two paragraphs from your own career materials. Attach one paragraph to each side of this sheet. Then number the sentences within the paragraph and identify each sentence as fact (F), opinion (O), or both (FO).

PARAGRAPH ONE SOURCE INFORMATION

Title: _____

Author: _____

Place of publication: _____

Publisher: _____

Copyright Date: _____ *Page(s):* _____

PARAGRAPH TWO SOURCE INFORMATION

Title: _____

Author: _____

Place of publication: _____

Publisher: _____

Copyright Date: _____ *Page(s)* _____

DETECTING PROPAGANDA DEVICES

Interpreting hidden messages is essential when an author uses one or more subtle devices intended to persuade you to agree with his or her point of view. In such a situation, the author is appealing to your emotions and trying to change your thinking or your behavior. If you are a person who doesn't think things through too thoroughly and who accepts what is written without adequately evaluating an author's purpose in writing the material, hidden messages may mislead you and cause you to accept his or her opinions. As a result, you may develop inappropriate ideas and behaviors.

The persuasive techniques used by authors to appeal to your emotions and cause you to make changes in your thinking or behavior are called propaganda devices. Seven commonly used propaganda devices will be discussed in this part of Chapter Eleven: **name calling, glittering generalities, testimonial, transfer, bandwagon, plain folks,** and **card stacking.** Although the emphasis is on the use of propaganda devices in written material, be aware that the same devices are often used by speakers as well as writers. They are particularly prevalent in both forms in advertisements and during political campaigns.

Each of the seven propaganda devices is described below. It is important that you become familiar with these devices and their effects so that you are able to read beyond written words to detect them in authors' hidden messages.

Name Calling and Glittering Generalities

Both name calling and glittering generalities are propaganda devices which involve the use of labels. In name calling, the labels are negative ones which are supposed to trigger negative emotions in the reader. You are being persuaded to hate, condemn, reject, or ridicule the individual, group, or other recipient of the negative label. For example, if a political candidate is labeled as a "wimp" during the heat of a campaign, you are supposed to view this person as ineffectual, weak, and easily led by others. The image is set by the label.

On the other hand, the glittering-generalities device makes use of positive labels. These labels are supposed to trigger positive emotions in the reader. You are now being persuaded to accept, adopt, or approve of an individual, group, or other recipient of the label because they are good: Any right-thinking person would believe in them. If you read that American astronauts have the "right stuff," you are supposed to think of this group as consisting of individuals who are fearless, bright, adventuresome, and far above the average mortal. Again, the image is set by the label.

Testimonial and Transfer

Two propaganda devices, testimonial and transfer, use the prestige of individuals or institutions to convince you to accept unrelated commercial products, ideas, or symbols. With these two devices, an author intends to create positive images which will trigger positive emotions in the reader.

The testimonial device utilizes famous persons to speak for whatever the author is trying to sell to you. A perfect example is an advertising campaign in which a well-known person claims to use a certain product or service. The idea behind the campaign is that your awe and respect for the famous person will somehow be transferred to the product or service and you will feel compelled to purchase it.

When using the transfer device, the author's message is again involved with prestige. In this device, however, the prestige is that of an institution or a symbol which is being used to create acceptance and to trigger positive emotions. When, for instance, the symbol Uncle Sam is used to sell hot dogs, you are supposed to transfer your trust of Uncle Sam and the positive emotions this symbol triggers within you to the hot dog. How could any hot dog endorsed by Uncle Sam be anything but worthy of your purchase?

Bandwagon

The bandwagon device appeals to your desire to be accepted as part of a group that has ideas, purposes, or other factors in common. This device is intended to trigger positive emotions that make you want to join in on whatever the author is selling. The bandwagon device can be used in appealing to you to join in positive groups—as, for example, when a political candidate urges you to join other environmentalists in support of his or her election. Bandwagon can also be used to appeal to negative emotions by stressing such things as prejudices and fears, so that readers will join hate groups. In such cases, you are urged to join with others who hate a certain group of people so that you can stand united against them.

Plain Folks

The plain-folks device is used to make you accept other persons because they are just like you. This device is often used by politicians or other well-known persons to create feelings of confidence regarding that person, feelings that are based on the idea that you share the same experiences. An example of the plain-folks device is the political candidate who puts on a hard hat when campaigning in an industrial plant. He or she attempts to look like the workers within that plant, thus becoming just one of the folks.

Card Stacking

When an author is willing to go to any lengths to convince you to believe in his or her message, the propaganda device of card stacking is often employed. In such cases, the author may use half-truths, present total lies that are disguised as the truth, sidestep issues, raise unrelated issues, or try to confuse you with the written message. The purpose of such tactics is often to divert you from seeking the truth, since the truth would be harmful to the propagandist. In other words, the author is trying to trigger positive emotions in situations where your emotions might be negative if you had the correct information and the ability to analyze and evaluate what you are being told. An example of card stacking is the advertising campaign which promises increased love, enhanced sex appeal, a great social life, and so on if you will only use the shampoo, deodorant, mouthwash, perfume, or other personal product being touted.

SAMPLE PRACTICE
Detecting Propaganda Devices

DIRECTIONS: Name the propaganda device used in each of the following statements. Refer to the descriptions of the devices as needed.

Name Calling	Plain Folks
Glittering Generalities	Bandwagon
Transfer	Card Stacking
Testimonial	

1. The governor of the state visited us while we were surveying for the new highway to be constructed in 1995. There he was, dressed in flannel shirt, jeans, and padded jacket. If you didn't know who he was, you'd think he was just one of the gang working out in the field.

   _____

2. "I have loved Mill's Tomato Juice since my college days," says Harry Cooper, executive officer of the Cooper International Restaurants chain. "It's the first thing I want to drink after a tough negotiating session."

   _____

3. Jay Long can't do anything more than simple arithmetic without a calculator. How can such a number-illiterate be treasurer of the A-One Services Corporation?

   _____

4. Vote for Sam Oberlin and I know you won't regret it. All of the best folks in our section of the factory are supporting him for union representative. He needs your support. Won't you join the group of the great people voting for him?

   _____

5. The Simpson Rock Company is by far the best company in town to work for. We get to wear great-looking uniforms—pink and mauve with the company name on the back. You can have your name put on over the shirt pocket if you'd like. The salary may not be great but the benefits are terrific. For example, look at our cafeteria. We must have the best-looking one in town, and the menu is just fantastic—more good things to eat than you thought possible in a company cafeteria.

   _____

6. Like the watchdog on our logo, Guardian's Home Security Systems are dependable and effective. Our electronic systems, in fact, are a home's best friend.

   _____

7. Sam Shade deserves to be promoted to supervisor of construction. His long record as a conscientious leader and tireless worker indicates that he is the man for the job. In addition, his A.A. degree from Uptown College indicates that he is bright and able to handle the paperwork involved in such a position.

   _____

8. Eliot Jamison bears a strong resemblance to George Washington. Lately, he has changed his hair style so that it looks just like the one you see in the paintings of Washington. Now when Eliot tries to sell stocks and bonds in his deep, serious, old-fashioned way of speaking, you could swear you are being sold by G.W. himself.

   _____

Check your answers. Be sure to read the explanation below each answer given below. If your answers don't match those given, be sure to analyze how they are different.

Sample Practice Answers

1. **Plain Folks**—The governor is trying to appear to be just like one of the surveyors on the job.

2. **Testimonial**—Harry Cooper is endorsing Mill's Tomato Juice. The message is that an important man drinks this juice after important events.

3. **Name Calling**—Calling someone a "number-illiterate" is not exactly complimentary.

4. **Bandwagon**—This is an appeal to join others in support of Sam Oberlin's election as union representative.

5. **Card Stacking**—The author of this description of life at the Simpson Rock Company is trying hard to convince you that this is a great place to work. The issue of low salary has been sidestepped and the unrelated issues of attractive uniforms and a super cafeteria brought up. Does the author really think that these "benefits" can overcome the effects of a poor salary?

6. **Transfer**—In this case, the symbol is a watchdog. It is used to give the illusion of safety, alertness, and security, which are the qualities one expects in a watchdog, to the company.

7. **Glittering Generalities**—Sam Shade is described with some glowing terms: "conscientious leader," "tireless worker," "bright."

8. **Transfer**—In this situation, the symbol being used is George Washington, who was known for his honesty, including never telling a lie. These qualities are supposedly found in Eliot, who tries to encourage this illusion by making himself look and sound like George Washington.

Now go to Skill Development Exercise 11–2 on page 313 for additional practice in detecting propaganda devices.

Then go to Skill Application 11–2 on page 317, where you will apply what you know about detecting propaganda devices to your own career material.

SKILL DEVELOPMENT EXERCISE 11–2
Detecting Propaganda Devices

A. *DIRECTIONS: Analyze each of the following statements and write the name or names of the propaganda device(s) used by the author below it.*

Name Calling	Plain Folks
Glittering Generalities	Bandwagon
Transfer	Card Stacking
Testimonial	

1. It is critical that we rid our union of the radical troublemakers who have come here from Detroit for the sole purpose of creating dissension among us. They are obviously financed by sneaky card-carrying Reds whose only desire is to destroy what we have gained from management.

   _____

2. During the week, Lucifer Lyons may be the executive corporate officer of the multimillion-dollar Happy Hours Corporation, but he spends his weekends just like the men who work on the assembly line. Every Saturday finds him dressed in shabby old pants, flannel shirt, and beat-up old boots. He heads for the fishing hole, where he spends lazy afternoons catching fish for dinner.

   _____

3. After years of intensive research, the Darby Drug Company has developed Pep Up!, a true miracle tonic. Indeed, Pep Up! may be the greatest boon to mankind since the invention of sliced white bread. Taken three times a day, Pep Up! has been found to be effective in the treatment of cancer, depression, dental plaque, sinus congestion, dandruff, and twenty-seven other serious conditions. Made up of 96 percent alcohol and 4 percent pure spring water, Pep Up! has been fortified with all the vitamins known to man. Pep Up! is guaranteed to bring immediate results; you'll feel better than you have in years.

   _____

4. The Alexander Hamilton Investment Plan is the financial plan endorsed by a number of prominent people. John Moses, mayor of Titleton, Fred Hannock, governor of the state, Marie Torrance, senator, and Lawrence Reeves, congressman, have been active investors since the Plan was

initiated. If they have complete confidence in the Plan, shouldn't you? Join these people in the know—enroll now!

_____

5. Elect Roger Burns as your representative to the salary negotiating team! He has much to offer us. His cool exterior hides a brilliant analytical mind that never stops working. Roger speaks with authority and has the respect of both management and labor. He will be a fantastic spokesman for our side. Let's go with Roger!

_____

6. Let Old Faithful Trucking Company move your industrial equipment. This reliable company makes sure that everything arrives as scheduled and is set in place with a minimum of lost assembly-line time. You can't go wrong with Old Faithful!

_____

7. The advertisement shows a high-priced automobile parked in front of an impressive mansion. A handsome, distinguished, and very well-dressed young man with just a hint of gray hair sits at the wheel of the automobile. Beside him sits a beautiful young woman wearing an obviously expensive gown, a fur wrap, and exquisite jewels. The advertisement says that "this is THE automobile for the rising young executive. This is the perfect automobile for you."

_____

8. We aren't going to take this mistreatment from the company any more! We are all going out on strike. We will be meeting at 7 a.m. in front of the gates to get our signs and final instructions. Let's make it a 100 percent strike effort! Be there to show your support for our cause.

_____

9. Don't go to work for the S, T, and U Construction Company. They are so cheap that you'll never get an honest day's pay from them. They'll manage to charge you for all kinds of damage you've never done and deduct it from your pay. Also, I wouldn't be surprised to find out they cheat their customers, too. Seems to me they are using inferior building materials and charging customers for top quality goods. How dishonest can they be?

_____

10. Did you see old J.D. at the company picnic last Sunday? What a great guy he is! There he was eating a hot dog and drinking a beer right along with all the guys who run the presses for him. Just to look at him you'd never guess that he's president of the Lumfield Publishing Company and worth more than just a couple of million dollars. What a down-to-earth fellow he is!

B. *DIRECTIONS: Read the following mock advertisement. Circle any propaganda devices you detect and name the device. Write the name of the device as close to your circle as possible.*

316

SKILL APPLICATION 11–2
Detecting Propaganda Devices

DIRECTIONS: *In this Skill Application you have two choices in how to apply what you know about propaganda devices.*

1. *Choose, duplicate, and attach two examples of the use of any of the seven propaganda devices from your own career materials.*

2. *Write two examples of propaganda that might occur in your own career. Again, use any of the seven propaganda devices discussed in this unit.*

SOURCE INFORMATION ONE (if you choose number 1 above)

Title: _____

Author: _____

Place of publication: _____

Publisher: _____

Copyright Date: _____ *Page(s):* _____

SOURCE INFORMATION TWO (if you choose number 1 above)

Title: _____

Author: _____

Place of publication: _____

Publisher: _____

Copyright Date: _____ *Page(s):* _____

TRANSLATING GOBBLEDYGOOK

There may be times when you read material and, although you apply everything you know about interpreting hidden messages, you cannot figure out what the author is trying to say. In such cases, the difficulty may be with the material and not with your skill as an interpreter. You may have come up against material that can be described as **gobbledygook.**

Gobbledygook is a form of writing that uses very difficult language when it is not necessary, uses pompous words when simple ones will do, and uses a number of words when one will do very well. It is obvious why the reader of gobbledygook finds it very difficult to interpret any message the author is trying to send.

Gobbledygook is not a new problem. People interested in proper use of the English language have been concerned with it for years. During his administration, President Carter tried to make government agencies and personnel write in simple, easy-to-understand terms. He had only limited success. In the summer of 1989, a California newspaper carried a report on the effort by lawyers in that state to simplify the language in legal documents so that they become more comprehensible to persons outside of the profession. The result of this effort is not yet known.

Although gobbledygook can appear in any kind of written material, it frequently is used in contracts, wills, and other legal papers. It also appears in government regulations, proposals, and reports of all kinds. However, its use is not limited to legal and government documents, since examples of gobbledygook also are easy to find in the written materials of private businesses and industries. Gobbledygook can also appear as jargon, that special career-related vocabulary used by persons employed in law, medicine, education, data processing, construction, management, or any other field. Finally, gobbledygook can be found in just about any reading material in which an author chooses to use difficult language when it is not necessary to do so.

The following examples of gobbledygook appeared in a recent newspaper column which used humor to decry the lack of plain English in speaking. They can just as easily be used as examples of gobbledygook found in written material.

"The canine which shares residential space with the humanoid population of the domicile is expressing, through a series of gyrations, tongue distensions and excessive salivations, an urgent desire to perform a basic bodily function; the mandatory restraining device (Stand. Issue-4-K9p) is operational and at your disposal." (Translation: "Rover has to go; here's the leash.")

"Conditions warrant the immediate disposition of an aggregation of refuse, non-edibles, unrecyclable waste material and discards." (Translation: "Take the garbage out.")

While the above examples are humorous, gobbledygook becomes a very serious matter when you encounter it in important material which you must translate accurately and react to appropriately. You may even sign important legal, professional, or personal documents that you don't fully understand. Obviously, this can have very serious results. It is, therefore, essential that you break the language barrier set up by an author when material includes gobbledygook.

The following steps should help you in the proper translation of gobbledygook.

1. Recognize gobbledygook for what it is; know that it is precisely what you are dealing with in the material.

2. Know that you must go beyond the written words in order to comprehend the author's message.

3. Read slowly and carefully. Translate as you go.

4. Use clues in context to simplify terms, or look them up in the dictionary if necessary.

5. Look for main ideas and for details that support these main ideas.

6. Map or chart if you think either technique will help to clarify the information.

7. State the information in your own words. If it makes sense, you have probably done an adequate job of translating the gobbledygook.

SAMPLE PRACTICE
Translating Gobbledygook

DIRECTIONS: Translate the following three examples of gobbledygook. Refer to the seven steps above for translating gobbledygook, as needed. Space has been provided for your translation under each example.

1. **From an application for funds for projects:**

All applications will be screened to determine their completeness and conformity to the requirements of this announcement for funding of projects. Applications that are not complete or do not conform to the requirements will not be considered for funding. This screening is intended to assure a level playing field for all applicants.

2. **From a health insurance form:**

   ASSIGNMENT OF BENEFITS: Except where my [insurance] plan provides for automatic payment of benefits to the provider of services, I authorize payment of benefits, otherwise payable to me, for services rendered by those physicians or providers described below and/or as indicated on the enclosed bills. I understand that I am financially responsible to the provider for the charges not covered by my benefit plan.

3. **From a government labor report:**

   Women's attachment to the labor market has increased dramatically since the end of World War II—especially for those between the ages of 25 and 54. More than 7 of 10 women in this age cohort are now in the labor force, up from about 3 of 10 four decades earlier. The rise in women's attachment to market work is clearly both a product and a cause of many profound social and economic changes that have occurred in the United States over the past 40 years.

   Check your translation of the above gobbledygook. Translating gobbledygook is, of course, expressed in your own words, so that it is unlikely that your translation will exactly match those presented below. However, the ideas in the original material should be about the same in any translation.

Sample Practice Answers

1. In order to give all applicants an equal chance for funding, applications that are not complete or do not conform to the requirements will not be considered.

2. When my insurance plan does not automatically pay providers of services, I authorize the payment to the physicians and/or providers whose bills are enclosed with this form. I understand that I will have to pay any charges not covered by my insurance benefits.

3. The number of women in the labor force has increased from 3 out of 10 women at the end of World War II to 7 out of 10 women now. This increase has had an effect on economic and social changes over the past forty years.

Now go on to Skill Development 11–3 on page 323 for additional practice in translating gobbledygook.

Then go to Skill Application 11–3 on page 327. There you will have an opportunity to apply what you know about translating this kind of writing in your own career materials.

SKILL DEVELOPMENT EXERCISE 11–3
Translating Gobbledygook

DIRECTIONS: Read each example of gobbledygook very carefully and translate it. Go back to the seven steps for translating gobbledygook on page 320 if you need help. Remember to map or chart on a separate sheet of paper as needed. Space has been provided for your translation under each example.

1. **From the bylaws of a condominium association:**

When more than one Person owns an interest in any Condominium Unit, all such Persons shall be Members of the Association. The vote for such Condominium Unit shall be exercised as the Owners of the Condominium Unit determine among themselves, but in no event shall more than one ballot be cast for or with respect to any Condominium Unit concerning any one vote of the Association. The vote for each Condominium Unit must be cast as a unit and fractional votes shall not be allowed. In the event that the joint Owners are unable to agree among themselves as to how their vote or votes shall be cast, they shall lose their right to vote on the matter in question. If any Owner or Owners cast a vote on behalf of a Condominium Unit, it will thereafter be conclusively presumed for all purposes that he/she or they was/were acting with the authority and consent of all Owners of the Condominium Unit. In the event more than one vote is cast for a particular Condominium Unit during a particular vote of the Association, none of said votes shall be counted and said votes shall be deemed void.

2. **From a union agreement with a government service:**

> *Section 5. Suspension of More Than 14 Days or Discharge.* In the case of suspensions of more than fourteen (14) days, or of discharge, any employee shall, unless otherwise provided herein, be entitled to an advance written notice of the charges against him/her and shall remain either on the job or on the clock at the option of the Employer for a period of thirty (30) days. Thereafter, the employee shall remain on the rolls (non-pay status) until disposition of the case has been had either by settlement with the Union or through exhaustion of the grievance-arbitration procedure. The employee who chooses to appeal a suspension of more than fourteen (14) days or his discharge to the Merit Systems Protection Board (MSPB) rather than through the grievance-arbitration procedure shall remain on the rolls (non-pay status) until disposition of the case has been had either by settlement or through exhaustion of his MSPB appeal. When there is reasonable cause to believe an employee is guilty of a crime for which a sentence of imprisonment can be imposed, the employer is not required to give the employee the full thirty (30) days advance written notice in a discharge action, but shall give such lesser number of days advance written notice as under the circumstances is reasonable and can be justified. The employee is immediately removed from a pay status at the end of the notice period.

3. **From a code of business conduct for officers and employees of a company:**

> Officers and employees are expected to devote full time to the business of the Company and must avoid situations that might result in a conflict or appearance of a conflict between their personal inter-

ests and the interests of the Company. All personnel who deal with suppliers, licensees, or persons contracting or doing business with the Company or who supervise anyone who has such dealings are prohibited from realizing personal profit or gain as a direct or indirect results of such dealings. At no time should an officer or employee jeopardize the Company's negotiating position for securing the best possible price, quality, or service. It is most important that all officers and employees avoid relationships which would be likely to impair objectivity or influence their judgment. All dealings with public officials, suppliers of goods and services, customers, other employees, and all other persons and organizations shall be conducted in compliance with this policy , and all officers and employees are expected and directed to perform their duties with complete honesty, candor, and integrity in the best interest of the Company, in accordance with this policy.

4. **From a call for bids: purchase of a computer system by a company:**

The successful bidder shall defend any suit or proceeding brought against the buyer so far as based on a claim on any equipment, or any part thereof, furnished under this contract which constitutes an infringement of any patent of the United States, if notified promptly in writing and given authority, for the defense of same, and the bidder shall pay all damages and costs awarded therein against the buyer. In case said equipment or any part thereof, in such suit held to constitute infringement and use of said equipment or part is enjoined [prohibited], the bidder shall, at his own expense, either procure for the buyer the right to continue using said equipment, or part, or replace same with noninfringing equipment, or modify so that it becomes noninfringing.

5. **From an employee agreement—large corporation:**

2.02 Efforts of Employee. Employee agrees that he will at all times faithfully, industriously and to the best of his ability, experience and talent, devote his full time to the performance of all duties that may be required of him and from him pursuant to the express and implicit terms hereof, to the reasonable satisfaction of Employer. Employee shall devote his full time and best efforts towards the promotion and development of Employer's Business. Employee recognizes that Employer's organization, business and relationship with suppliers, customers, prospective accounts and others having business dealings with Employer ("Business Relationships") are and will be the sole property of Employer and Employee shall have no separate interests or rights with respect thereto, except as an employee of Employer, and enhancement of the value of Business Relationships is a principle responsibility of Employee pursuant to this agreement. Employee shall actively develop or participate in the development of new product lines.

SKILL APPLICATION 11–3
Translating Gobbledygook

DIRECTIONS: *You have two choices in how to apply what you know about translating gobbledygook.*

1. *Choose, duplicate, and attach two examples of the use of gobbledygook from any source.*

2. *Write two examples of gobbledygook that might occur in your own career material.*

SOURCE INFORMATION ONE (if you choose number 1 above)

Title: _____

Author: _____

Place of publication: _____

Publisher: _____

Copyright Date: _____   Page(s): _____

SOURCE INFORMATION TWO (if you choose number 1 above)

Title: _____

Author: _____

Place of publication: _____

Publisher: _____

Copyright Date: _____ *Page(s):* _____

Chapter Twelve

Handling Business Mail

With the widespread use of computers throughout business and industry, it has been predicted that eventually a paperless occupational world will emerge. To date, this has not occurred. In fact, there is probably more career-related written material for you to read than ever before. While some of this material may be encountered on a computer monitor, much of it still takes the traditional paper form. Thus, during your working day, you will often be expected to read and respond to a wide variety of career-related messages, both electronically transmitted and in paper form. For our purposes, we will call these messages "business mail."

Business mail includes letters and memoranda (often called "memos"). Both letters and memoranda are kinds of career-replated communications frequently used in all sorts of work situations. Business letters usually bring you information from outside sources, while memoranda are used to share information within a company, organization, government agency, department, etc. Since business letters and memoranda share a number of characteristics, they are discussed together in this chapter.

When you read any business mail, ask yourself: **Can I handle this business mail more quickly and efficiently?** Upon completion of this chapter, your answer to this question should be yes, and then you should be able to apply what you have mastered here.

Both letters and memoranda give the receiver the advantage of gaining information before reading the first word of the actual message. A glance at the top and bottom of a business letter or memorandum will tell you something about the sender and prepare you for reading the contents of the communication.

In addition to transmitting information, both business letters and memoranda often require that the receiver perform some kind of action. Thus, it is important that you be alert as to what is expected of you as a result of the communication.

The following suggestions should help you to deal effectively with the greater number of business letters and memoranda which seem to arrive daily in just about every workplace.

1. Find out about the sender of the communication. If you are dealing with a business letter, quickly glance at the top of the letter and at the signature at the bottom to learn the date the letter was written, who sent the letter, in what company, association, department, etc. that person is employed, and the sender's position. If the communication is in the form of a memorandum, look at the identifying information that is usually found at the top: the date the memorandum was written, who wrote it, and sometimes, the purpose for writing it. If you have dealt with the sender before, you have some very general idea of the subject of the communication. If the present communication is part of a series of interactions between you and the sender, you may have an even more specific idea of what the letter or memorandum will be about. In addition, it is often helpful to know who else has received a copy of the same letter or memorandum.

2. Read quickly down the letter or memorandum until you arrive at something that is essential for you to know. The writer may begin with important information right in the first sentence so that you must focus your attention immediately on what has been written. Sometimes, however, the writer may begin with polite clichés, such as those that say your letter or memorandum has been received and read, or with introductory sentences that do not impart any important information. In these cases, read quickly until you find information that is important for you to know. At that point, begin to read carefully.

3. Read for blocks of related information. In other words, be alert for main ideas and the details that support them. Remember that it is easier to understand and retain written material if you organize it into blocks of related information.

4. Underline or highlight key points that require action on your part. Business letters and memoranda often require you to respond or to perform some kind of action. When you accent such parts of a letter, you do not need to reread the information when you are ready to react to the communication. Just look at what you have underlined or highlighted and do what needs to be done.

5. Write trigger words. If a letter or memorandum is lengthy, you may find it very helpful to develop an informal index of the communication's content in its right-hand margin. As you read important information, mentally ask the first question used to identify the main idea of a paragraph: **What is the topic of the paragraph?** Write the answer to this question, which should be no more than a word or two, in the margin directly next to the original information. These words are "trigger words" since they trigger your memory as to the important subjects covered in the communication. If you need to refer to a lengthy letter or memorandum later, you can find specific information that you need by simply glancing down the right-hand margin.

6. Simplify complex information. If the information within the letter or memorandum is difficult to understand, map or chart any part(s) or all of it. Remember how these two techniques aid in simplifying material so that you can understand and retain it. In this particular kind of application, in which you are not planning to study from a map or chart, you might want to take some shortcuts—especially since you probably won't be keeping this material much longer than it takes to simplify it. Instead of the more formal kind of map and chart you made in earlier chapters in this textbook, simply make rough maps or charts. Don't bother with rulers and formal boxes for the information. However, keep in mind that you need to be able to use that map or chart, so be sure it is clear enough for you to read. The time it takes to draw a map or design a chart in such an informal way certainly pays off by reducing the time that you probably will need to ponder the content of the letter or memoranda. A map or chart also can help you to compose your response to the sender.

How many of the above suggestions you will follow for any given letter of memorandaum will depend on how much information is included, how difficult it is to read, and how much of the communication you need to react to. You decide.

Keep these six suggestions for reading a business letter or memorandum in mind as you examine the following samples. Sample A represents a typical business letter and Sample B a typical memorandum. For demonstration purposes, all of the six steps have been followed.

SAMPLE A: A Business Letter

COLUMBIA BANK
1243 Harrison Street
New York, N.Y. 10015

June 10, 1990

Mr. Mark Roberts, President
Uptown Manufacturing Company
8762 North Jordan Road
Middletown, NJ 05087

Dear Mr. Roberts:

We are writing in response to your recent correspondence
regarding the Uptown Manufacturing Company account   *account #*
726-55-0130.

Please be advised that we are unable to comply with
your request to transfer your account balance into a
Joint Tenancy account, as we require a letter of
instructions signed by the registered owner. That   *signed letter of instructions*
signature must be guaranteed by an officer of a   *signature guaranteed*
commercial bank or trust company, located or having
a correspondent bank in New York City, or from a
member firm of a National Securities Exchange.

Kindly note that we require the enclosed application   *enclosed.*
to be signed by the registered owners of the new   *application instructions*
account and completed in its entirety, making certain
that all desired features are designated.

We trust this information proves helpful. Should you
have any questions, please do not hesitate to contact   *telephone #*
Customer Service at 1 (800) 274-9100.

Sincerely,

Hadley Sturgis

Hadley Sturgis
Commercial Accounts Department
HS:jb
c: Walter Hennings, Supervisor, Commercial Account
   Frank Barker, Branch Manager

enc.

When you read the information at the top and bottom of the letter in Sample A, you can discover some facts about the writer, Hadley Sturgis. Mr. Sturgis is employed in the Commercial Accounts Department of the Columbia Bank in New York City. He probably is not part of management in the department since he did not include a title under his signature and he has sent copies of his letter to a supervisor of the department as well as to the manager of the bank's branch.

The first paragraph of the letter can be read over quickly; Mr. Roberts certainly knows the reason why this letter was sent since he initiated the correspondence. Move to the second paragraph, in which instructions are given for transferring the bank balance into a Joint Tenancy account. All of these instructions should be underlined or (highlighted) as shown in Sample A, since they require action from Mr. Roberts. If Mr. Roberts so desires, he could write trigger words next to important parts of the letter. This is also shown in Sample A.

Even though this is a brief letter, the receiver could clarify its multiple instructions by drawing an informal map such as the one below.

The only important information in the last sentence is the telephone number. It should be underlined since it does involve an action if Mr. Roberts has questions about what he is to do.

SAMPLE B: A Memorandum

DATE: January 21, 1990
TO: Samantha Collins
FROM: Margaret Upshaw
SUBJECT: Customer Data Base

This is just one of those times! We are only two weeks away from the annual departmental planning session and I still have not been able to pin down all of the effects, pro and con, of actually initiating a customer data base. I need your help.

Please check with Jack Morgan in the Computer Department about the three data base programs he suggested to the Advertising Department. Why does he think each will be appropriate for our department needs? Get information from him on the advantages and disadvantages of each program. Be sure to also get information on the following specifics:

contact J. Morgan re: data base programs, advantages, disadvantages

1. cost of computer system
2. cost of program
3. cost of other materials/equipment
4. time needed to input information on 6500 customers
5. number of computer personnel required
6. training needed for program users

} get information

Write the information in a report that we can later share with top management. Send it to all department personnel by the 27th of January so they have time to analyze it before the planning session. Thanks.

report by 1/27

c: Bartlett Jenson
    Harry Stokes
    Martha Cooper
    Sally Fountain

When you quickly cover the information at the top and bottom of the memorandum, you can find out who has sent it to Samantha Collins, the subject of the communication, and the other persons who received a copy of it. When time is an important factor, as it probably is in this case, a glance at the top of the memorandum will let you know when it was sent. If Samantha Collins has difficulty following the instructions in the memorandum, the time she was given to do the task might become an issue.

The first paragraph of the memorandum can be read quickly; the information in it is not critical to what Ms. Collins must do. Move to the second paragraph, in which instructions are given for gathering information about a customer database. Additional instructions are provided in the last paragraph, where Ms. Collins is told to write a report and to send it to all department personnel by the 27th of January.

All of these instructions should be underlined (or highlighted) as shown in Sample B, since they require action from Ms. Collins. If she thinks it important, Ms. Collins could write trigger words next to important parts of the letter as is shown in Sample B.

As you read this memorandum, you begin to see how the instructions given set the direction for gathering information about the three database programs and for then reporting that information. A chart would be an appropriate way to handle all of the required information, and it certainly would be an outstanding graphic to supplement the narrative in a written report.

If you examine the underlined parts of both samples, they strongly resemble a telegram. In both samples, the instructions have been reduced to the essentials. In addition, the trigger words in the right-hand margin provide an index to the important points in each communication just in case the receiver wishes to check to see if all instructions have been followed without consulting the original material.

SAMPLE PRACTICE
Handling Business Mail

> DIRECTIONS: Read the following sample business letter and sample memorandum and follow the instructions found after each one. Refer to the suggestions for handling business mail on pages 330 and 331 and Samples A and B above to help you.

ARIZONA DEPARTMENT STORES, INC.
147 Hunter Street
Phoenix, AZ 84016
(602)945-6100

April 4, 1990

Mr. James Rollins, Manager
Accounting Department
Boutiques Unlimited
8976 North Boulevard
Jenkintown, PA 19046

Dear Mr. Rollins:

Thank you very much for your letter inquiring about
employment with Arizona Department Stores, Inc. At
present we do not have any openings in our Accounting
Department. Our retention of employees in this
department is very high so there are rarely positions
to be filled.

I have, however, taken the liberty of forwarding your
letter to Ms. Sally Compton in our Personnel Office and
requested that she keep your letter on file for future
reference. You should make further inquiries to
Ms. Compton at that office since she is in a position
to be the first to know about potential employment
opportunities.

Good luck in your search for employment in the Phoenix
area. I can understand your reasons for possible
relocation to the Southwest; it is a great place to live
and work.

Sincerely,

Roger Dawson

Roger Dawson
Supervisor,
Accounting Department

RD:bt

c: Ms. Sally Compton

1. Circle the first word of information that is important for James Rollins to know.

2. Underline or highlight any part of the letter that requires action on the part of the receiver.

3. Write trigger words in the right-hand margin to indicate important points covered in the letter.

4. Write the main idea of this letter from Roger Dawson.

DATE: November 21, 1989
TO: Bryan Parker
FROM: William Shaw
SUBJECT: New Feature -- Corporate Money Market Account

Beginning on January 1, 1990, the Corporate Money Market Account will become more flexible and convenient for our customers. Deposit capabilities will be expanded to allow customers to deposit more than one check per deposit.

The price schedule for this new feature is $0.49 per deposit for each deposit with more than one check and $0.06 per check. Note that these charges do not apply to single item deposits.

Although these changes allow for more deposit capabilities, you are aware that federal regulations still restrict the number of transfers or withdrawals per month from the Corporate Money Market Account.

We are very anxious to publicize this new feature with the intent of increasing the number of Corporate Money Market Account customers. Therefore, we will shortly be initiating an advertising campaign. You will be receiving cardboard displays to be placed in areas of the bank and drive-in where they can be easily seen by potential account-openers.

Refer any questions you or the branch managers may have re the new feature and the proposed ad campaign to George Landis and Olivia Sanchez at the Main Office.

c: George Landis
    Olivia Sanchez

1. Write trigger words in the right-hand margin to indicate important points covered in the memorandum.

2. Underline or highlight any key points that require action on the part of the receiver.

3. Write the main idea of this memorandum to Bryan Parker.

Check your responses to the instructions given below each sample of business mail.

Sample Practice Answers

LETTER TO MR. JAMES ROLLINS

The following copy of the letter has been marked with the four things you were told to do. Your trigger words may not match the ones written below, but the same content in the letter should be represented in the margin.

ARIZONA DEPARTMENT STORES, INC.
147 Hunter Street
Phoenix, AZ 84016
(602)945-6100

April 4, 1990

Mr. James Rollins, Manager
Accounting Department
Boutiques Unlimited
8976 North Boulevard
Jenkintown, PA 19046

Dear Mr. Rollins:

Thank you very much for your letter inquiring about
employment with Arizona Department Stores, Inc. At
present we do not have any openings in our Accounting
Department. Our retention of employees in this
department is very high so there are rarely positions
to be filled.

Begin careful reading here

I have, however, taken the liberty of forwarding your
letter to Ms. Sally Compton in our Personnel Office and
requested that she keep your letter on file for future
reference. You should make further inquiries to
Ms. Compton at that office since she is in a position
to be the first to know about potential employment
opportunities.

further inquiries to Ms. Sally Compton, Personnel Office

Good luck in your search for employment in the Phoenix
area. I can understand your reasons for possible
relocation to the Southwest; it is a great place to live
and work.

Sincerely,

Roger Dawson

Roger Dawson
Supervisor,
Accounting Department

RD:bt

c: Ms. Sally Compton

Implied main idea of the letter (wording will vary): Although there isn't an opening at present, Mr. Rollins should keep in contact with Ms. Sally Compton, who can advise him on future available positions.

Note that the last paragraph does not require trigger words.

MEMORANDUM TO BRYAN PARKER

DATE: November 21, 1989
TO: Bryan Parker
FROM: William Shaw
SUBJECT: New Feature -- Corporate Money Market Account

begins 1/1/90

Beginning on January 1, 1990, the Corporate Money Market Account will become more flexible and convenient for our customers. Deposit capabilities will be expanded to allow customers to deposit more than one check per deposit.

more than one check/deposit

The price schedule for this new feature is $0.49 per deposit for each deposit with more than one check and $0.06 per check. Note that these charges do not apply to single item deposits.

49¢/deposit
more than one check
6¢/check

Although these changes allow for more deposit capabilities, you are aware that federal regulations still restrict the number of transfers or withdrawals per month from the Corporate Money Market Account.

still restrict transfers/withdrawals

We are very anxious to publicize this new feature with the intent of increasing the number of Corporate Money Market Account customers. Therefore, we will shortly be initiating an advertising campaign. You will be receiving cardboard displays to be placed in areas of the bank and drive-in where they can be easily seen by potential account-openers.

ad campaign

Refer any questions you or the branch managers may have re the new feature and the proposed ad campaign to George Landis and Olivia Sanchez at the Main Office.

refer questions

c: George Landis
    Olivia Sanchez

The main idea of the memorandum is stated in its heading. It is all about the new feature of the Corporate Money Market Account. The body of the memorandum consists of details which support that subject header.

Now go on to Skill Development Exercise 12 on page 343 for additional practice handling business mail.

Then go to Skill Application 12 on page 347, where you will apply what you know about handling business mail to your own career materials.

SKILL DEVELOPMENT EXERCISE 12
Handling Business Mail

DIRECTIONS: Mark the following letter and memorandum as if they had been sent to you. Then answer the questions under each.

```
                    BUSINESS ASSOCIATES, INC.
                   12894 South Lincoln Avenue
                     Silver Spring, MD 20902
                        (302)469-0085

March 14, 1989

Ms. Joanna Winters
Winters Gift Shoppe
6920 Buckhill Drive
Silver Spring, MD 20902

Dear Ms. Winters:

We have received your letter of March 7, 1989 and note that
you inquired about the services of Business Associates, Inc.

Each year thousands of businesses are expanded by hopeful
entrepreneurs.  Unfortunately, many of these businesses
fail because expansion has not been planned adequately
and carried out in the best way possible.  Let us help
you to be one of the successful owners who are able to
expand and operate a business.

Business Associates, Inc. has personnel and resources to
help you expand your business here in Silver Spring or any-
place in the United States.  We also have twenty years of
experience in advising business owners like yourself.

You can lay the groundwork for success by working with our
company on extensive planning, on selection of a site for
the new addition to your business, on a survey of potential
competition, on marketing techniques, and on arranging
for creative financing.

Please contact our New Client department at 469-0086.
We look forward to working with you.

Sincerely yours,

Alicia Strong

Alicia Strong, President

AS:rm
```

1. What is the main idea of this letter to Joanna Winters?

    _____

    _____

    _____

2. Were you able to read this letter quickly and efficiently.
    Why or why not?

    _____

    _____

    _____

3. Did you follow all of the suggestions for reading letters?
    Why or why not?

    _____

    _____

    _____

DATE: October 8, 1990
TO: Arnie Neal
FROM: Sarah Jones
SUBJECT: Staff Meeting -- October 6, 1989

We discussed a number of important issues at the meeting
on the 6th. Since you had to be out of town on that date,
here is a brief recap of what was covered.

Everyone's major concern was the coming Christmas rush.
We remember too well what happened last year and would like
to avoid the pressures we all felt. The following
suggestions were made:

> 1. Hire new staff who will remain on a permanent
>   basis--1 chef, 2 bakers, and 3 waiters.
>
> 2. Rearrange the dining room so that more parties
>   of 4 or more can be accommodated.
>
> 3. Extend the restaurant hours for maximum seating.
>
> 4. Accept reservations.
>
> 5. Hire an extra truck and driver for faster
>   delivery of catered foods for home parties.

As you well know, we are all interested in becoming the
top restaurant/catering service in the city. If the
above 5 suggestions will help us to attain that goal,
they need to be carried out as soon as possible.

We need your input on these suggestions. Please write
out what you see as advantages or disadvantages of each,
the cost factors and the amount of time it will take to
put each into operation. Share your information with the
rest of the staff by next week so that we can read and
analyze the points you make before we have our next meeting.

1. What is the main idea of this memorandum to Arnie Neal?

_____

_____

_____

2. Were you able to read this memorandum quickly and efficiently?
Why or why not?

_____

_____

_____

3. Did you follow all of the suggestions for reading memoranda?
   Why or why not?

   _____

   _____

   _____

SKILL APPLICATION 12
Handling Business Mail

DIRECTIONS: Write one business letter and one memorandum on this sheet. The content of these pieces of business mail should be appropriate for your own career. Then show how you would handle these business mail samples efficiently by following the steps presented on pages 330 and 331.

BUSINESS LETTER:

MEMORANDUM:

Chapter Thirteen

Reading Reports and Articles from Professional Journals

In today's occupational world, many fields are characterized by rapid and frequent changes. Thus, one of the most important things for persons working in any career to do is to keep up-to-date. This can be accomplished in a number of ways, including in-service training, attending conferences, or enrolling in classes away from the workplace. Another way to keep abreast of changes is to read widely in your field. Two sources of information which will enable you to acquire up-to-date information about what is happening in your specific career field are reports and articles from professional journals.

In many career areas, there seems to be an overwhelming number of such reports and journals which need to be covered. Just keeping up becomes a real chore. However, there are ways to meet your own specific career-related reading needs. When you read such materials, ask yourself this question: **Can I read this report or article from a professional journal more quickly, more efficiently, and with more than adequate comprehension?** When you know how to apply the skills covered in this chapter, you will be able to answer yes to that question.

REPORTS

Reports are a way to communicate a great deal of related information. Such reports usually result from a need to pull this information together to answer a specific need or to answer a specific question. Reports are written in a number of different formats depending upon the profession, the kind of report it is, and the purpose of that report.

Generally, reports look very formal and even a bit intimidating when you are unaccustomed to reading them. Two important factors will make reading your own career-related reports easier. First, you will most likely be reading in your own field. Thus, the vocabulary and concepts presented should be relatively familiar to you, and this should lead to increased comprehension. Second, many fields seem to prefer certain kinds of reports over others. Once you have mastered the kind of report(s) used most often in your own field, you will become accustomed to the specific format used in such reports and it should be less difficult for you to comprehend and retain the information found in them.

Although there are a number of types of reports, five kinds are commonly used in business and industry. They are briefly described below.

- A **feasibility report** discusses the possibility of completing a project and what it will take in terms of time, cost, material, resources, and so on to bring the project to successful completion. For example, if an engineering firm is hired to build a bridge over a specific span of water, it needs to know and relate to the client whether the project can be done, and it needs an estimate of time and labor costs. This information would be included in a feasibility report.

- A **progress report** tells how a project is developing. It is usually written for and submitted at regular intervals to persons responsible for the project. Using the same example of an engineering firm, a person supervising the project may be asked to submit monthly progress reports to the firm and to the client on how the bridge-building project is moving along.

- A **review of the literature** is a research-based report on information located in books and periodicals that pertains to a single subject. Again, in the case of the bridge, engineers working on it might review the literature to find out all they can about a particular kind of material which is used for such projects. This would be written as a review of the literature and could be submitted to other engineers at the firm for their information or to the client as an explanation for using that specific material in building the bridge.

- A **financial report** is usually compiled and distributed to clients, stockholders, partners, or other interested parties. It describes the financial health of the company. It also usually includes descriptions of factors, positive or negative, which could affect the company's profit. The formats in which financial reports are presented may range from very glossy, fancy booklets complete with various photographs and graphics to letters to interested persons which contain only critical profit-and-loss information.

- A **research report** can have several functions. You may find that a research report describes controlled experiments and their results written by the experimenter; or a research report may describe the results of a survey and be written by the person(s) who designed and administered that survey; or a research report may be descriptive in that it presents details on a specific situation.

There is a structured way, or technique, which will help you to read any kind of report. It will enable you to decrease the amount of effort you must use and increase the amount of information you can understand and retain. You have already mastered some parts of this technique, so it is only a matter of reminding yourself to apply them when appropriate. The technique for interpreting reports is described below.

1. Read and analyze the title of the report. Ask yourself what you already know about the subject mentioned in the title. Since the report is written about some factor in your own field, you should know something about the subject. Analyzing the title in this way brings this information to mind and prepares you to read the report.

2. Read the abstract or summary. An abstract is found at the beginning of the report and the summary, of course, is at the end. Both serve the same purpose: They point out the critical aspects of the report for the reader. If the report has a summary, it is a good idea to treat it as though it were an abstract and read it before you go into the body of the report. Getting a preview of information to come establishes the foundation for what you will read later.

3. Look for structure or format in the body of the report. Some writers divide the report into sections and provide a subtitle for each subdivision. The subtitles and the division of material make it easier to understand different aspects of the report.

4. If the body of the report looks as though it might be difficult reading, preview its content before you read it from beginning to end:

   - Read the first paragraph or two.

   - Read the first sentence of every paragraph in the report.

   - Read the last two paragraphs before the summary.

You are, by following this previewing procedure, getting the gist of the report and, thus, establishing the foundation for a more thorough reading of the entire report. You are gambling that main ideas are present in the parts of the report you preview and will help you to comprehend the report in its entirety.

5. If the report has a bibliography, read it quickly to get a sense of the kinds of information and the selection of sources found within the report.

You may stop here if the above steps fill your need for a general idea of what is in the report. If you need to know more about the specific content of the report, go on to step 6.

---

6. Read for main ideas and details that support them. As you read, write trigger words in the margin which will enable you to refer to specific parts of the report if neccesary. Remember that these triggers can serve as an index for the material presented in the report.

7. Apply what you know about using graphics in combination with written text. As you learned earlier, graphics can be valuable aids to comprehension when a great number of facts are presented.

8. Map or chart as aids to comprehending complex information. These aids may be formal, such as those presented in Chapters Eight and Nine, if you are going to use them over time, or informal as described in Chapter Twelve.

9. Read beyond the written words. Watch out for opinions disguised as facts and propaganda devices that should be detected. Since there isn't any place for either of these techniques for changing your behavior or emotions in an objective report, be on the alert and stick with the facts and only well-supported opinions.

10. Translate any gobbledygook that may be in the report.

11. Check to see whether the writer has provided you with additional aids to understanding the report. There may be a glossary to help you define terms you might not know, or a list of the meanings of abbreviations or symbols used in the report.

SAMPLE PRACTICE
Reading Reports

DIRECTIONS: Read the following report using all eleven of the steps described above. Answer the questions at the end of the report.

TITLE: AUTOMATED CONTROL SCHEME FOR REFRIGERATION SYSTEM

AUTHOR: Mike Oliver, Head of Refrigeration Engineering Company

TO: Engineering Department, Marshall Dairy, Pacer, Georgia

DATE: September 16, 1989

I. INTRODUCTION

This document proposes a control scheme that will efficiently manage an ammonia refrigeration system for Marshall Dairy located in Pacer, Georgia. The present control scheme employs operators to monitor the system and start and stop equipment accordingly. This scheme of control imposes the problem of wasted energy and manpower. With today's technology, an automated control scheme can manage the refrigeration system to its maximum efficiency and minimize manpower requirements.

To design a control scheme that will accomplish the prescribed objective, a proper approach must be selected. A systems approach is used by Refrigeration Engineering Company, which helps ensure that the control scheme design supports all the requirements set forth by the user and the system.

The proposed control scheme will entail programmable controllers interfaced with the necessary machinery. Using both analog and digital inputs/outputs, the control scheme will monitor and manage the refrigeration system and its supplemental equipment.

II. OBJECTIVE

The objective prescribed by Refrigeration Engineering Company is to design an automated control scheme that will monitor and manage the refrigeration system to its maximum efficiency. The scheme must contain all the existing safety requirements and additional checks preferred by Marshall Dairy. The control scheme would be designed in accordance with an economic analysis that is compatible with the company's recommendations.

III. BACKGROUND

To complete a successful control scheme as proposed, a knowledge of ammonia refrigeration systems is required. Refrigeration Engineering Company, headed by Mike Oliver, offers sufficient background in the refrigeration field including six years experience with ammonia systems. This background assures that a feasible control scheme will be designed.

1

IV. METHOD OF APPROACH   2

A systems approach will be used in designing the control scheme. The systems approach consists of five major steps: systems analysis, general systems design, systems evaluation, detailed systems design, and system implementation.

Systems analysis will result in defining the user's requirements. Knowing the requirements, the scope of the system must be established. The facts and information must be gathered at this point, and then analyzed to complete the first step.

Next, a general systems design is established. Broad design building blocks are constructed with only the bare essentials included. This step includes a presentation of alternate designs.

System evaluation is the third step. Technology selection and vendor evaluation are accomplished in this step. A cost effectivity analysis is done comparing technologies and vendors to help in selecting the best system.

Following system evaluation, the detailed systems design involves writing the detailed specifications of the building blocks prescribed in step two.

Presuming the previous steps are accepted, the final step would be the system implementation which concludes the task. In this task, the design is tested. Conversion to the new system is done; and after installation the system is retested. This step of the approach is not included in the proposal.

V. SCHEDULE

The schedule for completing the proposed control scheme, based on the approach described herein is as follows:

SCHEDULE

Step Completion	Date
1. Systems Analysis	10/01/91
2. General Systems Design	10/15/91
3. System Evaluation	11/01/91
4. Detailed System Design	11/20/91

VI. ANTICIPATED BENEFITS   3

Numerous benefits are anticipated from the proposed automated control scheme for the refrigeration system. The major benefit is a savings on energy costs from a reduction of inefficient power usages by refrigeration compressor motors. Another immediate saving will be the reduction in current labor costs involved in manually controlling the refrigeration system. The accurate automatically recorded documentation of machine hours will improve preventive maintenance scheduling.

VII. SUMMARY

The current control scheme used to operate the refrigeration system causes costs that could be reduced with the proposed automated control scheme. The automated control scheme would use programmable controllers and a microcomputer that will interface with the necessary machinery for complete control over the system. Using both analog and digital I/O, the control scheme will monitor and manage the refrigeration system to achieve its maximum efficiency. The saving of energy and labor costs will result in a short payback period that will make the significant investment well worthwhile.

1. What kind of report is this? (progress, feasibility, research, review of the literature, financial)

_____

2. Has the author of this report divided it into sections? If so, what are they?

_____

_____

3. Does this report have an abstract or summary? If so, did you read that part before going into the report itself?

_____

4. What is the objective of the proposed automated control scheme project?

   _____

   _____

5. Does the report tell how the project will be carried out? If so, where in the report can you find this information?

   _____

6. Is there a timed plan for carrying out this project? If so, where in the report can you find this information?

   _____

7. After reading this report, how would you describe its purpose?

   _____

   _____

   Check your answers to the above questions. If your answers do not agree with those given below, analyze the differences. If you need to, go back to the report and recheck your answers.

Sample Practice Answers

1. This is a feasibility report, since it describes how the project can be successfully completed.

2. The report is divided into seven sections: Introduction, Objective, Background, Method of Approach, Schedule, Anticipated Benefits, and Summary.

3. The report has a summary which you should have read before reading the report.

4. The project objective is to design an automated control scheme that will monitor and manage the refrigeration system at Marshall Dairy with maximum efficiency.

5. Yes, the description of how each step of the plan will be carried out is found in Section IV, the Method of Approach.

6. Yes, Section V, Schedule, provides dates for each step in the Method of Approach section. The final step, testing of the system, is not included in the schedule.

7. The purpose of the report is twofold. First, the author of the report has spelled out exactly what must be done in order to provide the refrigeration system needed by Marshall's Dairy. Second, the Anticipated Benefits section is trying to convince Marshall Dairy to go ahead with the project and to hire the author to complete the project. The latter point is indicated by the inclusion of the Background section, in which the author of the report states his qualifications.

Now go on to Skill Development Exercise 13–1 on page 359 for practice with another kind of report.

Then go to Skill Application 13–1 on page 365, where you will apply what you have learned about interpreting reports to your own career materials.

SKILL DEVELOPMENT EXERCISE 13–1
Reading a Report

> DIRECTIONS: Read and analyze the following research report from Arthur Andersen and Company, using the steps for reading such material presented on pages 351 and 352. Then answer the questions at the end of the report.

November 1988

Results of the 1988 Arthur Andersen Small Business Survey

Small businesses continue to play a vital role in the economic expansion of the American economy in the development of innovative technologies, industries and ideas. The driving force behind these small businesses is their chief executives — the owner-managers. Arthur Andersen & Co. has conducted this nationwide survey of small business chief executives annually for the past three years to provide focused insight into the economic and business climate from the entrepreneur's perspective. This study is designed to communicate and promote the interests of enterprising businesses.

Executive Summary

The survey results present the views of some 21,000 small business owner-managers on a range of governmental, economic and business issues. Respondents represent companies in a variety of industries and regions, with sales ranging from $1-$120 million. Approximately 127,000 businesses received the 1988 Arthur Andersen & Co. survey, and the results represent the views of 16.5% of this audience — an unprecedented response rate.

The newly elected administration must address two critical issues as it leads our economy into the 1990's. **The Federal Budget Deficit was identified by 66% of those surveyed as the most important issue the new administration faces. Spending cuts are the best way to attack the deficit, say 55% surveyed.** Respondents believe these cuts should be made without corresponding tax increases. Income taxes were named as the second area of concern, as most executives anticipate that corporate and individual taxes will increase under the new administrations.

Overall, small business reported an excellent year in 1988, as forecasted in the prior year, and they project that 1989 will be similarly successful.

☐ **Over 70% surveyed experienced an increase in sales over 1987,** with more than half realizing over 10% growth in sales. Three out of four companies predict continued increases next year.

☐ **Nearly half of the respondents expanded their work force during 1988.** Approximately the same number of businesses expect an increase in the number of employees in 1989.

☐ This year, **employee compensation is up in 85% of the companies surveyed.** Eighty-four percent expect an increase in 1989.

Local Results

Arizona business owners are not as optimistic about Arizona's economy as they have been in prior years. Only 11% of the survey respondents see the economy improving, while 43% say it is stable and 46% say it is declining.

The majority of Arizona businesses showed an increase or a leveling off in sales between 1987 and 1988, indicating that the State's economy is still growing but at a slower pace. Nearly one-third of the survey participants are forecasting a 10% increase in sales between 1988 and 1989.

Anticipating or reacting to the slowdown in the local economy, over one-half of Arizona companies had either a decrease in employees or had the same number of employees between 1987 and 1988. Approximately the same number of businesses expect employees to decrease or stay the same between 1988 and 1989. This is in contrast to the national survey results which showed nearly half the respondents expanding their work force in 1988.

Profitability among the surveyed companies was mixed this year. 37% of the companies said they were more profitable, 36% said they were less profitable, while 27% said they had about the same profit level as last year.

Overall, Arizona businesses continued to grow and create jobs in 1988 but the pace seems to have slowed from prior years.

While exporting remains steady (at the same rate as in 1987), **83% of small business exporters believe certain barriers, namely lack of information, should be reduced or eliminated.** If incentives are established to help exporters overcome these barriers, it would provide opportunities to create significant economic and job growth.

Despite increasing health care insurance costs, almost all small businesses surveyed provide health and medical insurance to their employees, with over two-thirds paying at least 75% of the insurance premiums. A digest of the most significant concerns raised by executives participating in our survey follows. Complete survey results are on pages 6 and 7 of this booklet.

America — The 1990's

As America approaches an era of change — with a new administration and tough choices ahead — **the small business sector warrants governmental support and attention.** The small business agenda, revealed through our survey, highlights the policies the administration must work toward as we approach the 1990's. Small business owners' number one concern is the Federal budget deficit, followed by income taxes. All other issues (domestic programs, foreign policy and defense spending) are of less importance.

Federal spending is too high and it should be cut according to almost all — ninety-nine out of one hundred — executives surveyed. **Foreign aid (65%), welfare (56%) and defense spending (49%) were most often cited as areas where spending should be reduced.** Small business owners, in general, do not perceive their companies gaining much benefit from expenditures in these areas.

Spending Cuts for Federal Budget

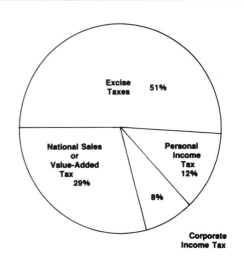

Foreign Aid   65%
Welfare   56%
Defense Spending 49%

Small Business Concerns for the Future

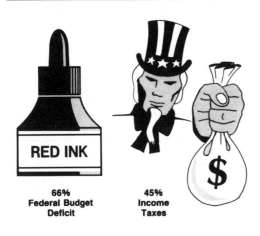

66%	45%
Federal Budget	Income
Deficit	Taxes

If taxes must be raised, our respondents view excise taxes, such as alcohol, gas or cigarette taxes, as the most palatable choices. A national sales tax or value-added tax is favored by just less than one-third, while the remaining 20% feel an increase in corporate or individual taxes would be appropriate.

Tax to Be Increased to Generate More Revenue

Over half of responding CEO's believe cutting spending on existing federal programs is the most effective way to reduce the deficit. Almost all other executives support cutting spending combined with tax increases.

Most Effective Method to Reduce Deficit

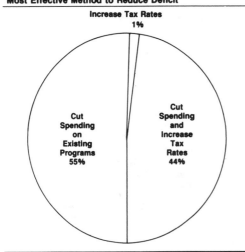

Increase Tax Rates
1%

Cut Spending on Existing Programs 55%

Cut Spending and Increase Tax Rates 44%

Excise Taxes 51%

National Sales or Value-Added Tax 29%

Personal Income Tax 12%

8%

Corporate Income Tax

Operating Insights and Results

Small businesses' strong performance in previous years has established a solid foundation for present and future growth. **Small business enterprises continue to prosper and expect future success, as they experience their third straight growth year.** This year, profitability will increase or stay the same as last year at three out of four companies. Sales, employee compensation and number of employees also exhibited positive growth over last year. These trends continue to reflect the good health of U.S. small businesses and the importance of these enterprises to the continuing prosperity of this country.

This year, 71% of small businesses report sales increases over last year. Remarkably, 42% of all companies increased their 1988 sales more than 10%, achieving the increases projected in last year's survey. Given their track record, **1989 should be another good year for small businesses.** Three out of four companies forecast sales increases, with one out of four expecting sales increases of greater than 10%.

Small Business With Increased Sales By Region

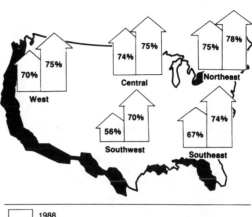

| | 1988 |
| | 1989 |

Small Business Sales Growth

Sales Growth as a Percent Increase over the Previous Year

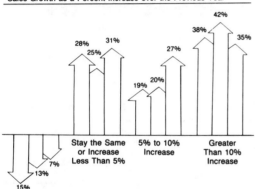

	Actual 1987 Over 1986
	Actual 1988 Over 1987
	Estimated 1989 Over 1988

The outlook for the nation's small business employees is positive. **Eighty-five percent** of responding small businesses **report an increase in current employee compensation** over the previous year. Of those companies that increased salary levels, almost half increased wages between 5 and 10%. Employees should continue to share in the growth and profitability of small businesses, as **84% of small businesses anticipate wage increases next year.** This realized growth is creating job opportunities in the small business sector, as evidenced by the 1.3 million new jobs small business accounted for in 1987. This trend should continue as **almost half of the executives increased their employees during 1988,** versus only 13% who decreased their employees. Approximately the same results are predicted for next year — 48% expect increases and less than 10% expect decreases.

Breaking sales out by industry, almost half of all manufacturers report current-year sales increases over 10%, while only 29% of responding retailers realized such increases. Expectations for next year follow the same trend, as 41% of manufacturers and 22% of retailers expect sales increases greater than 10%.

Achieved and projected sales are similar for businesses in all regions of the country, except the Southwest. This region varies primarily due to its oil- and gas-based industries. Only 57% of Southwest companies report current-year sales increases, versus the national average of 71%. Projections for these businesses are more optimistic for 1989 but they are still approximately 5% below the national average of companies expecting sales increases.

Employment Change Among Small Businesses

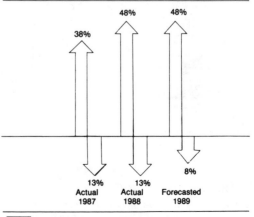

| | Increased Number of Employees |
| | Decreased Number of Employees |

Foreign Competition

The U.S. trade deficit, the weak dollar and international trade restrictions all impact the exporting climate and the overall economy. **Twenty-eight percent of the survey respondents currently export,** and exports account for more than 5% of total revenues for one out of ten businesses. However, manufacturers export substantially more than others. **Half of all manufacturers currently do business abroad,** and nearly a fifth rely on exports for more than 5% of their revenue. Lack of information and cost competitiveness, 31% and 29%, respectively, are the most significant barriers to expanding export revenues for manufacturers. Greater availability of information on doing business abroad (45%) and tax incentives (32%) would be the most effective incentives to encourage manufacturers to export. If barriers were removed and incentives established, 65% of manufacturers could start exporting or increase current export levels.

This potential for increasing exports, through reduced barriers and increased incentives, could expand both profitability and employment. The manufacturers that comprise over 30% of our survey population estimate they can increase revenues by $24 billion if effective incentives are established and export barriers reduced. According to the U.S. Department of Commerce, a $1 billion increase in export revenues creates 25,000 jobs. Given a $24 billion increase, over 600,000 jobs could be created. Certainly, efforts to eliminate barriers and establish further incentives should be a priority for the new administration.

Increase in Employment if Export Incentives Are Established

Employee and Labor Issues

Contrary to popular belief, small business employees are provided with a variety of benefits by their employers.

Almost all **(97.2%) of the small businesses surveyed provide their employees with health/medical insurance.** Two-thirds of the companies pay more than 75% of the insurance premiums; however, 90% of the small businesses report an increase in health insurance costs over the past year's. Over 70% also provide employee bonuses, and 54% offer retirement plans. Other popular items include dental insurance, flexible hours and tuition reimbursement.

Percent of Responding Companies with Health/Medical Insurance

The majority (70%) of small businesses surveyed have been affected by fair labor laws. Two-thirds of the companies affected by these laws report that the laws have resulted in the retention of employees that the companies might otherwise have terminated. This may burden those small businesses affected. At a minimum, the increased record keeping would require a company to spend more time on nonrevenue-producing activities.

Small Business Profile

Virtually all owner-managers surveyed say they **enjoy running a business, are interested in expanding market share and consider themselves to be innovators.** These and other attributes may be the reason small business CEO's are the driving force behind this vibrant sector of the economy. The executives describe themselves as **hardworking** and **concerned about the well-being of their employees.** The majority are not active in politics or local business organizations. They are also not interested in investing their personal assets in stocks or bonds. It is not surprising that these executives are minimally active outside of their companies. Hard work leaves little time for political or local business organization activities. Stocks and bonds are not of interest as most small business executives reinvest their assets in their companies where they feel they can achieve the highest return and continue to grow the business.

1. Does this report have an abstract, a summary, or both?

   _____

2. What five major areas are included in the survey?

   _____

   _____

3. What percentage of businesses that received the survey responded?

   _____

4. Whose views are represented in the survey results?

   _____

   _____

5. Why do you think the Local Results are boxed on the first page?

   _____

   _____

6. What is the greatest concern of small businesses for the 1990s?

   _____

   _____

7. If taxes are to be raised in the 1990s, how would most of the persons surveyed approve of it being accomplished?

   _____

   _____

8. According to the text and map on page 361, which region of the U.S. showed the smallest increase in sales from 1988 to 1989?

   _____

9. What percentage of companies that replied to the summary provide their employees with health/medical insurance?

   _____

10. The text on page 362 says that 70% of the small businesses surveyed have been affected by fair labor laws. How has this affected two-thirds of this 70%?

    _____

    _____

11. What is your opinion of the graphics provided in the report?

    _____

    _____

12. How do executives describe themselves in the Small Business Profile section of the report?

    _____

    _____

SKILL APPLICATION 13–1
Reading a Report

DIRECTIONS: Duplicate and attach a copy of one report from your own career field. Then briefly answer the general questions about that report.

REPORT SOURCE INFORMATION

Title: _____

Author: _____

Place of publication: _____

Publisher: _____

Copyright Date: _____ *Page(s):* _____

1. What kind of report is it? (review of literature, feasibility, financial, progress, research)

   _____

2. What is the purpose of the report?

   _____

   _____

3. Was the report divided into sections to make it easier for you to read? If so, what are they?

   _____

   _____

4. If this report describes methods, what are they?

   _____

   _____

5. If this report discusses results of any kind, what are they?

   _____

   _____

6. Briefly summarize the report on the following page.

REPORT SUMMARY:

ARTICLES IN PROFESSIONAL JOURNALS

Since journals (also called periodicals or magazines) in nearly every career area are published frequently, they are a valuable source of current information. If you are serious about keeping up-to-date on changes in your career area, you may soon find yourself trying to catch up on the number of articles you want to read. There are techniques for reading these articles which will help you to reduce your reading time and also help you to better comprehend and retain what you read. The following suggestions for reading any kind of article will do both of these things for you. (Note that some of the steps are similar to those presented as suggestions for reading reports.)

1. Read and analyze the title of the article. Ask yourself what you already know about the subject mentioned in the title. Since the article is written about some area in your own field, you should know something about the subject. Thinking about the title in this way brings the information to mind and prepares you to read the article.

2. Look to see who wrote the article. Since it is in your own field, perhaps you have heard of the author, met him or her, or read other articles he or she may have written. If any of these are the case, you have a head start on the article. You know the kinds of ideas that the author has previously expressed, so you come to this new article prepared for the direction it will probably take.

3. Read the introduction to the article, if there is one. Also read the summary if that has been included. Both of these parts highlight the essential aspects of the article for the reader. Getting an idea of information to come establishes the foundation for what you will read later.

4. Preview the article by reading the first two paragraphs, the first sentence of each of the following paragraphs, and the last two paragraphs. This should give you a good idea of what is included in the article.

You may want to stop here if you only need a general idea of the content or if you elect to read only sections that are of importance to you. But if you need more specific information about what is in the article, go on to step 5.

---

5. If you decide to read the article more thoroughly, you have a foundation of information acquired in the above steps. Use the structure or specific format in the body of the article. Some writers divide the article into sections and provide a subtitle for each subdivision. The subtitles and the division of material make it easier to understand different aspects of the article

6. Read for main ideas and the details that support them. As you read, write trigger words in the margin which will enable you to refer back to specific parts of the article if necessary. Remember that these triggers will serve as an index for the material presented in the article.

7. Apply what you know about using graphics in combination with written text. As you learned earlier, graphics can be valuable aids to comprehension when a great number of facts are presented. Take advantage of the fact that they are there to either clarify or substitute for written text.

8. Map or chart as aids to comprehending complex information in the article. These can be informal maps and charts.

9. Read beyond the written words. Watch out for opinions disguised as facts, and for propaganda devices that should be detected. There isn't any place for either one in a periodical article.

10. Translate gobbledygook if there is any in the article.

11. Check to see if the writer has provided you with additional aids to understanding the article. There may be a glossary to help you define terms, or a list of the meanings of abbreviations or symbols used in the article. There may be a bibliography (also called references or sources) that you can use to find books or articles with additional information on the same subject as the article.

SAMPLE PRACTICE
Reading an Article from a Professional Journal

DIRECTIONS: Read the following article, "Examining Our Telephone Manners," using the first four suggestions (page 367) for reading articles from periodicals to guide you. Then go to the end of the article and answer the questions.

EXAMINING OUR TELEPHONE MANNERS

by Richard D. Cornell
Human Research Manager
Cray Research Inc.

The way we and our staff answer a ringing phone can significantly affect our business. When we pick up that phone, we leave an impression with the person on the other end of the line of the quality of service or product he or she can expect. The person who answers the phone represents, to the caller, the entire department or company. Consequently, as managers, we have a considerable responsibility to do it right ourselves and see that those reporting to us also have good telephone manners.

Inside and Outside Customers

To improve the image projected through phone conversations, it's helpful first to consider such communication as an *inside/outside* relationship. The caller is on the *outside* and the receiver on the inside. In some cases, the outside person may be a customer who receives goods or services and in turn pays the company money resulting in us being paid. But the idea of customers goes beyond the people outside of our organization. We have customers inside the organization as well, people within our company to whom we provide services.

So, when it comes to the quality of telephone communications, everyone is important. Because almost everyone who calls us is in a sense a customer, everyone who calls us is a person who deserves to be treated right. Not only is it simply the right thing to do, it is profitable to our company and us personally.

Assuming we want to give our telephone manners a checkup, where do we begin? Basically all telephone conversations fall into two categories—incoming and outgoing—so let's begin by placing ourselves in the position of a caller.

What are the factors that determine how pleasant or productive a call we place will be? After some consideration, we will likely choose the tone of the person's voice who picks up the receiver as the main factor. Does the person sound friendly and sincere? Does the person sound hurried?

If the person sounds the latter, it might be appropriate to ask, "Is this a good time to be calling" or "Do you have a few minutes, or would it be better if I called back at another time?" It is not a good idea to force one's way in. In face-to-face conversation, we can see what is going on around the person to whom we are talking. We sense what is appropriate to do and say and what to avoid. When it comes to the telephone, though, we are in a situation in which we can only make judgments by tone of voice. The phone can be an incredibly intrusive technology if it rings at the wrong time. So, when making outgoing calls, the number one rule for us is to respect the other person's situation and respond accordingly.

Incoming calls are something else. If there is a number one rule here, it is, if you answer a ringing phone, that caller becomes your responsibility. That means, for instance, we must never transfer a call and hang up before the other person answers. The person calling is relying on us to guide him or her to the right place. How well we fulfill our responsibility is in our hands.

Training and Development

Training and developing people to care about and be effective on the phone can do much to help our department and career. What can we do to train and develop our people? As always, the best training is to set a good example. We need to observe our own telephone behavior and be aware of our attitude when it comes to dealing with people.

Increasing our awareness of how we act on the phone can be a powerful step in improving departmental performance. When we walk by a ringing phone during a busy time of day, do we answer it or do we think that it is our secretary's job? How does our voice sound? Do we take responsibility for calls we take? Do we respect the space of the person at the other end when we place a call?

There is also training. Much can be accomplished with a little bit of training. In two to three hours, a skilled communication trainer can help make everyone aware of how he or she sounds over the telephone and provide tips for dealing with difficult people. If we don't have the budget for training, we can hold a meeting on the topic to increase awareness of this important public relations tool. Time might also be spent describing problem situations, like dealing with disgruntled customers, and what to do about them.

Dealing with Difficult People

We have all had to deal with difficult people at one time or another. They may even be yelling at us.

Under such circumstances, we have to avoid being trapped into a win-lose frame of mind. It is a contest we can never win and maintain good relationships with customers outside or within our organization.

To keep from getting hooked into an "I'll show you" frame of mind, we should slow down our response time and listen. Let the person ventilate. We shouldn't take responsibility upon ourselves for events over which we had no control. Nor should we get into a "you think you have problems!" frame of mind. The right thing for us to do is to do what we can to help solve the problem.

It helps in such situations to remember difficult people are having a difficult time. We shouldn't take their remarks personally. They are directed at the problem, not at us. If we can separate the two, then we can approach the circumstance in a helping mode. At all costs, let's be a part of the solution, not a part of the problem.

If we can be effective role models in these difficult situations, we will be helping our people. We can also help them by taking the time to discuss how to deal with difficult people and the reasons they become difficult. There will be cases in which people become difficult because our department or organization made a mistake. These mistakes, if discussed, can be used very effectively as tools for training and development.

Telephone Tennis

In these hectic times, one of the favorite games we get into is "telephone tennis." We call again and again, leaving message after message to call back. The telephone can be a great time waster and a great time saver. Like any tool its application is the key.

There is no real way to totally avoid telephone tennis unless we stay at our desks at all times. But we can keep it to a minimum by leaving clear messages ourselves as well as taking messages for others. For some reason, unless an offer is made, the idea of leaving a message doesn't seem to occur to callers.

Finally

In the midst of today's rapid technological change, the phone continues to look pretty much the same and work pretty much the same. It is the one piece of technology with which we are probably most comfortable. It is also the one to which we pay the least attention.

Telephones assist us in doing the big communication job necessary to deal with the complex world we face. Paying attention to the little human details like a friendly greeting and a sincere tone of voice can do nothing but pay dividends.

You did not have to go through all eleven suggested steps to answer the following questions. They are based on what you have done through step 4. Note how much information you are able to retain just by previewing the article.

1. Does the article have an abstract, an introduction, or a summary?

2. According to the article, why do managers and their staffs have a responsibility to have good telephone manners?

_____

_____

3. What is the first thing suggested to improve the image projected through phone conversations?

_____

_____

4. Why is it important to train and develop people who care about being effective on the phone?

_____

_____

5. How can you keep from getting hooked into an "I'll show you" frame of mind when dealing with difficult people?

_____

_____

6. What other two ways are suggested for dealing with difficult people?

_____

_____

7. The author offers a final suggestion for communication on the phone. What is it?

_____

_____

If your interest in the article has been aroused by what you did in steps 1–4, go back and finish following the rest of the suggested steps for reading an article in a professional journal.

Check your answers to the questions. Your answers may not exactly match the wording of those given below, but the content of the answers should be the same. If your answers do differ, go back to the article and recheck what you have written.

Sample Practice Answers

1. The article doesn't have sections labeled abstract, introduction, or summary. However, the information before the first subtitle would serve well as an introduction. The subsection entitled "Finally" is not a summary.

2. To the caller, the person who answers the telephone represents the department or company.

3. Consider a phone conversation as a relationship, an inside/outside relationship.

4. (1) Train and develop people who care about the use of the phone to help themselves and the department.
   (2) Increase employees' awareness of the importance of how they act on the phone.

5. Slow down your response time and listen to the caller.

6. (1) Remember they are having a difficult time.
   (2) Serve as a role model.

7. Pay attention to details like a friendly greeting and sincere tone of voice.

Now go to Skill Development Exercise 13–2 on page 375 for practice in reading another article from a professional journal.

Then go to Skill Application 13–2 on page 381, where you will apply what you have learned about reading articles from professional journals to your own career materials.

SKILL DEVELOPMENT EXERCISE 13—2
Reading an Article from a Professional Journal

DIRECTIONS: Read the following article from a professional journal and answer the questions that follow it. Use the suggestions on pages 367 and 368 for reading such articles. See how quickly and effectively you can read this article on time management. Although the author of the article may be in a field which is different from yours, his suggestions on time management apply to any work situation.

TIME MANAGEMENT . . . OR LEARNING HOW TO SAY NO

by Jose L. Gonzales

In seven years of public accounting, all my training and experience in time management has centered around mastering two basic principles: planning and organizing.

The object of time management is using time effectively. To achieve this objective you must manage interruptions, control crises, and practice prevention. Although your time is affected by those around you, you alone can control what you do with your time. Crises must be controlled and interruptions must be managed to minimize the impact of those things that are beyond your control.

Manage Interruptions

Minor interruptions can be time-consuming if the interruptions are not kept in perspective and the cause of the interruption is not dealt with immediately. When interrupted, you must set a time limit and stick with it as much as possible. When people ask for a minute, tell them that they can have five, but not more.

Set the stage early to let those around you know that you are truly busy. If you keep a pencil in your hands, stay standing when people drop in, meet visitors in conference rooms so that you can leave when the meeting is not productive, and avoid small talk when people interrupt, you can prevent short interruptions from becoming long ones.

Most interruptions are caused by people. You must deal with this fact and be gracious with people. Recognizing that a certain diplomacy is necessary in an office environment, you must avoid showing annoyance and give the interrupter your undivided attention. Through your responses you can lead the interrupter to get to the point immediately.

As a manager you must deal with interruptions and the problems that come with them. You cannot let the interrupters go away empty handed. If necessary, promise that their problem will be taken care of later, and fit it into the day's schedule. Explain that there are other priorities and that they might call someone else in the company. Consider having the interrupter come back and give an update later after he has had a chance to think some more about the problem.

Some managers tend to use interruptions as an excuse to procrastinate. You cannot react to interruptions by complaining or taking a break. It is important to get back on track after interruptions and not lose the momentum built before the interruption.

Control Crises

Despite your efforts in planning and controlling time, unexpected crises arise which must be controlled. If you are more concerned about what people will think of you rather than coping with the problem, you may become unglued and lose your cool, things will tend to get worse, and you will undoubtedly make enemies. Managers who do not effectively control crises are not really managing.

A tremendous amount of energy is expended in dealing with even a minor crisis. Allocate time to think about a problem and channel your energy to find solutions. Develop and maintain a plan of action to deal with the crisis in stride. For example, take a moment to think and consider options, relax before preparing mentally and then tackling a problem, and continue to delegate to subordinates while the crisis is around you.

By running the crisis instead of letting the crisis run you, you can maintain the necessary awareness to solve problems and reduce the time spent on crises.

Practice Prevention

It is difficult to manage time effectively without establishing your own strategic defense initiative screen. By organizing your office you can communicate subliminally that your office is a functional workplace, not a hangout. Visitors to your office should be clearly aware of the need for short concise analyses of problems or situations that must be dealt with. Although a closed-door policy can be damaging to every manager, an open-door one can be a very serious time killer.

In performing your job, plan your schedule carefully to prevent wasted time. Minimize the number of trips out of the office to visit peers, or to get a cup of coffee. The more you unload on others, the more they will unload on you. Do not try to avoid peers but rather stress the importance of keeping idle conversations in perspective.

The work environment provides additional distractions to effective time management. Exterior noise, although slight, can have a distracting effect on the ability to concentrate and complete the task at hand. Very often distractions can be prevented by going to a conference room or library, working half days at home, if possible, and setting aside periods of the day where interruptions such as phone calls are diverted. Asking a secretary to take calls and screen visitors goes a long way in deciding who can interrupt and who can't.

Organizing

With the many demands facing each of us, it is easy to throw up our hands and say, "I just don't have the time!" The question really is not whether you have enough time, but how you will spend the time you already have. You must learn to: diagnose time, arrange all tasks, and implement a plan to complete tasks.

To rid yourself of nonproductive, time-wasting activities, you have to ask yourself:

1. What am I doing that is nonessential?
2. What is the best use of my time now or what activities could be done by somebody else just as well if not better?
3. How am I wasting the time of others?
4. What are my major time wasters and what could be done to avoid them or perform more effectively?

Often you are confronted with different projects on an ongoing basis throughout the day. You attend meetings, receive phone calls, get visits from your subordinates on many different accounts or customers. After each of these events, make a note that will help to define the problem so it may be dealt with at a later point in time. Arrange files and correspondence in a logical manner.

By maintaining a folder or divider for each of my customers or clients, I am able to place all similar, relevant notes in one location for easy retrieval.

Rank your many different tasks by priorities. A "to-do" list is useful in organizing thoughts and dealing with tasks on a priority basis. If you anticipate known deadlines and avoid procrastination, you can act while you still have available options. You should check with your subordinates and superiors on a daily basis and make contingency plans to prepare for the absence of key subordinates. This practice will ensure your "to-do" list does not get longer and longer.

The key to organization is implementing the plan to complete all tasks on a timely basis. Managers who organize effectively but procrastinate on completing tasks are often frustrated and find themselves taking work home to complete tasks prior to the stated deadline.

Time management skills are difficult to learn and implement because of the environment in which we work on a daily basis. To perfect time management skills, you must consistently practice them. Some other aids to effective time management:

- Make the most of unexpected time. If you commute some distance by car, listen to tapes on current issues. If you have unexpected waiting time, have some reading material in your briefcase.
- Perfect the art of dictation.
- Get some time alone or quiet time. To the extent possible, set aside time to sit and reflect on the situation around you.
- Make the best use of your weekend. You can be more effective on the job if you enjoyed a weekend of exercise, relaxation, and hobbies. Moreover, you can become more interesting as a person by pursuing nonwork activities.
- Learn to say "no!" We all want to be highly successful. Highly motivated individuals have a tendency to accept any work handed down by superiors. Only you can control your time, and only you know how much time you have available. Learn to say no or be prepared to deal with the consequences.

1. According to the author, what are his two basic principles of time management?

_____

_____

2. What are four things the author suggests for managing interruptions?

_____

_____

_____

_____

3. What does the author mean when he says that you should run the crisis instead of letting the crisis run you?

_____

_____

_____

_____

4. How does that suggestion help in a crisis?

_____

_____

5. Why is it important to establish your own "strategic defense initiative screen?"

_____

_____

6. What can be done about distractions in the work environment?

_____

_____

_____

_____

7. How does the author suggest that you rid yourself of nonproductive, time-wasting activities?

_____

_____

_____

_____

8. What is the purpose of maintaining a filing system?

_____

_____

9. According to the author, what is the key to organization?

_____

_____

10. How can you perfect time management skills?

_____

_____

SKILL APPLICATION 13–2
Reading an Article from a Professional Journal

DIRECTIONS: Duplicate and attach a copy of one article from a professional journal related to your own field. Then answer the questions. Be sure to give the source information

ARTICLE SOURCE INFORMATION

Title: _____

Author: _____

Place of publication: _____

Publisher: _____

Copyright Date: _____   *Page(s):* _____

1. Why did you choose this particular article?

    _____

    _____

2. What is your opinion of this article?

    _____

    _____

3. What three things did you learn from the article that you feel will be of most value to you?

    _____

    _____

4. Write a brief summary of this article on the following page.

ARTICLE SUMMARY:

Index